Jake!

THE LAST SOUTHERN POPULIST MAYOR
WHO TRANSFORMED JACKSONVILLE, FLORIDA
FROM A SLEEPY CITY WITH AN INFERIORITY COMPLEX
INTO A DYNAMIC METROPOLIS WITH A CAN-DO ATTITUDE

Mike Tolbert

outskirts
press

TABLE OF CONTENTS

Chapter 1

From Public Housing to Public Adoration

THIS IS A book about the life and times of Jake M. Godbold, a Jacksonville, Florida political behemoth and last of the southern populists who has remained at the top and in the forefront of the political flow of his city for fifty years, despite last holding elected office in 1987.

My mission has been to chronicle Jake's outsized personality, his political and communication skills, and his passion for Jacksonville and tell the story of how this one individual pushed, pulled and led Jacksonville from being a sleepy city with an inferiority complex to become a dynamic southern metropolis with a can-do attitude.

A lot of things happened in Jacksonville between July 1, 1979, when Godbold became an elected mayor, until he left office 8 years later because of term limits, on June 30, 1987. Hopefully, after reading this book you will learn more about what happened, how it happened and why.

I came to Jacksonville in September 1969 as a political reporter for *The Florida Times-Union*. My job was to cover the new consolidated city government, including the mayor and 19-member City Council. My feet had barely walked on Northeast Florida land when I first met Jake Godbold, a young, brash and funny member of the year-old council.

I'll be honest. I was smitten right away.

Jake was a 35-year old dynamo who had already demonstrated a great propensity for leadership. It started in the north Jacksonville public schools he attended as a kid and continued when he joined the large and effective Jacksonville Jaycees organization for young men, which led to his election to the old Jacksonville City Commission in the mid-sixties.

Jake was a salesman first and foremost. As a kid, he stood outside ball parks and entertainment venues to sell bags of boiled peanuts.

In his early professional life he peddled insurance on a debit for Independent Life Insurance Co., which was headquartered in Jacksonville. Every day in every situation, Jake sold ideas and causes. His passion for whatever had his attention at the time was ever-present and it was catching, as infectious as sunshine breaking through on a rainy day.

That passion, along with his leadership skills, caused him to collect a large army of friends and associates like bees are drawn to honey, a loyal army of people who have loved him as a brother and would follow him into hell.

Jake Godbold is a master communicator, whether he's one on one, sitting close, leaning in and putting his hand on your arm, speaking to a group of 20 community leaders in a conference room to convince them to put their influence behind an issue, or making a speech to 1,000 people. He commands the room and attention.

Holding court over food is his specialty. He loves good food and good company. Sometimes it has been a small group gathered in a booth or at a table in one of his favorite restaurants like The Pig, Toby's, Jackie's Seafood Kitchen, Cotton's Barbecue, Piccadilly's, the airport Holiday Inn, and these days, River City Brewery in downtown Jacksonville. Often 30-40 people will show up at his Gateway Chemicals office at Friday lunch to eat and talk politics. Each December, he organizes and hosts a quail dinner at River City Brewery on the river that draws 400-500 friends, followers and associates.

He naturally attracts a crowd. Many of his loyal supporters and friends show up at a moment's notice to hang onto every word, even if they've heard the same stories over and over.

In 1995, after he lost a third bid for Mayor, we attended an annual cookout at friend J.B. Coxwell's 1,200-acre Thousand Oaks Ranch. Jake is an avid fisherman and never bypasses an opportunity to put his line in the water. Usually he throws in several lines at one time.

Late in the afternoon, Jake was out in the gazebo on Lake Helen. He had three rods with their lines in the lake trying to catch one of the trophy bass swimming in the water. As usual, he was surrounded by a group of his guys, and as usual, Jake was telling stories. His three rods were propped up against the gazebo wall, hooks well-hidden beneath the blue lake. Jake was not paying attention to his rods.

All of a sudden, a huge bass hit one of the lines and the rod flew up and over the wall into the lake. With the bass towing, the rod skimmed across the top of the lake. Nobody moved.

I looked at him and said, "Now you know the difference between winning and losing." "What do you mean?" he asked.

"Well," I replied, "if you had won the election, every one of these bastards standing here would have jumped in the lake to get your rod."

Author Mike Tolbert talks with Jake after 1995 election loss.

When speaking to a group, he's never been hesitant to call out individuals who might be chatting while he is speaking. He even did it to Donald Trump (yes, that Donald Trump). It happened in 1984 on the occasion of a USFL football game in the Gator Bowl between Jacksonville's Bulls and the Trump-owned New Jersey Generals. As was normal, before the game Jake had an overflow crowd of people in his box for a pre-game reception. Trump was in attendance, standing in the back of the room.

When Jake got up to speak, the room got quiet…except for Trump who was talking to the person next to him.

Godbold stopped, looked out at Trump and said, "Mr. Trump, this is not New York City. In Jacksonville when the Mayor speaks everybody listens." The Donald stopped talking.

JAKE!

I've often thought his very favorite place to speak to an audience is from behind the pulpit in an African American church. It's where he has practiced moving the masses or reaching that lone person who truly believes he or she is the only one Jake is talking to.

As a 25-year old reporter, I quickly knew several important things about Jake. He was great copy, always a go-to-guy for a good quote. He was a great source. I think he instinctively knew the value of trading good information to the media to build close and helpful relationships. He was totally unafraid of controversy or confrontation and he was outspoken.

When John Lanahan was president of the City Council he grew tired of Jake's constant presence in the press. Lanahan was an ex-Marine who expected his commands to be obeyed. He ordered Jake to stop holding news conferences without his advance permission. If Jake continued, Lanahan threatened to remove him from all of his committee assignments.

It was a perfect opening for Godbold. He called a news conference. Obviously, it pissed off Lanahan. That was followed by Jake refusing to call off a public hearing on a controversial zoning issue. Lanahan removed Jake as committee chair and yanked his committee assignments.

It was a dumb act and politically tone deaf. Jake was not fond of committee assignments anyway. His response? He said it cleared his calendar so that he had more time to increase his presence in the media and drive Lanahan nuts.

Godbold was a natural foil for Consolidated Jacksonville's first mayor, Hans Tanzler. Tanzler was the face of the "White Hats," a group of city leaders who fought the winning fight to throw out the inefficient and often corrupt city and county governments to form a new kind of local government with a strong mayor and 19 independent members of the

City Council. Tanzler was also a favorite of the blue bloods who lived in the upper-class neighborhoods on Jacksonville's West and South sides of town along the river.

While Jake supported creating the new government, he was certainly no favorite of Jacksonville's political or social elite. He grew up and lived "on the Northside." That was the wrong side of the tracks in Jacksonville.

Tanzler was a 6-foot-6-inch lawyer who had been a star basketball player at the University of Florida. He was a judge before being elected Mayor. He spoke the king's English, sometimes eloquently.

Jake stood about 5-feet 7-inches, and while he also sometimes talked eloquently, he spoke the language of the north Florida red-neck more than that of somebody's king.

I think Godbold personally liked Mayor Tanzler. Tanzler was a man's man. Like Jake, Tanzler loved to hunt and fish. Jake appreciated and admired Tanzler's integrity.

But while Tanzler was smart, he was politically slow against a political gazelle like Godbold. And Jake was often quick to publicly challenge the mayor. Many city employees disliked Tanzler, particularly his chief administrative officer Lex Hester. Most loved Godbold and were foundational to his political life.

Godbold was council president in 1978 when Tanzler resigned to run for governor with six months left on his term. Godbold was automatically elevated to the mayor's office.

Jake grew up poor. His family lived in public housing and his father was blind at one time. In his childhood Jake was always working, whether it was with his mother to boil, bag and sell peanuts, collect empty soda bottles to sell back to grocery stores, deliver the daily newspaper or work as an usher at the neighborhood theater.

Jake didn't attend college. He was an okay student at Andrew Jackson High School, but school work was not his favorite thing. He joined the Army and went to Korea. When Jake mustered out of the military, he got married to the love of his life, Jean Jenkins, and started working for Independent Life Insurance Co.

He sold life insurance on a debit, calling weekly on mostly African Americans to collect payments in northside neighborhoods near where he grew up and still lived. He developed lifelong relationships that would later help propel him to a successful political career.

For the sake of transparency, you should know that after leaving the *Times-Union,* in 1971 I ran Godbold's re-election campaign to the City Council and assisted Tanzler's re-election efforts behind the scenes. In 1975, I managed Godbold's re-election and I also ran Tanzler's third and final campaign for mayor. I then became an aide on Tanzler's staff.

In 1979, when Godbold ran for mayor for the first time, I ran his campaign. After he won, I became a member of his staff. When he sought re-election in 1983, I'd started my own public relations business and took a role as the campaign's strategic advisor.

Over the years, Jake and I have remained very close.

I think both of us would say our long relationship has been both a blessing and an aggravation: a blessing for me because he is such a bigger-than-life individual who can lose his breath at the sight of a beautiful bird in flight and will lose his unbuttoned falling pants rather than give up the battle to land a large bass.

Watching him work his persuasive magic to get Jacksonville a front row seat at NFL owners meetings (which eventually led to Jacksonville getting a team), convince the U.S. Olympic Gymnastics Federation to hold its U.S. Olympic Trials in Jacksonville on two occasions, and get the owners of the NFL's New England Patriots to bring the Michael Jackson Victory Tour and the Jackson Five to Jacksonville for three nights of sold-out concerts at the Gator Bowl has been pure joy.

It was also a blessing because he's empowered me to do things with and for him that have embedded themselves into the history of Jacksonville.

The aggravation? I've long had a reputation for speaking truth to power. It comes naturally. But sometimes, I don't deliver the message with great grace and civility. While Jake appreciates frankness, my tone has caused problems. I'm a little better now, I think.

Because I grew up as a journalist, I am deadline driven and anal about being on time. That's something Jake has often cared little about. The result is many of us have spent a collective lifetime waiting on him to show up. Sometimes, he doesn't. Once in the nineties, when he was to speak at a large banquet, I anticipated his absence and stood a life-size cut-out at his chair on the dais.

In his aging, he is doing better. That's probably because he is thinking none of us has as much time left to wait.

Through it all, we've stuck together. We respect each other. We trust each other. And, we love each other.

For those reasons, I believe he asked me to write this book.

I'll be honest. This has been an adventure that has been intimidating, especially the research. I was involved in much of Jake's life. I was there for many of the big and small events. As a witness and sometimes participant, I know a lot about the eight and one-half years he was Mayor. Until I had to digest it all in doing this book, I had forgotten just how much was done and how vast the impact.

One last confession. Because I have been intimately involved in some of the events described here, I have been cautious to make sure this is not an account of me. This story is not about me. It's about Jake. While I spent days interviewing Jake, I've also interviewed about 60 individuals who were part of this history to collect their own memories and impressions. There are more than 1,500 pages of transcribed notes.

While Jake was Mayor, his aide Martha Barrett kept huge, card table sized scrapbooks of every mention in the newspaper, every day, providing a wealth of research.

Finally, my one regret in doing this work is that so many people very important to helping Jake in his great success for Jacksonville are no longer with us on this earth. They took their memories and stories with them. However, I'm confident that through their tales they preparing their new friends to meet their old friend, Jake Godbold.

Mike Tolbert

Chapter 2

Turn Out the Lights-
the Party's Over

WHEN JAKE GODBOLD cut out the lights in his City Hall office on June 30, 1987, his last day after eight and one-half years as Jacksonville's mayor, he walked away knowing he had lived up to the new consolidated government's intention of having a strong mayor.

The list of accomplishments during Godbold's leadership was impressive by any standards. It was especially significant when compared to the previous first twelve years of Consolidation. A partial list of achievements includes:

- Construction of J. Turner Butler Blvd. from I-95 to the beaches.
- JEA $1.6 billion coal-fired plant.
- The Mayo Clinic.
- Metropolitan Park.
- The Jacksonville Landing.

- The Southbank Riverwalk in downtown.
- Saving and restoring the historic Florida Theatre.
- Renovating and expanding the Gator Bowl.
- Saving the historic Jacksonville Terminal and converting it into the Prime Osborn Convention Center.
- $1 billion in downtown development.
- Building four regional libraries, seven community centers, seven swimming pools, six miles of sewer lines a year, a $330 million road and drainage program, $1 billion in downtown development, creation of 10,000 new jobs each year.
- Merger of University Hospital with University of Florida's Shands Teaching Hospital.
- Mayor's Older Buddies (M.O.B.)
- The Jacksonville Jazz Festival, the Spring Music Festival, and the Michael Jackson Victory Tour.
- Launched the quest and laid the foundation for Jacksonville landing an NFL team.

Prior to Consolidation, in the 1950s and 1960s, Jacksonville often was its own worst enemy. The city and county governments were inept, ineffective and corrupt.

During the early sixties, 11 city and county officials were indicted on 142 counts of bribery and larceny. Included in the sweep were four city councilmen, two city commissioners, one county commissioner, the city's auditor, the county's purchasing agent and the executive secretary of the city recreation department.

In 1965, the Florida Legislature created the Local Government Study Commission that started the process to get rid of the corrupt governments and replace them with something new and hopefully better.

With Jacksonville civic and business giant J.J. Daniel leading the way as chairman, the fifty-member commission comprised of business and civic leaders (no elected officials or government employees) started its work on October 1, 1965. The Legislature gave it until May 1, 1967 to finish. Within 15 months the commission submitted a Consolidation proposal. It was called *Blueprint for Improvement.*

After some adjustments, the Duval County Legislative Delegation ordered it to be put on the ballot as a referendum.

The political war that followed between the forces for Consolidation, called the "White Hats," and those who opposed creating a new government, the "Black Hats," was intense and often ugly.

On August 8, 1967, county voters approved the referendum 54,768-29,768 and the people of Jacksonville celebrated, believing it was a new day in their town.

No longer would local government be shackled by costly duplicate purchasing agencies, public works departments, and recreation departments. The days of having both a Sheriff's Office and a Police Department would be over. Instead, law enforcement would be under one roof, the Sheriff's Office, with an elected sheriff.

Jacksonville was christened "The Bold New City of the South." The City limit signs were picked up and moved out to the county borders. Overnight, with its 841 square miles, Jacksonville became the largest city in land area in the lower 48 states.

Old Jacksonville's dwindling population of 200,000, due to white exodus to the suburbs, all of a sudden exploded to 500,000 as the new Jacksonville was born.

It felt like the clouds hovering over the city might be lifting. There was hope. The city had a heady feeling.

The new government opened for business on October 1, 1968 with Hans Tanzler as mayor and Jake Godbold sitting on the 19-member council as an at-large member.

For the most part, in the early years the government seemed to work well. Tanzler stocked his appointed department heads and division chiefs with retired military officials (Jacksonville is a major Navy town and the talent was available) and other experienced government pros. Cutting government costs and keeping taxes low was a major commitment made during the referendum election, and Tanzler made sure the "White Hats" kept their promise.

Year after year after year, the mayor and others in the new government bragged about reducing property taxes, cutting costs and eliminating city jobs. As a result, little money was spent to fix infrastructure or invested in economic development.

Tanzler led the effort to flush the stinking St. Johns River of its foul and destructive pollution, caused by 18 million gallons of raw sewage flowing directly into the river each day through 77 downtown outfalls. It was a monumental achievement that cost $150 million in municipal bonds, all paid for by Jacksonville taxpayers with no help from the state and federal governments. When the seven-year project was finally finished in 1977, a giant celebration was held downtown and attended by an estimated 100,000 people. Standing 6-6, Tanzler skied with the world-famous Cypress Gardens Skiers to demonstrate that when he fell from his skis he would not die of disease because the river was now clean.

Still, something was missing. It was as if there were some kind of deficiency in the heart and soul of the city.

- Race relations were raw.
- Public high schools were disaccredited.

- Economic growth was stagnant, due in part to an oil embargo and national recession.
- The city stank from air pollution caused by paper mills and chemical factories.
- Other Florida cities were adding population, but not Jacksonville.
- The city owned its own electric utility plant which was totally dependent on high cost imported foreign oil. Electricity was very expensive and the public was highly upset.

Nothing seemed to work.

The luster of the new government was beginning to wear off.

Everything collided to seemingly cause an entire Jacksonville to have an inferiority complex. Simply put, the people who lived in what was labeled "The Bold New City of the South," didn't feel very bold and most of them shared negative feelings about their hometown.

That was the city Godbold inherited when he was sworn into office on July 1, 1979 as Consolidation's second elected mayor.

Two early events had a history-shaping impact on the new mayor and the direction he would follow.

Three days after Godbold was elected, Albert Ernest and Preston Haskell came calling. Ernest, civic leader and president of Barnett Bank, and Haskell, owner of a design-build engineering firm who started becoming a Jacksonville icon in the early 1970s, were there representing the Chamber of Commerce, most of whose leadership had opposed Godbold. Ernest was about the only Godbold-backer in the chamber.

Godbold remembers the meeting as if it were just yesterday because it was so defining for him. "Jake, you are now in charge and I came over here to talk to you representing the chamber," Ernest said. "You know that most of the chamber supported Brantley (Lew, the former Florida Senate president who was his major opponent)." Ernest told the new mayor that because he had supported Jake from the beginning, he was selected, along with Haskell, to speak with the newly elected mayor. "Now, you need to make up your mind what you want to do. What are your goals? What do you want to accomplish?"

Ernest acknowledged that it would be tempting for Godbold to be vindictive against those who had opposed him. Then, Godbold said, Ernest hit his sweet spot. "He told me, 'You can choose to sit up here and be a ceremonial mayor, kiss babies and cut ribbons. You can choose to kick a lot of people's asses. I don't think that's what you want to do. I hope that's what you don't want to do. That's what the chamber hopes that you don't want to do, even though they are afraid you may very well do that.'"

The chamber realizes, Ernest continued, that for the last 12 years, "We've just been going in and out, in and out, like the tide." The chamber, he said, had one agenda and the mayor had another agenda. The chamber believes Jacksonville's consolidated government must have a strong mayor. "We all need to form a partnership and this form of government won't work unless you are willing to take the lead." Ernest promised the mayor that if he would lead the chamber would follow.

"That really made a deep, deep impression on me," said Godbold. "I told him I was inspired and I was very excited in what he said and the way he said it. I believed what he told me."

Shortly after that meeting, the chamber hired Washington D.C. political pollster William Hamilton to conduct an issues survey in Jacksonville. The results of that poll became foundational in shaping Godbold's agenda. Hamilton reported to the new mayor that Jacksonville's biggest obstacle was the negative attitude of its citizens. There is no pride in Jacksonville, he said, and until that was reversed Jake would get very little accomplished.

In 1986, a young John Peyton, son of Gate Petroleum icon Herb Peyton, interned in Godbold's City Hall office. In 2003, Peyton would be elected the sixth mayor of Consolidated Jacksonville. Looking back on his days as an intern, Peyton reflected, "The thing that mystified me the most was how a man who absolutely butchered the king's English garnered so much loyalty among his staff, his key supporters and the key stake holders in the community. What I learned over time is Jake's passion and his energy and his vision made the day. That's what brought everybody together, regardless of who it was or what station in life they were in. His love for Jacksonville superseded any shortcomings he had. That was fun to watch."

When Godbold left office in 1987, the *Jacksonville Journal*, a newspaper which had supported his opponent in 1979, wrote this in an editorial under the headline of "Godbold lifted city's spirit and listened to the people":

> *"Jake Godbold will go down in the history of Jacksonville as one of its most effective mayors, the man who presided over the city government during one of the city's headiest periods of population growth and economic development.*
>
> *"There are a remarkable variety of brick-and-stone monuments to his eight years in office. But we suspect that Godbold is proudest of a contribution that cannot be seen, touched or measured, but which tens of thousands of Jacksonville people instinctively credit him for.*

"It is the spirit that abounds in Jacksonville today—a spirit of optimism, hope, community pride, willingness to aspire and a determination to achieve."

The editorial concludes:

"The man and the city and its people did well together during the Godbold years. How do we apportion the credit? Let the historians figure it out. Meanwhile, the people of Jacksonville express their opinion in a telling way. When they see Godbold, they smile and shout, 'Hi Jake!' And Jake beams and waves back."

Chapter 3

———❧———

LEARNING ABOUT PROFITS FROM BOILED PEANUTS

YOU COULD ARGUE that the best day in Godbold's life was the day as a child when he first learned to talk. That gave him the tool he needed to create a successful life; one in which he has used his God-given gift of communication to move and motivate others to act, or sometimes to refrain from acting.

Jake was born during the Great Depression on March 14, 1933 to Charles and Irene Godbold and the poverty and despair that began in 1929 with the collapse of the stock market. Jacksonville was not exempt. Charles Godbold was lucky to have a job, making $1 a day at the water works facility in Riverview on Jacksonville's northside.

The Godbolds had four children. Jake was the first-born, followed by Fay, Charlene and the youngest, son, Len.

When Jake was only six-years old, and as the Great Depression was winding down, his father lost his eyesight and was unable to work. The family lived in the downstairs of a small house near downtown Jacksonville for two years. "Those were some trying times," Godbold recalled. It was so trying, he said, the house's owner, Minnie Oliver, who lived upstairs, often helped out by not charging rent and buying the family groceries.

The Godbolds moved into the government subsidized Brentwood Projects apartment #3657 in 1939 and remained in that townhouse unit for 11 years before moving into a smaller unit, #3651 for three more years. Afterwards, Charles and Irene moved into a small house in the Brentwood area, not far from the projects. After Charles passed away, Irene remarried W.L. Whitfield and she lived in that house until she died shortly after Jake was re-elected Mayor in 1983.

His dad, Godbold says, "was a very gentle guy who never cussed or raised his voice." During his period of blindness, which lasted almost three years, Charles would spend most of his time each day in his room listening to the radio. The room faced the east and the windows had shades to keep out the morning sun. One morning when young Jake was getting ready to ride the church bus to Sunday School at Beaver Street Baptist Church he heard his dad hollering.

"I ran in there. The shade had a little hole in it and he could see some light coming through the shade. That was the first sign his sight was coming back."

An excited Jake raced into the kitchen where his mother was preparing breakfast and told her the good news. Afterwards, he remembers, "She sent me off to Sunday School." Charles' sight never completely returned, but it was good enough for him to function. He slowly began working again.

Jake and his father bonded over baseball, especially the old Jacksonville

Tars who played their games at the ballpark on Myrtle Avenue. His dad, says Jake, "loved baseball and he knew baseball." When they could save up enough money, on weekends the two would walk from the Brentwood projects, down Brick Road that separated the black and white neighborhoods, then cut over to the railroad tracks and follow the tracks to Eighth Street and to the ballpark on Myrtle Avenue. "We went right through the minority community. We got where we knew all those people and they knew us," Jake says. "After the games and on the walk home the people would holler and ask us, 'Who won?'"

When the Tars played games out of town, Jake and his dad listened to the games on the radio.

Charles Godbold got a job painting and repairing Brentwood Projects apartments after tenants moved out. He eventually became foreman.

While painting the unoccupied apartments, Charles would often find and collect empty soda bottles and put them in a sack until the sack was full. Then he'd send young Jake to Silver Front Grocery on the corner where he'd sell the bottles for two cents each. Jake always returned home with a Party Pack Cola and two 15 cent Tampa Nugget cigars for his dad.

As an adult, Godbold is often seen with an unlit cigar in his mouth, one of his favorite treats in life. "I wish my dad would have lived long enough that I could buy him a box of cigars," he says.

Jake was born to sell. That would be his ticket out of the housing project. He knew early on that he had to work to help his family. Selling empty soda bottles back to the store was the first of many jobs he had as a boy. "I was always an entrepreneur, a kid out on the streets doing anything I could to make a little money." Before he was old enough to have a paper route, Jake convinced other tenants in Brentwood to pay him $1 a week to take their garbage out to the end of the block for the garbage man to pick up. "There were some old people who couldn't do that, so before school I'd take out their garbage and bring the empty cans back in after school."

Living in Brentwood Projects "was a privilege," he said. "It was not a God-given right to live in the projects at that time. Everybody was fairly poor, but they were all good people. It was very strict and you had to follow the rules." Jake remembers a manager at Brentwood named Mrs. Thompson. "She was like a first sergeant. She had the right to go into your house anytime she wanted to. Once a month she inspected the whole house. No bugs, no roaches. If you didn't live by the rules you had to move out. You get in trouble or your kids get in trouble you have to leave."

One of the rules said tenants had to keep their yards mowed regularly. From what he earned taking out garbage cans, Godbold saved enough money to buy a lawn mower. "I had a line of customers to cut their yards. There was always something you could hustle and make a little money."

When Jake was nine he was given a wagon for Christmas. Across Brick Road from the Brentwood Projects was a well-populated black community. "So many of them had a field next to their house with sour weed growing in it. There would be a milk cow tied up with a rope." Jake learned there was a shortage of lawn fertilizer so he plastered some signs on his wagon, crossed Brick Road and loaded up the wagon with cow manure. Then he'd take his wagon full of manure over to another nearby neighborhood where the families had more money. "I'd sell it to the wives for their flowers and plants. I had more customers than I had cow manure."

While he was peddling cow manure, Jake also had a peanut business. He and his mother would buy peanuts at the Silver Front Grocery and take them home where she would boil them. Then, she and Jake would count out the peanuts on the kitchen table, put an equal amount in each bag, roll up the bags and place the bags of freshly boiled peanuts in a cigar box. Then he'd take bags out and sell them for ten cents a bag "all over the place."

After selling out, Jake would rush home with his money, full of the excitement that comes with being a successful entrepreneur. "I'd lay all of the money out on the table and count it out. Then I'd tell mother how much I had and what I wanted to do with the money."

That's when Irene Godbold taught her young son a lesson about economics that he never forgot. "She'd say, 'That's not your money.' And I'd say, 'Yes, it is. I sold those peanuts.'" Then, Irene got her pad and had Jake write out what she told him. "On one side I had to write 'overhead.' That's when she made me write down how much the bags cost, how much the peanuts cost, how much the salt cost. I wrote down all those numbers and then she helped me add them all up." That, his mother said, "is called overhead."

Then, she had Jake count the money. "Now," she said, "take your overhead and deduct it from your money. That is what you call profit," she said.

His mother, Jake says, "taught me you have to sell enough to make a profit. A lot of people never learned that, but I learned it at an early age on a kitchen table."

Jake's mother, he says, "was very tough. She was a disciplinarian who kept the family together. She was the one who paid the bills. She was the leader of the family." Godbold says his father only gave him a whipping once, "but my mother was the enforcer. She made things happen and she was very particular about things being done right. Everything had to be in order." Jake says Irene continued to inspect his ears for cleanliness until he was 15-years old.

"Mother took a little bit of money and made it go a long way. We never went hungry." The Godbolds ate a lot of vegetables and starches. There wasn't much meat, he recalls. "She knew how to cook lima beans, rice and tomatoes." On Friday nights the family ate hamburgers, and on Sunday they ate chicken.

Irene was always cautious that Jake not let being poor and living in a government funded housing project impact his outlook or zest for life. "My mother always said, 'You have to remember that you are as good as anybody else.' Nobody resented that we were all poor. I always learned not to put people down."

All of his life, Godbold has told of his upbringing in Brentwood with great pride and strong memories. "After I got elected, my mother didn't like it that I said I came out of a housing project. But, I always used that to tell other little guys they could do the same thing," he says.

"I've always had this great compassion for poor people because I've never forgotten those times and where I came from. There weren't a lot of agencies or safety nets out there at that time. It was people, your neighbors, who helped you."

When he was old enough, Jake got a paper route delivering the *Jacksonville Journal* on his bicycle each afternoon. By then he already had plenty of work experience. "A great part of my life was my paper route. I made a lot of money." His route included many prominent Jacksonville citizens; lawyers, doctors, the northside pharmacist, judges, a golf pro, and teachers. "I knew all those people."

When he told his dad he wanted a paper route, Charles admonished him, "If you take this route, you're going to deliver it, six days a week. I'm not going to deliver it. I don't ride a bicycle." He reminded Jake that a paper route came before baseball and other activities.

It was a lot of responsibility, but like most things, Jake attacked it with a passion. Every Saturday morning, he would go to each house on his route and collect for the week's newspapers. At 2:30 p.m. he would pay his *Journal* route manager for the papers, then collect papers for the afternoon delivery. Jake was making about $25 a week, as much as his dad.

Godbold has always been about relationship-building. It's as natural to him as breathing. His paper route gave him a great life's lesson about serving others well and making friends. "I saw them every Saturday morning. They appreciated the way I delivered their paper on the porch and always dry. They would give me lemonade and cookies when I came around on Saturday, and at Christmas I got cards and tips. I loved working with those people and they loved me."

The first automobile the Godbolds ever had was bought with the money Jake made on his paper route. It was a 1939 Plymouth. Jake wasn't old enough to have a driver's license. "My dad and I walked up to a car lot on Main Street." Charles was a good mechanic and Jake says, "He kept up that car real good."

As a 16-year old, Jake held down two jobs. He continued with a paper route, delivering the *Florida Times-Union* each morning. But, he came up with a scheme to deliver his papers in a car. He teamed with good friend Tommy McCrone whose route included Panama Park, while Jake's route was North Shore. The two knew each other's route and early every morning, one of them would drive while the other rode in the back seat and threw the papers out the window. "He knew my route and I knew his. It was a big route and we made more money."

When Jake was still in high school, Brentwood Theater opened and a friend of Jake's helped him get a job there as an usher, three or four nights a week. Later, he became a doorman, taking tickets from movie goers. Jake would work one night and his friend worked the next night. Jake was also responsible for closing the theater at the end of the evening. When the box office closed after the last movie of the night started playing and the manager left, "I let all of my friends in to see the movie. The manager inventoried the popcorn boxes, so I would get some boxes that people had thrown on the ground and then make popcorn for everybody."

Later, he was hired by Jacksonville Shipyards, a job that Jake did not enjoy. He took the job in large part because the Shipyards would let him pitch for the company's softball team. "I had a tough job, working underneath those ships. I was drilling holes and hot lead was falling all over me." One day after work, Godbold complained to his dad about how bad the job was. "The only thing he had to comfort me was, 'If you don't want to work, don't hire out. And if you're going to work, do the job and don't complain about it.'"

It wasn't all work and no play for young Jake Godbold at Brentwood Projects. While he was always working to help his family, he was also encircled by close friends who grew up in Brentwood. Jake was always ready for a good time. "Life was exciting. You're poor, but you didn't know. Nobody looked at the labels in your shirt to see where it came from. Everybody thought they were as good as everybody else."

His social life was centered around Brentwood Park, which was across the street, only 50 yards away. It was both beautiful and active. Flowers were in abundance. There were tennis courts, basketball courts and a field where you could play baseball. The best part: the park was open at night. "In the summer we played out there until 10 o'clock."

Brentwood Park was where Jake first rubbed up against the raw Southern racism of the 1940s. Even though he grew up in an all-white housing project and attended all-white schools, Jake lived across the street from blacks and the northside of town was where most of Jacksonville's black population lived. "We've always lived near the minorities and we always got along good. My father worked with a lot of black people who respected him." Then, one hot summer day, a group of young blacks came over to Brentwood Park to see if Jake and his buddies wanted to play a game of baseball. "We started to play and the park director came over and told us we couldn't do that. The black guys walked off disappointed and we walked off disappointed."

One afternoon, when 8-year old Jake was walking home he saw a cab parked by the curb waiting to pick up someone. Two young black boys came walking by, carrying baskets of peaches to sell. The white cab driver got out of his cab, stopped the boys and told them he would give them a dollar to fight each other. "Those two little boys put down their peaches and started beating the hell out of each other. They were bloody. When they finished, the man gave them a dollar and they picked up their peach baskets and walked away. I was terrified. I had just witnessed evil racism at its worst."

The centerpiece of Brentwood Park was its bandstand with classic Doric columns where the kids skated and watched free movies on Friday and Saturday nights. It was also where the annual May Day Parade was held. "One year I was King in the May Day Parade and my mother had to go to a thrift store and get a little black jacket that she had to work on so I could wear it. It was the first time I had a sports coat. Mother put it on me and told me how good it looked, and she said not to let anybody say anything about that jacket."

Jake says he didn't understand then what his mother meant. "But, I do now. She just didn't want me to have a complex about where I came from."

As a kid, Jake joined St. Marks Methodist Church in his neighborhood, where he is still a member today. "I had to be baptized so I could pitch baseball for them." One night, after pitching an inning he returned to the bench. There was another Brentwood kid sitting on the end of the bench who wasn't on the team. It was Arnold Tritt. "He came over and started rubbing my arm and saying, 'You've got to keep that arm warm.'" The two became best friends for life.

Summers were also special for Jake because it meant a chance to spend a week at Y.M.C.A. Camp Immokalee in nearby Keystone Heights, Florida. "It was one of the greatest things I looked forward to every year." The Y.M.C.A. had nine Boys Clubs scattered around Jacksonville. One of the clubs was behind the Brentwood Projects office. Each month, the club took a field trip. "You would pack a lunch and go all day. You would get to swim, hike in the woods, and do things that boys like to do." Jake was very engaged in all of the club's activities and he participated in meetings because it meant racking up important points that would qualify him in the summer to be one of just 30 boys selected from the nine clubs to spend a week each summer at Camp Immokalee.

"I loved that atmosphere. They had a big lake and we could swim and the chapel was next to the lake. That's where I learned to swim." It's also where each summer he met boys 13, 14 and 15-years old from all over Jacksonville. The camp director was an older boy named Lou Ritter, who would later become the last mayor of Jacksonville's old city government.

As a junior and senior high school student, Jake was not the best, but he loved school. "I wasn't on the honor roll. I did what I had to do to get by and that was all. I was sleepy because I worked so much." But, he says, "I was a good person and all my teachers loved me and helped me."

Once again in his life, school was about building relationships. "I loved the action. I loved being there, the girls, the guys and the excitement."

Mike Houser was the Dean of Boys at Andrew Jackson High School. "He was a big part of my life. He kept you straight. He'd beat your ass, but we always loved him. Everybody respected him." Irene Godbold had meetings with Houser, says Jake, and she would always tell him, "Don't send Jake home. You work him or you spank him, but don't send him home."

Over his life, Jake has been part of many organizations, and more often than not, he has played leadership roles. "I've never been a joiner, but I've always been civic minded." Jackson High School had fraternities and sororities. Jake joined and became president of one of the strongest fraternities, Sigma Omega Tau. "We had our parties and our fund raisers and our week at the beach." Before Jackson would schedule a school dance, Jake says the school would check with Sigma Omega Tau to make sure the fraternity was not having a dance at the same time.

"It was a good place to be with good people. You couldn't be in there if you weren't a good person because they'd vote you out."

Chapter 4

———∽∽———

"THE SADDEST DAY OF MY LIFE"

AFTER JAKE GRADUATED from Andrew Jackson High School in 1953, the U.S. Army wanted him for the Korean War. He attempted to join the Navy and then the Marines, but he was rejected by both because of an inner ear issue.

Godbold enlisted in the Army with a friend and the two of them left Jacksonville on a bus bound for Fort Jackson in Columbia, South Carolina. "Our parents were at the bus station. My mother didn't cry at all, but my daddy cried. The only advice he gave me was, 'Jake, you act like a man and they'll treat you like a man.'"

After basic training at Fort Jackson, Jake was shipped to Fort Rucker near Dothan in south Alabama where he was placed in Supply. He was 18-years old. After Supply School, the Army let Jake come home to Jacksonville for Christmas where he was joyfully united with some of his closest buddies. After Christmas, he was to be shipped from Seattle to Korea. His pals were in the Navy and were returning to California, so Jake hitched a ride.

From California, he caught a bus to Seattle, then shipped to Japan. From Japan Jake was put on a torpedo boat to Korea. That was followed by a train ride to Kimpo Air Base in South Korea where he remained for 15 months.

It was a miserable but life-toughening experience. "We didn't have any food and no electricity, only a generator. The only time we had meat was on Friday or Saturday night. There was snow and ice. I missed electric lights. You had to light a lamp and there was an old pot belly stove. The thing I missed most was a phone, just to hear a girl's voice."

While Jake was serving in the Army in Korea, he sent all of the money the Army paid him to his father. His dad bought a 1956 Ford to replace the 1939 Plymouth Jake had purchased for his dad using his paper route earnings.

Jake's dad, Charles Godbold, had a weak heart which eventually claimed his life at age 49. "I remember when he had his first heart attack and one of the black guys who worked for him came to visit. I was just a young fellow. He said, 'Mr. Charlie, you've got to get better. You've got to take it easy.'" His dad replied, "Yea, but I've got to get back to work."

"But, Mr. Charlie, that work's going to be there when we're gone."

"Yea, that's right," Charles said. "But, when I die I want my part of it to be finished."

After he returned home from Korea, 21-year old Godbold continued to live at home for a while. His mother had a night job. One evening, his sister Fay called out to him. "She said, 'Something is wrong with daddy.' I ran up to his room. He had the nitroglycerin beside him on the table." Jake tried to get the glycerin on to his father's tongue, but his teeth were tight. "He died in my arms. That was probably the saddest day in my life because my daddy meant a lot to me."

Charles Godbold had lived the life of a good man. Raised in nearby Lake City, Florida, and high school educated, he started a family in the middle of the Great Depression, went blind for three years when Jake was only six-years old, and he worked hard. Years after his death, Jake would recall, "I love him more today than when I was a kid because I know all of the things he stood for. What compassion I have comes from him. He had a helluva work ethic."

When Charles' eye sight returned three years after he lost it, Jake's dad joined the Main Street Baptist Church and attended Sunday School and church every Sunday. Jake recalls one Sunday in particular. "There was a luncheon for his Bible class at the teacher's house. He told me how this man had these T- bone steaks and this grill and he cooked the steaks on the grill." That was brand new to Charles. "He didn't know anything about that. The only time he had a steak it was cheap and tough. He was excited about how good that steak was. He was a grown man with four kids and had never had a grilled steak."

Jake didn't handle the day of his dad's funeral very well. "It was the saddest day of my life. That Men's Sunday School class was a very important part of his life. I really got mad about all of those people coming to the house and I got mad at my mom for letting them come. You have to remember that my daddy died in my arms. I fell apart and there was nothing I could do."

Chapter 5

FUELED BY INDEPENDENT
LIFE AND THE JAYCEES

IN EVERYONE'S LIFE you can probably find, at most, maybe half a dozen major events that altered or set its direction. Several stops on Jake Godbold's life's journey set the course his own life would take. None are more important than his first meaningful job out of the Army with Independent Life Insurance Company, and his membership in the Jacksonville Jaycees, an organization of young men civic minded and politically motivated. Independent Life and the Jaycees were connected in powerful ways.

When Jake got back to Jacksonville from military service, he started asking himself what he was going to do with the rest of his life. From the time he was a child everyone close to him had said he would be a salesman. "They said, 'You've got the personality, people like you, and you are an extrovert. Don't bother going to college because you can make a lot of money as a salesman.'"

For a brief time, he ignored the advice he was receiving and enrolled in Jacksonville University. But then he remembered he really wasn't a great student, and "I knew I had to make a living." He heard that Fred Brooks Cigar Company was hiring people to work in the warehouse and also call on small stores selling smokes and candy. It wasn't exactly Jake's thing, but he took the job.

One of his Brentwood childhood friends, David Balanky, had been hired to sell insurance for Life of Virginia and he convinced Jake to file an application with that company. Jake did. He studied for his license and he started selling Life of Virginia insurance. In the first two weeks he made $70 plus his commissions. "I learned a lot and began to grow up."

His manager and mentor at Life of Virginia was a veteran salesman, Mr. Hughes, who Jake says really taught him the insurance business and about how to enjoy a different quality of life. "I began to learn about things I'd never had. I never had a boat and they were into boats and the river and picnicking and water skiing." Mr. Hughes "picked me up like a son," Godbold said.

Also during this period he met Jean Jenkins, the young lady who would become his wife and lifetime partner. Some mutual friends arranged for the two to get together and they began dating. After Jake and Jean had been seeing each other for over a year, Mr. Hughes intervened. "On Fridays we got our commission sheets and one Friday Mr. Hughes and I were taking a walk and we went by Kay's Jewelers. "See those engagement rings in there?" Mr. Hughes said to Jake. "You're a fool if you don't go in there right now and buy that Jean one of those rings. If you don't, you're going to mess around and she's going to marry somebody else."

But Jake was not ready to get married. "I just got back from Korea," he said. And, after all, he was just getting a little taste of what life was like: water skiing, boating and taking trips to places like Silver Springs. "I was living like an individual."

But Hughes was not budging. "I'll be damned if he didn't talk me into buying the damn ring."

While Jake was making a living at Life of Virginia, he was reminded by his friends that the company's headquarters were not in Jacksonville, while two other major life insurance companies, Gulf Life and Independent Life, had buildings that dominated the downtown skyline. "Some of my friends said if you're making money at Life of Virginia you should go to work for Gulf or Independent because they are hometown companies." So, Jake put in an application at Gulf Life. "But, they wouldn't hire me because I was single." His close friend Bill Mouro urged him to try Independent Life, where he worked. He applied. Jake said he was engaged to be married and he was hired.

"That was a different life," Godbold says. He started working for Independent when he was 22-years old. For two years, he was successful working a debit (collecting cash payments weekly) in Woodstock Park where he mostly called on white middle-class families.

Dickie Burnett was about four years younger than Jake. He got to know Jake when the future mayor delivered the Burnett's newspaper. About the time Jake went to work at Independent Life, Burnett got a job with Life of Georgia. "We both had a Woodstock Park debit," Burnett says. "The first year I was top salesman in my office, but I couldn't touch Jake Godbold out there. He was a selling son-of-a-bitch."

Within two years, Independent Life promoted Godbold to superintendent with six people working under him. One person who eventually joined his team was J.F. Bryan IV, son of the company president, J.F. Bryan III. Jacob Bryan III was a business and civic giant in Jacksonville.

He was a humble man who believed when you are an important person, you don't have to tell people you are important, Godbold said.

Mr. Bryan took a strong interest in all his employees, especially the young men who worked for the company. He urged them to get involved in Jacksonville civic and political issues, and he especially pushed them to join the Jacksonville Jaycees, where Independent would pay their dues.

After three weeks working under Godbold, J.F. Bryan IV said Jake told him, "Come on J.F., we're going to a Big Brothers meeting. I'm the incoming president and I want you to go with me."

"So, I got out to Lem Turner Boulevard where they're meeting. It was a group of old men, some of the original founders," J.F. IV said. "Other than me, Jake was the youngest there. Three weeks later I get a letter from Big Brothers and I'm on the letterhead as a board member." J.F. IV went to see Jake. "How the hell did that happen?" he asked. "Son, your daddy is always telling us to be involved in the community and you might as well get started." Three years later, J.F. IV was president of Big Brothers and then he served on the organization's national board for 14 years.

Bill Mouro, who had convinced Jake to apply at Independent Life, was a Jaycee and he began urging Godbold to join. Jake also knew that Mr. Bryan wanted him to sign up. "I kept telling Bill I was just interested in feeding my family and doing a good job at Independent. I didn't know if I could do both." Then, Mr. Bryan interceded, explaining to Jake that he could, indeed, "do both. I want you to go in there."

In the 1950s and into the 1970s, the Jacksonville Jaycees was probably the town's top organization producing young civic leaders as well as a major political machine. The members who served alongside Godbold became a Who's-Who of Jacksonville politics. Former State Attorney and Mayor Ed Austin and Mayor Godbold. Florida Senate President Lew Brantley. City Council members John Lanahan, Walter Williams, Johnny Sanders, Charley Webb, Bill Basford, Don Davis, Henry Cook and Lynwood Roberts. Public Defender Lou Frost. Judges like Charlie Mitchell and John Southwood. At its zenith, Jaycee membership probably numbered around 1,000.

"We did a lot of great things," says Godbold, "probably 100 projects a year." The projects ran from the Soap Box Derby to Toys for Tots with the Marine Corps. The club conducted the Miss Jacksonville Pageant and it sponsored a Christmas shopping tour for kids living in the Baptist Home for Children, where Mouro had grown up. "I remember the kids always wanted to buy something for their mothers, despite them living in the Baptist Home because their mothers couldn't or wouldn't care for them."

The largest project the Jaycees managed was in partnership with the Duval County Medical Society. The Jonas Salk vaccine for polio had been developed and the president of the Medical Society approached Godbold and Jaycee President Henry Cook to enlist help from the Jaycees. "They needed a large group of young people who would get out in the community and do the leg work to make this happen," said Godbold. The plan was to get the vaccine to every child in Duval County during one weekend. All of the schools in the county were opened on a Saturday and Sunday. The Jaycees put Salk vaccine on tens of thousands of sugar cubes." The children flowed into the schools over the two days and the Jaycees made sure each child was vaccinated. "We did it and we did a heckuva job."

The Jaycees also placed collection boxes at each vaccine location so that people who wanted to do so could donate money. "Thousands of dollars were donated and that money did some good things for the community."

The Jaycees also became a driving force in getting Duval County's public schools reaccredited.

"The whole thing about the Jaycees was to teach good ethics, how to get things done, and leadership. We learned to take a project from the bottom to the top and make it work. When it was done, you knew you'd done your best."

Jake's life followed a pattern. Just as he had in other circumstances, he was encouraged to take leadership positions in the Jaycees. He was elected second vice president, which meant that he would probably advance to first vice president and then to president of the organization. As always, Jake was well-liked and very respected by his peers. Unfortunately, first vice president Tony Bates was not too popular, so a group of Jaycee leaders urged Jake "to jump over Tony and run for president."

A grass roots political campaign sprang up and longtime friend Arnold Tritt was his campaign manager. "Tritt got the name of every member of the Jaycees and where they worked. Then, he called their bosses and asked them to give me five minutes to talk to each employee while they were working." Tritt and Godbold then went from business to business, to City Hall and the County Courthouse, wherever there was a Jaycee working. "We were campaigning."

Jaycee Lou Frost, who would later be elected Public Defender (a post he held for 36 years), wrote Jake's campaign speeches.

On the night of the big vote, around 1,000 Jaycees showed up in the auditorium of the Seminole Hotel in downtown. "There were signs everywhere. It was like a real political convention." Each candidate was to give a ten-minute speech. Godbold was nervous. He was backstage thinking about his speech and drinking a bottle of Coca-Cola. Jake was holding the soda bottle so tight that it burst in his hand. His hand was bleeding. Frost wrapped a towel around his hand, and then Frost said, "These are your people. They belong to you. They favor you. You just go out there and tell them what you want to do, the kind of person you are and how you love the Jaycees. You just talk to them like you talk to me now. You're never short on words. This is a big audience but cut the audience out and figure you're one on one and you're talking to your best friends."

All of a sudden, Jake recalls, the fear inside of him went away. "That was a big step. Lou thought it was a little thing, but it was a big thing to a young man. I went out there and did a terrific job and I was elected."

Chapter 6

—◆◆◆—

SERVING ON THE OLD,
RUNNING FOR THE NEW

JACKSONVILLE'S CITY AND county governments were in turmoil and disruption in the early 1960s. Corruption was rife and incompetence was the norm. Mr. Bryan wanted Jake to campaign for the nine- member Jacksonville City Council. "He thought it was a good idea because I had just been president of the Jaycees and we had a lot of young supporters." He challenged Council incumbent Elbert Hendricks, a pressman at the newspaper. "He wasn't a bad guy and was not mixed up in any of the trouble, but he had been there when a lot of stuff went on," said Godbold.

Godbold and Hendricks ran citywide to serve Ward 1, a northside district that included Panama Park and North Shore. On June 20, 1967 Jake won, along with fellow Jaycee Johnny Sanders and African American community leaders Mary Singleton and Sallye Mathis.

It was the last council of the old government, which voters replaced with Consolidation one year after Jake was sworn in. "We had to then make up our minds if we were going to run for one of the new consolidated seats." Campaigning and being a member of the council had already drained Jake of his $2,500 in savings and any vacation time he had at Independent. Plus, he had six people working for him. His supervisor, Mr. Motley, was against Jake running again. He told Godbold he didn't want him to spend any more time away from the people he was supposed to manage.

One day, Mr. Bryan called Jake into his office to talk about whether or not he was going to run for the consolidated council. Mr. Bryan called Godbold "Jacob," which was also Mr. Bryan's first name. "Jacob," he said, "I understand you aren't going to run again." Jake explained that he had just run and won and had spent his savings and had no vacation time remaining. "On top of that, Mr. Motley doesn't want me to run again. My number one priority is to make a living for my family, and I've got a responsibility over here for six people working for me," said Jake.

Mr. Bryan was unconvinced. "Yes. But you have a responsibility to the community and you have a responsibility to me. I run the company. Motley doesn't run the company. I want you to run and I want you to run at-large. You're appreciated all over the community, not just in that northside district," he said.

Then, Mr. Bryan picked up his phone and called Mr. Motley. He put Motley on the speaker. "Mr. Motley, I'm here with Jacob and he tells me he doesn't think you want him to run again for the council, but I feel like he should be part of this new council and he should run. I'm going to get together with Mr. Carroll (the company's director of managers) when we finish here and I'm going to get Mr. Carroll back with you to work something out so he can take time-off and he can run. Do you understand?" Motley replied that he understood.

But, Jake was still concerned. "I told Mr. Bryan that Motley is a vindictive guy. I can't go back over there and work for him. He'll make it real hard on me." Once again, Mr. Bryan wasn't moved. "Son, you don't worry about that. I'll take care of that." Mr. Bryan told Carroll that he wanted something worked out where Godbold could take as much time as he needed to campaign for the new 19-member City Council as well as serve after he is elected. Jake became a floating superintendent. "I didn't work for anybody. If I had some time I came in and worked, and if I didn't, it was alright."

In that 1967 campaign, Godbold had two strong opponents for one of the five at-large seats. Carl Ogden, the Democrat, would later be elected to the Florida Legislature and become House majority leader. Tiger Holmes was a well-known and wealthy lumber baron who was a political force in the Republican party. Godbold defeated Ogden in the Democratic primary and then turned away Holmes in the general election.

Jake won the election for several reasons. He is a political workhorse who not only does his job as a candidate, he makes sure everyone else is doing theirs. Even from the earliest days of his political life, he always maintained the best and the largest campaign organization that was the result of friendships he made as a young kid living in the Brentwood Projects, his days as a student at Andrew Jackson High School, and his deep involvement with the Jacksonville Jaycees. When it came time to campaign, he had an enthusiastic army of volunteers. "We didn't have the most money but we always had the most people and the best organization."

There was also the force of his personality which drew people to him, and his ability to communicate with people in all levels of life. He knew how to capture the hearts and minds of voters.

In that first election to the new council—and all future Godbold campaigns—there was also another factor. It grew out of his long-time relationship and identity with the black community. Because Jake spent his youth in Brentwood and his days as a young man selling insurance for Independent Life in Jacksonville's northside middle-income white and black communities, people there knew and trusted him.

In those days, white candidates seldom—if ever—personally campaigned in black neighborhoods. Instead, they paid significant money to at least one so-called black political leader to get their names out in the community. Frank Hampton, Josh Hilman, Otis Speights and Ed Holt were the biggest black operators.

"They had a set up out there where everybody thought you had to buy into this black machine." Each leader had an election ticket and if you wanted to get on it, you paid a hefty price. The higher the office, the more you paid. "I couldn't get on those tickets because I didn't have the money," said Godbold. "We had to figure out a way to get around that."

Godbold also knew that it was mostly a scam. "All they were doing was taking money from a candidate, maybe opening a store front and putting some signs in it, and then the day before the election they hired some kids to put their tickets in mail boxes."

Labor lawyer Al Millar, who was in the Jaycees with Jake, created his own ticket called "Nine Steps to Heaven." It was also called the Kennedy ticket because pictures of John and Bobby Kennedy were on it. It was a post card. The names of the candidates being endorsed, including Jake, were listed on each of the nine steps. "Al took those postcards to Washington D.C. and then he mailed them back to black voters in Jacksonville."

Godbold also bypassed the old system. He and his organization campaigned in black neighborhoods the same way they campaigned in white neighborhoods. They went door to door, visited the churches, put volunteers on street corners to wave at motorists, and drove people to the polls on election day.

All those tactics served Jake well in that first campaign for an at-large seat on the new consolidated City Council, and they continued to serve him well in every election afterwards.

"After the election we're at a big victory celebration at the Northside Women's Club on Pearl Street," remembers J.F. Bryan IV. "Jake didn't drink, but he had about five Cokes and he was supercharged." When he spoke to the gathered crowd, Godbold was pumped up from his victory. "One day," he roared, "I'm going to run for mayor." Bryan recalls saying, "Come on Jake, get over it. You just got elected to the council."

His friends from the old council, Sanders, Singleton and Mathis were also elected to the new council, as was fellow Jaycee Bill Basford, who was chair of the Duval County Commission.

The new City Council was sworn in on March 1, 1968 and became official when Consolidation took place on October 1. That meant that for seven months, both the old City Council and the new City Council were holding meetings until the old council disappeared and Consolidation took over. Godbold was attending meetings for both legislative bodies. "It wasn't easy on me. I would tell one of the people at Independent I'd be out to work with him that night and I'd never show up because those meetings would go on and on. That went on for a year."

Being absent from Independent Life was beginning to eat at him. "I couldn't keep my promises and do my duty at Independent." He went to see Mr. Bryan and told him, "I don't feel good about it." Mr. Bryan said he would take care of it. Jake continued to spend most of his time working with the two councils and going to Independent whenever he had some time. Independent was mailing him his pay checks.

The arrangement of working for Independent and serving on the council continued for two years, but it ate at Jake's insides. Finally, after 16 years with the company, and after much prayer, he left Independent Life to work for Misco Products Company, a janitorial chemical maker out of Chicago. "I had the experience of being a good salesman and knowing everybody. Misco sent me a big book and told me to read it. And, they sent three or four boxes of chemicals so I just started selling chemicals."

Chapter 7

———— ⚬⚬⚬ ————

CONSOLIDATION AND
COALITION BUILDING

THE FIRST CONSOLIDATED council in 1968 was impressive. It included two Republicans, seventeen Democrats, four African Americans and two women. All had supported Consolidation in the referendum.

After he won a special election to replace resigning councilman Bill Basford, Lynwood Roberts became a member of the council coalition that included Godbold, Johnny Sanders, Mary Singleton and Sallye Mathis. "We were a minority, but not because we wanted to be a minority. We generally saw things the same way," said Godbold. Often, Jake's coalition was joined by Walter Williams, a fellow Jaycee alum, and Earl Johnson, an African American attorney. Williams and Johnson both were elected at-large. "If it had remained city and county governments, Earl probably would have been mayor of the city," said Godbold. Even so, he served on the government study commission, campaigned for Consolidation, and helped write its charter.

Other members of the council were what Jake called, "the silk-stocking group." It included John Lanahan, I.M. Sulzbacher, Wallace Covington, Earl Huntley, Don McLean, and Ted Grissett. "I had great respect for most all of those guys," said Godbold. "One of the most respected was Sulzbacher. He was very bright and he was very organized. He worked hard and he always had his details done." Sulzbacher, however, was one of the council members who underestimated Godbold and Roberts, often to his regret. "He was always cordial but he was the kind of guy who put himself a little above other people."

The "silk-stocking" crowd represented a different group of people from those Godbold often fought for. "I represented middle class and poor people. At that time, they didn't think I was as oriented to the business community as I should have been."

In his heart, Godbold was a little resentful. "But, it was fun battling those people because they looked down at us. We didn't take orders very well and we didn't follow the line. They wanted to set the course for the new government and they thought we should do it their way."

The council wild card was insurance agent Joe Carlucci, who could always be counted on to vote "no," no matter the issue. Carlucci, elected at-large, was a popular maverick who seldom was on the winning side of issues. It was a position he relished.

One of the councilmembers Godbold crossed swords with was John Lanahan, a former Marine and tough Irish-Catholic who had played center on the Notre Dame football team. Lanahan was among those who wanted to run the council his own way. "I had the best of times and the worst of times with Lanahan. He was a strong person. He was a leader," said Godbold.

When Godbold first ran for council president in 1971, Lanahan tried to defeat him. "He did everything he could to beat me. Once it was over, John was the type of guy who would always back the chair, no matter who was in the chair. If anybody challenged me, he stood with me." After Godbold was elected president, Lanahan told him, "As long as you have that gavel you run the meeting. If somebody is out of order you rule them out of order. If they object I'm going to be with you and try to get others to back you."

On the night of his swearing in as council president, Godbold admonished his fellow members in a classic Godbold way with remarks that became the stuff of lore. "We are going to have to buckle down and put our shoulders to the wheel and our noses to the grind stone and bite the bullet."

At the end of that one year as president, over 1,000 people, including three former Florida Governors, attended a testimonial for Godbold at the Robert Meyer Hotel. Former Gov. Fuller Warren said of Godbold, "He is a bright young man who has come a long way, does a lot of good, and still has a bright future ahead of him."

Times-Union reporter Bill Foley wrote, "After that night it was a fore-gone conclusion that Godbold would run for mayor."

Godbold and Lanahan often butted heads.

As council president, Lanahan made Godbold chair of the zoning committee. "He put a bill into my committee to hold a public hearing." American Bank on Beach Boulevard, just up from the police union headquarters, wanted to put in a new driveway so its customers could enter a different way, putting traffic into an adjacent neighborhood. Godbold instructed the city's director of public works, Jim English, to do a traffic study to determine how many automobiles would be going into that neighborhood when coming to the bank. Then he called a public hearing. When time for the hearing arrived, English didn't have the traffic count. "I got upset about it and called the meeting off. I reset the hearing in two weeks and said I wanted the traffic count numbers."

Jake with former governors Fuller Warren, Haydon Burns and Farris Bryant.

When Godbold left City Hall, Lanahan met him in the parking lot. "He said he wanted me to call the hearing off. I said, 'John, I can't do that. We're already set up.'" Lanahan responded by telling Godbold he was chair of the committee and he can do whatever he wants to do. "You call that meeting off. I don't want to have it."

"Well, you shouldn't have put it in my committee," said Godbold. "I've advertised it, and I'm involved. These people need to have a hearing."

"No," said Lanahan. "You're going to do what I tell you to do. You're going to pull that thing and cancel the meeting."

"No, I'm not going to do that," Godbold responded. "As council president you have a right to cancel it. I'm not going to do that. I set up the meeting and I'm going to have the meeting as long as I'm chairman."

Lanahan said, "Well, tomorrow you won't be chairman." The next day Lanahan put out a notice that he had removed Godbold as committee chair and jerked him from three other committees. When the media asked Godbold about it, he said, "The president gives and the president takes away."

With no committee assignments, "I had plenty of time to look at everything. It put me in a position to be against everything he wanted to do. I spent the rest of the year doing nothing but staying on his ass," said Godbold.

Lanahan was known as a fun loving Irish boozer. Often, late in the afternoon, he would have some of his council friends gather in the council president's office for cocktails and closed-door meetings. The press was all up in arms. Sensing it was a political opportunity, council secretary David McNamara suggested to Godbold that he have his office door removed. Godbold called City Hall's building maintenance office and McNamara called the press. The following day *The Florida Times-Union* ran a photograph of Godbold and the city workers taking his office door off its hinges as he announced his open-door policy and invited the media, the public and other councilmembers to visit him.

Lahanan fumed.

The next election, Jake was returned to the council without opposition.

With city employee assistance, Jake removes door to his council office.

JAKE!

Chapter 8

TIMING IS EVERYTHING

GODBOLD'S FINAL TERM on the City Council became a political chess match as his close friend Lynwood Roberts actively sought to position himself to take advantage of the expected resignation of Mayor Hans Tanzler, who was planning to run for Florida Governor in 1978.

Tanzler kept his plans tightly held. While Roberts and Godbold expected Tanzler to resign, no one knew when it would happen, especially members of the City Council. When it did happen, whoever was sitting in the council president's chair at the time would automatically become mayor for the remainder of Tanzler's term, getting a leg up in a 1979 campaign to be elected to a full four-year term.

"Lynwood and a few of his friends were trying hard to get Hans to commit when he would resign so that Lynwood could be in the right place at the right time," said Godbold. "I had no idea and really didn't care and I was willing to just let Lynwood play that hand out. I tried to help Lynwood make sure he had his target right."

Roberts, who was retired from Southern Bell and had been a member of the Duval County Budget Commission, joined the City Council almost by accident. When the council started to organize itself to begin operations in 1968, Roberts was not a member. Bill Basford, a Jacksonville attorney who had been member of the Florida Legislature and the old County Commission, was elected to one of the five at- large seats. Basford, always politically ambitious, wanted to be the new council's first president. He was challenged by another lawyer, Ted Grissett, Jr. Grissett won and Basford resigned from the council shortly afterwards.

In a special election, Roberts ran for and won the at-large seat that had been held by Basford. Insurance executive Tommy Gay was his opponent. Godbold took a month's vacation and campaigned hard for Roberts, especially in the black community. The two were friends.

(Basford would return to the City Council as an elected member when Godbold was mayor. Eventually, he was elected council president.)

Following the 1975 elections, Councilman Charlie Webb—who was a close friend of both Roberts and Godbold—started engineering a strategy so that his two friends would serve a term as council president during the next four years. Webb called on Godbold.

"He wanted to know if I wanted to be president during the last four years. I told him all I wanted to do is serve these last four years and call it quits." But Webb insisted that Godbold take the helm one more time. "He said that it looked like Earl (Johnson) had the votes to be president in the first year. Everybody thought he deserved that." Roberts was then slotted for the second year and Godbold was inserted into the third year. Roberts and his friends had been hard at work to figure out when Tanzler would resign. They thought it would be earlier rather than later, probably during the term of the council president in the second year.

But, when Johnson had a publicly embarrassing misstep that prompted the council to remove him as president, Roberts, the vice president, was moved up to serve the time remaining in Johnson's term. John Lanahan wanted to serve another term as council president and he was actively opposed to Roberts serving the second year right after filling Johnson's slot. "Lynwood came to me. He knew I had the written and verbal votes to be president in the third year," said Godbold. Roberts said, "It looks like I've got half a term here so I'd like to be president again."

"I told Lynwood that it didn't make any difference to me. I said I wasn't going to help him run for president two years in a row. If he wanted to do it for the third year, I said I would release all my votes and he could go talk to them." Godbold decided to take the fourth year as council president to appease Roberts.

"Lynwood missed out on his time table," said Godbold. Tanzler announced his run for Florida governor in 1978. However, he delayed resigning as mayor until January 2, 1979, the very last minute required by Florida law. That meant that Godbold was elevated to mayor for the first six months of 1979 after he opened the way for his friend Roberts to capture the presidency in year three and make Godbold president the fourth year.

While he did not get to be mayor, Roberts served as council president an unprecedented three times. In 1979, the year Godbold was elected mayor, Roberts became Duval County Tax Collector, an office he held without opposition for 20 years.

Chapter 9

Political Connection
to Stop the Stink

Six weeks after Godbold was sworn in as interim mayor, the U.S. Marshal served notice on Jacksonville that it was being sued by the Environmental Protection Agency (EPA) over the long-plagued Buckman Street Sewage Plant. The city had to show cause why the plant shouldn't be closed. "We all went crazy with that," said Godbold. Shutting down the plant would derail Godbold's drive to bring new industry and jobs to Jacksonville.

The sewage plant, which was built in 1958 and expanded by the new consolidated government in 1968, never really worked properly. Over the years, Buckman's issues were a continuous story in the media as water and sand pushed through two hundred miles of decaying sewer lines, forcing the plant's pumps to falter and sewage to overflow.

The plant discharged waste into the St. Johns River, and the odor for neighbors was unbearable. "We've got to where we can't take walks. It saturates our noses," one neighbor told *The Florida Times-Union*. "We live like hermits," said another.

The Rev. Ken Owens lived two blocks from the plant, and his church, East 11th Street Baptist, was also in the neighborhood. "Someday I'll get up in the morning and I'll open up the door and take a breath and it just ruins the whole day," he said. "It permeates the inside of your house. Friends, when they come over to visit, the first thing they say is, 'How can you stand living here?'"

Sverdrup & Parcel (S&P), a St. Louis engineering firm, had partnered with Jacksonville firm Flood & Associates to project manage the plant and solve its issues. Godbold was fed up and called the head of S&P. "I'm tired of every night on the 6 o'clock news showing raw waste running into the river and every day at dinner people have to watch this. You're going to have straighten this out or you are never going to do any business with the city as long as I'm here," Godbold said.

In the meantime, Godbold had to find a way to stop the feds from shutting down the plant and bringing commercial construction to a halt. Plus, the city was facing a fine of $10,000 a day. On February 21, 1979 Godbold and his team met with Atlanta EPA chief John White for two hours. After the meeting, White said he wanted Jacksonville to plead guilty, agree to a compliance schedule to correct the problems and accept a token fine. Godbold was not happy about the guilty plea, but he didn't have any room to argue further. White insisted on the guilty plea and said he was not interested in exacting heavy fines from Jacksonville. He recommended a $50,000 penalty.

White sent his recommendation to the Presidentially appointed EPA Penalty Board in Washington, which rejected the recommendation and proposed heavy $300,000 fine on the city. It was very rare that the Penalty Board didn't accept an EPA region's recommendation. "The guy in charge at the region (White) said we had every right to take the matter to our senators and congressmen," said Godbold. "That's what we did."

In the meantime, Godbold was hot under the collar with the two engineering firms, S&P and Flood & Associates, who had been consultants on Buckman for several years. He said he wanted to fire S&P. That prompted S&P to request a sit-down with the mayor in an effort to save its contract. Godbold accepted the meeting, then threatened to cancel it.

Bob West, the chairman of S&P, flew into Jacksonville and offered to furnish experts to manage operations at the plant for six months without any overhead. If Buckman was not operating properly within six months, then Godbold should terminate S&P's contract, West said. Godbold agreed to consider the proposal if West would put it in writing.

"The reason you were hired was to keep us out of trouble with that design and we have some serious problems. How did you let the city get into the position we are in, in overloading that plant?" the mayor asked. "If you want to stay on Jacksonville's payroll, then get your people out there…make a detailed study and tell us why it isn't operating well."

S&P vice president H.G. Schwartz told the *Times-Union*, "The mayor kind of hit us in the head with a two by four." A week later Godbold appointed a ten-member panel to determine if the city should hire a firm "with a national reputation" to operate Buckman and the city's District 2 sewer plant, which was also plagued with problems.

In mid-March, Godbold accepted S&P's proposal and a management team, headed by S&P's brightest young engineer, Alan Williams, started running Buckman. They reported that Buckman employees were working in offices surrounded by sand bags to keep out the water and sewage.

Jacksonville was represented in Washington by two congressmen, Rep. Charles Bennett and Rep. Bill Chappell of Ocala. Two weeks before the Democratic primary election, in mid-May, with engineers and lawyers in tow, Godbold first called on Chappell to seek some relief from the EPA Penalty Board's decision to fine the city heavily. Chappell took the team over to Bennett's office. "Bennett didn't feel good about us being there and I got upset with the way he handled things," said Godbold.

Chappell said, "Charlie, the Lord Mayor (which is what Chappell called Godbold), a young mayor, has just become mayor and finds this on his desk. We need to help him do something about it. I don't know how the Lord Mayor can handle this. This is a big problem, a major sewer plant that can close the whole city down."

Bennett responded that he didn't know much about the EPA. "If it was the Navy, I might be able to help," he said.

"I wanted to throw up," said Godbold.

Chappell said he knew EPA Administrator Douglas Costle and would call him. Bennett didn't like the idea. "I was really upset at him," said Godbold. At that point, Chappell went to Bennett's secretary and told her to get the EPA chief on the telephone. When he was on the line, Chappell put the administrator on the speaker phone. "Mr. Administrator, this is Congressman Chappell. I'm in Charlie Bennett's office."

"No, no, don't tell him you're in my office," Bennett told Chappell. "That really made me mad," said the mayor.

Chappell then told the administrator, "You got the Lord Mayor Jake Godbold and he just took office and you got this big problem. Are you familiar with this problem?" Costle replied that he was very familiar with it. "I think we ought to help the Lord Mayor," said Chappell. He doesn't know where in the world he's going to get the money to pay this kind of fine."

Then Chappell went to the bottom line with the EPA administrator. "You know I'm the subcommittee chairman on your budget. When he asks me where in the world he's going to get the money to pay these fines and I don't have any choice but to help the Lord Mayor. Then I've got to go into your budget for places to cut so I can send him money."

Costle interrupted Chappell. "Congressman, I know where you're going. Let me call you back and we'll get something done." Godbold and his team returned to Jacksonville. A few days later, the administrator phoned the mayor. "He said, 'Mayor, come back up here tomorrow with your people and talk to me about your plan. I have something I think you are going to like. It's called the 'Philadelphia Plan,'" Godbold recalled.

Godbold asked why it was called the "Philadelphia Plan?" "Because we just did it in Philadelphia and we're going to do it for you," Costle replied. Instead of fine money being stent to Washington, it stays in a trust fund and the money is used to work on solving local environmental problems.

After Godbold had been elected mayor, on July 24, he returned again to Washington to meet with EPA administrator Costle. This time it was to discuss programs the city would adopt in lieu of the $300,000 fine.

"With the stroke of a pen they worked all that out and we went back to no fines." In the end, Jacksonville transferred $2 million to an environment trust fund to be used for "environmentally beneficial activities above and beyond the requirement of the law."

S&P engineer Williams, who put his bed in the sewage plant and remained there until it was fixed, got Buckman working properly. Godbold then hired Williams away from S&P and put him in charge of Jacksonville's water and sewer division.

Chapter 10

THE LOVE BUG BIT ME

COUNCILMAN LYNWOOD ROBERTS had guessed that Mayor Tanzler would resign sometime during his tenure as president, between July 1, 1977 and June 30, 1978. When Tanzler announced officially that he would be a candidate in February 1978, he still didn't unveil when he would resign from office. By law, he had until January 1, 1979 to walk away. That was more than a month after the gubernatorial election in November 1978, meaning Tanzler could continue receiving his salary while a candidate for governor.

After Tanzler made his announcement, Godbold, who was slated to become council president on July 1, 1978, told the press, "It (when Tanzler resigns) won't make me run or not run. I'm just not that ambitious. It would be fine with me if he resigns before July and Lynwood takes over. I just don't think about it (running for mayor). It's like falling in love. The love bug hasn't bit me yet."

On July 6, 1978, Godbold was unanimously elected president of the council and the shift in power from the outgoing Mayor Tanzler to

Godbold began. He started receiving the messages and being invited to the meetings that would normally go to the mayor and his staff. By Halloween the shift was complete since everyone knew that on January 1, 1979 Godbold would be the new mayor.

Once he was ensconced in the mayor's office on the 14th floor of City Hall, his lack of ambition to run for the job in the spring vanished. The love bug bit him. Godbold immediately continued to hone his image of being accessible and his reputation for being "champion of the little man," the *Times-Union* wrote.

He was feeling comfortable in his new job and even told the newspaper, "There's no reason to run a P.R. (public relations) campaign for mayor. Most people know me. If you don't want me I will accept that."

The fact was that most people in Jacksonville did know him. Polls showed he had 90 percent name recognition.

As council president, Godbold continued his assault on the JEA's mismanagement and its decision to hire Atlanta engineering firm Ebasco Services to design and project manage the utility's plans to build two coal fired plants. Because of private information he had received from a competing local engineering firm, Reynolds, Smith & Hills, Godbold was convinced the $57.5 million Ebasco contract was overpriced. Godbold thought the JEA board was rushing to approve the deal with Ebasco. Always the consummate politician, he also knew that taking on the unpopular JEA with its astronomical electric rates was good politics.

Just after Labor Day, council president Godbold wrote a letter asking the JEA to delay a vote on the contract, "until such time as the council has passed a resolution supporting the JEA in this endeavor."

On September 9, 1978, 44-year old Godbold opened his campaign account for mayor at the Jacksonville National Bank and designated lawyer R. Lee Smith as the campaign's treasurer. Smith was a former law partner of Tommy Greene, who would be Godbold's chief fund raiser.

Greene, along with his brother Ray, was committed to support former Florida Senate president Lew Brantley. "We were attending Henry Kramer's funeral at the Jewish Center when McNamara (Dave) and Jake got me aside and told me he was going to run for mayor. I didn't know Jake was going to run. Lew was a good friend of mine," recalled Greene. "I had to leave a good friend of mine for a better friend of mine." Ray Greene continued to support Brantley.

On September 18, 1978, Godbold again called on the JEA to delay action on the Ebasco contract pending an investigation by the council's finance committee. "We have no motive whatsoever," he said, "in delaying this contract or killing this contract except that when we get ready to sign it, we want to know that we're doing the right thing, we're going in the right direction."

The JEA board voted to postpone any action on the contract until the council finished its investigation.

All of the back and forth between mayor to-be Godbold and the JEA was constantly in the press. At the same time, outraged customers of the city-owned utility were receiving outrageous electric bills each month. It was one of those times when good policy and good politics dove tailed.

The council finance committee hired Warren Gartman, a Houston engineering consultant, to examine the Ebasco contract.

One day in November 1978, Godbold called me to come to his council office. I was an aide to Tanzler and handling the transition between

Tanzler and Godbold. When I arrived, Godbold was on the speaker phone with Gartman. Also, in the office were City Council auditor Bob Johnson and assistant general counsel Gerald Schneider. As I walked through the door toward a chair, Godbold told Gartman to tell me what he had just shared with the others about the Ebasco contract.

"In my opinion it's $20 million too high," said Gartman. I dropped to my knees, looked up at council president Godbold and said, "Congratulations, 'mayor'."

Just after Thanksgiving, the finance committee said, "We recommend JEA start over again and seek new proposals from engineering firms."

Godbold then pushed the JEA to ignore its managing director William Irving and hire Gartman to negotiate a new contract.

At 10 a.m. on Tuesday, January 2, 1979, the day after Tanzler resigned as mayor, Godbold was sworn in to replace him. The ceremony was in the auditorium of Independent Life Insurance where Godbold had worked for 16 years, and where his political career was launched. "I have a lot of friends there," he said. Four hundred and fifty people attended the swearing-in.

In his twenty one-minute speech, the new mayor promised to "take a practical approach," and said he doesn't "believe government can be everything to everybody." He said he would have open government and strong cooperation with the City Council.

Godbold also took time to praise his predecessor and sometime adversary Tanzler for keeping Jacksonville free of financial problems. "Hans Tanzler has the one quality I admire most in a man and that's his character. I hope that you can say about Jake Godbold when he walks away from this office, he had character."

In closing, he said, "I promise enthusiasm, honesty, integrity and a great desire to help you find solutions to our problems."

Godbold didn't lose sight of the fact that while he was now mayor for six months, he was also a candidate for mayor looking at a spring election. A $25 a ticket reception followed the ceremony. It, too, was held in Independent Life, downstairs, where an estimated 2,700 people crowded in to celebrate the new mayor. Godbold friend Bill Mouro, who was in charge of the reception, said that over 10,000 pounds of ice were used, and party-goers consumed enough liquor to make 7,000 drinks along with $3,000 in food.

One of those who attended was Brantley, Godbold's chief opponent in the upcoming election. He was there to see who was supporting Godbold.

A week later, Godbold filed his first finance report as a candidate for mayor. It showed he had raised $49,412.

Godbold instinctively knew that if he performed well as mayor and continued his enthusiastic and aggressive style, a lot of the politics would take care of itself. He had to handle problems with urgency, but also manage to look at the long term, as if he were going to be there for another four years.

A month after he was sworn in, Hank Drane, the *Times-Union*'s veteran political editor, interviewed Godbold. He told Drane, "A lot of people see my life as part of the American dream. They realize if I can be mayor, then their sons or daughters can attain the same goal."

Looking toward the upcoming primary election on May 22, Drane wrote, "They (the business establishment and social elites) may admire his propensity for hard work and his reputation for honesty. But, they wonder what sort of impression he will make in the sophisticated environment of Washington, New York and other areas where key decisions are made on disbursement of tax funds, bonding and location of industry."

Godbold was the last of the candidates for mayor to qualify, four hours before the noon deadline on the final day, February 27. His qualifying fee was $2,000. The mayor was accompanied by over 150 supporters. Other Democratic candidates who qualified for mayor were Brantley, former Tanzler chief aide Lex Hester, C. Lee Daniels, Ray Reaves, Lee Robertson and Republican Don Brewer.

After qualifying, Godbold walked to a breakfast at Independent Life, where 450 supporters joined him. Breakfast was $5.

If there was any question that the race between Godbold and Brantley was going to be intense, it was probably erased when the Brantley campaign leased a billboard adjacent to and looking directly down at the Godbold campaign headquarters on Riverside Avenue, just across the street from the *Florida Times-Union*. Rather than upset the Godbold campaign staff and volunteers, the billboard was a daily reminder they were in a hard-fought campaign.

At the second finance reporting, Godbold had collected $81,661 and Brantley had raised $77,142.

One Sunday morning in late March, the *Times-Union's* front-page main 72 pt. headline screamed, "Katz Raises Funds for Godbold." Nobody knew Katz. I was campaign manager and strategist. To me the headline could not have been any more harsh or alarming if it had said "Al Capone Raises Funds for Godbold" instead of Katz. Allen Katz was deputy Florida Insurance Commissioner and the top assistant to Commissioner Bill Gunter, and would later become U.S. Ambassador to Belgium. The report said he had been making calls to Tallahassee lobbyists to contribute to the Godbold campaign.

"I don't know the guy. I've never met the guy," said Godbold. "Maybe it deserved a story somewhere back in the paper, but not that kind of display."

In the meantime, candidate Godbold continued to make big headlines with his assault on the JEA. Two months before the primary election, he jumped on managing director Irving again, this time for paying $30,000 to employ a public relations executive while failing to hire a fuel supply manager. "Last week the JEA's fuel supply got down to a critical three-day supply. Know why?" Godbold asked. "Because Mr. Irving failed to hire someone to manage our fuel supplies, but did hire a $30,000 public relations man to tell us we're running out of oil." He repeated his call for the JEA to fire Irving.

In a speech to the Arlington Rotary Club, Godbold accused the utility of poor business practices for failing to bill the city for more than a year for $360,000 the city owes the JEA. "I'm not trying to get Irving's head on a platter, but we need a tight-fisted businessman to run the JEA and I don't think engineers make good businessmen. They're talking about raising rates and forgot to bill us for over a year!"

Chapter 11

VOLUNTEER-RICH, HUMMING MACHINE

THE GODBOLD CAMPAIGN was a humming machine. The headquarters were overrun with eager volunteers: city employees, firefighters, former Jaycees, workers from Independent Life, and old friends from Jackson High School, along with others who had grown up with Godbold in the Brentwood area.

Volunteers were there all the time, stuffing envelopes, making phone calls and planning for campaign events at senior centers.

Showing up for campaign activities on city time was forbidden for city employees, members of the mayor's executive staff and other city administrators. Godbold said the best way they could help their boss was to do their jobs in City Hall. But in off hours and on weekends, they showed up in droves.

Paul McCormick, a public relations consultant, was from South

Carolina and new to Jacksonville. He had worked on Florida U.S. Senator Richard Stone's campaign and had also worked for presidential candidate George Wallace. Godbold had expected me to be his campaign manager, but I left Jacksonville in the summer to take a job as political director for newly elected Alabama U.S. Sen. Donald Stewart. In November 1978, Godbold hired McCormick as his campaign manager.

"It was my exposure to the largest organization," said McCormick. "Everybody was involved in it." McCormick once told Godbold that the campaign didn't need to make yard signs. "Signs don't vote," he told the mayor. "I foolishly convinced him," McCormick recalled. "Brantley put out hundreds of signs and he (Godbold) went crazy. Within 48 hours the sign shop was making thousands of signs. It was the most amazing thing I'd ever seen. It got more people to working, especially the guys."

After Christmas, I returned to Jacksonville to take over managing Godbold's campaign.

Saturday mornings were special at the headquarters. Several hundred volunteers would arrive early in the morning to hear a roaring pep talk by Godbold, receive their literature and marching orders, then head out to various targeted neighborhoods and shopping centers across Jacksonville.

"Those meetings in '79 were something when hundreds of people came over there," said Godbold. "It surprised me how many people came out to work, and work hard."

The campaign knew where it had to mine for the votes to win and it wasn't in the well-to-do neighborhoods along the river in South and West Jacksonville. Godbold voters lived in the blue collar and black communities mostly in the West and North sides of town. Senior citizens were also a major target. That's where the volunteers were sent.

In 1979, Godbold sworn in as mayor by Judge John Southwood.

Linda Sullivan, a former congressional aide in Washington and a newcomer to Jacksonville, took charge of the senior vote. "She got along with everybody and she brought people together," said Godbold. "She taught us a lot about how to work with seniors. It was a big party every day, balloons and ice cream. I loved it."

The campaign was tightly organized, primarily because of Tom Poston, a jovial multi-talented man with an eye for detail who Godbold first met when Poston ran the Big Brothers organization. Poston knew little and cared less about politics. But he was a people-person who knew how to make the most from any moment and helped shape a large group of people into an effective campaign machine.

Denise Lee was in her early twenties when she was hired to be the campaign's minority coordinator. Freshly home from Tallahassee where she had worked in field operations for Democratic candidates, Lee was told to go to City Hall to meet with Godbold aide Betty Holzendorf, an African American who was the mayor's liaison with the City Council and his representative to the black community.

"This man and lady get off the elevator," Lee recalled, "and this lady looked at me." It was Betty and her husband, King Holzendorf. "They put me in this Cadillac and took me over to the campaign headquarters. She told me that the Alpha Kappa Alphas (black sorority) were going to support Jake, but they wouldn't support anybody that didn't have a black person on their campaign staff."

Lee was like finding a diamond in the rough. Cautious because of her youth, she was also aggressive, relentless, fearless and a strong communicator. She looked at Jacksonville's black community as her village and her mission was to deliver it to Godbold. Lee is also headstrong and a person who knows what she wants, which helps to explain why she later spent 27 years on the City Council and four years in the Florida Legislature.

Before I returned to the campaign, McCormick fired her. Upset, she phoned Holzendorf and told her what had happened. "Goddammit, who hired you?" Holzendorf asked Lee. "You did," she responded. "Well, take your ass back over there."

Lee thought, "This woman curses all the time."

"What I remember about the campaign was it was structured," Lee said. "The resources were there for what I was doing." She took her job seriously. "I was given responsibility and I was expected to deliver."

In addition to Poston, Sullivan and Lee, I added Rick Catlett and Pat Craig to my staff. I put Catlett in charge of Arlington, where he had just run and lost a primary election for the council. The two fit what I wanted like fingers in a glove.

Godbold and his team knew that black voters favored him by far for mayor. But they also knew they needed to get the community excited and motivated to turn out and vote for him.

Godbold, Holzendorf, and three white members of his mayoral staff—Martha Barrett, Fleury Yelvington and Glen English—spent every Sunday morning in black churches. Sometimes, others supporters went with them.

Finance chair Tommy Greene recalled one visit. "We were at a church at U.S. 1 and Division Street," he said. "Lew (Brantley) was there. It was a whole church full of black preachers. Lew talked about the American dream." When Godbold spoke, Brantley left the church. "Jake said, 'You know what? Mr. Brantley talked about the American dream. Mr. Brantley doesn't know anything about the American dream. You know what the American dream is? Working so you can get out of the projects. That's the American dream. Make enough money so you can get out of the projects.' They went crazy," said Greene.

At black churches, there is always at least one pass of the collection plate and often more than one. "I'd almost have a stroke," said Holzendorf. "When preachers see a politician, they take up ten collections. Jake would never have money. Every time the plate came by, we had to give him some money."

This next story has two different versions, one by Holzendorf and another by Godbold and Barrett.

According to Holzendorf, one Sunday at St. Paul's A.M.E. on Myrtle Avenue Godbold told the congregation that he and his team would return the next Sunday and the ladies with him, Holzendorf, Barrett and Yelvington, would sing with the choir. He committed them to going to choir practice in the middle of the week, said Holzendorf.

Outside the church, Holzendorf remembers she said, "I ain't no fool. I know I can't sing." Barrett, however, said "Yea, yea, yea," according to Holzendorf. "I told Martha, 'You don't live in the black community, but I do. If you get up there and embarrass me I'm going to whip your ass.' Jake fell out. 'Oh,' he said, 'we're going to see Betty beat up Martha.'"

Godbold remembers that Barrett was not so enthusiastic about singing with the choir. A day or so after they had attended the St. Paul's service, as a joke, the mayor said, "I told Martha that the minister had called me and said he wanted her and Fleury to sing at the service the next Sunday. Martha said, 'No, I can't sing.'" The mayor then reminded her of something. "Martha, you're working for me. This is like the big chief asking you to smoke the pipe and you won't smoke the pipe. That will be an absolute insult to him."

While Godbold had not spoken to Pastor Abraham Chandler, Sr., when Barrett phoned the preacher he went along with the joke. "He said, 'Yes, you're on the program and its Girl Scout Sunday,'" she recalled.

On Sunday morning, Barrett and Yelvington went to the church with Godbold, Holzendorf and English. "When we got there, they said, 'Where are you going?' I said, to sing. The mayor looked strange."

Barrett and Yelvington joined the other members of the choir and put on their robes. "Off we go out with the choir. I see the mayor having a fit and Betty going, 'son of a bitch.' The preacher said he was happy to have us both," Barrett said.

Godbold remembered, "The choir came walking out and there are these two white girls up there. The preacher said, 'We have this great pleasure of having two ladies from the mayor's office who are going to sing with the choir.'" According to Godbold, Holzendorf was in shock. "You know I'm going to kill those bitches if they get up there and embarrass us."

"We get up to sing and their faces are so funny," said Barrett. Still thinking Godbold had told her the truth when he said the preacher wanted Yelvington and her to sing with the choir, she said, "I still didn't get it."

"I just put my head down on the rail," said the mayor. When they began singing, he said, "The choir came in behind them and drowned them out and it sounded pretty good."

The choir sang, "The Battle Hymn of the Republic."

Afterwards, Holzendorf admitted, "They were good. They marched in with the choir and they rolled. I said, 'Well, y'all made me proud this time, but I'm not going to church with y'all anymore.'"

Chapter 12

———∞∞———

THE RING-NECKED DOG WINS

THREE WEEKS BEFORE the primary election on April 10, 1979, the *Times-Union* reported on a Bill Hamilton poll that showed Godbold with a comfortable lead over Brantley, 42 percent to 22 percent. Hester was at 6 percent. Hank Drane, the newspaper's political editor, wrote, "Godbold started as the ring-necked dog (strong front runner). With three months remaining nobody has budged him from his position."

Both Godbold and I made sure the campaign staff and volunteers didn't look at the poll results and start thinking they had the election in the bag. The goal was to push as hard as possible to top 50 percent on election day and avoid a runoff.

Godbold continued to blast the unpopular JEA in speeches, press releases and television commercials. On March 20 he said the JEA failed to comply with a six-year old city ordinance that mandated the utility combine water and sewer bills, which the mayor's staff said would save $500,000-$600,000 a year. "Why haven't they done anything, where you're talking about half a million dollars in savings?" Godbold asked.

The next day, he jumped on the JEA for spending $37 million for studies, additions and "unneeded acquisitions during the last few years, rather than needed maintenance."

On March 27, *Jacksonville Journal* reporter Lloyd Brown wrote, "Everywhere he goes, Godbold shakes hands, strokes backs, clutches arms and pats shoulders. Almost everyone calls him 'Jake,' not mayor or Mr. Godbold. If they do not (call him Jake), he tells them to."

Candidate Godbold, wrote Brown, "enters every store, but is attracted to beauty shops and barber shops." He even once tried to leave literature in a Port-O-Let, Brown said. "They don't have anything to read in there," quipped Godbold.

Godbold was unrelenting in campaigning among black voters. "They identified with me. They felt like anybody that came out of the projects would understand their problems," Godbold would later say. "It just grew with my passion. I know how to communicate with them."

Black ministers have a great deal of political persuasion with their congregations and Godbold made sure he talked personally with them all, in addition to visiting their churches on Sunday. "I set up meetings with every black minister in town. I told them who I was, where I came from and what I wanted to do," he said. "We got on our knees and prayed with them."

Godbold revolutionized the way white candidates campaigned in black precincts. He and campaign volunteers knocked on doors and went block to block in black neighborhoods; they visited black shopping centers and had their share of barbecue campaign events.

Black coordinator Denise Lee said the battle in black neighborhoods sometimes got personal and hot. "I'm in the median on the corner of 20th Street and Myrtle Avenue with Jake signs and Marsha Dean and

Corrine Brown (who would later be elected to Congress) were working there for Brantley," she recalled. "Marsha Dean came up to me and said, 'Get your ass off this corner.'" Lee said she walked off the median and went to the other end. "Then Mrs. Jan Wilson and Mr. Leonard Atwater were riding around in his camper campaigning for Jake." (Mrs. Wilson and Mr. Atwater were both highly respected in the black community). "I told them what happened. Mrs. Wilson said, 'I'll be damn. You get back on that corner. You can stand any place you want to. If you have a problem with them just call me.'"

When the candidates filed their final finance reports before election day, Brantley had passed Godbold in cash collected, $153,662 to $140,299, which was expected because of Brantley's strong support from the business community.

Also, as anticipated, on April 10, Goldbold garnered 43 percent of the primary vote to Brantley's 29 percent, 34,654 votes to 23,551. Hester, who was endorsed by the *Times-Union* and *Jacksonville Journal*, received 11,425 votes. That meant that Godbold and Brantley would face off in a May 1 runoff.

An analysis of the first primary vote broke like predicted. Godbold won the black precincts 3-1. In all- black precinct 9M, he defeated Brantley 183-55. Brantley, on the other hand, won the upper-crust vote. In Deerwood's 4K, he beat Godbold 219-108. In precinct 5A, where most voters were elderly, Godbold sacked Brantley 72-19. They ran neck and neck in Arlington, which would become key in the runoff.

A week after the primary election, Brantley contributed $30,000 of his personal funds to his campaign, pushing his total contribution to $47,000. On April 18, when the first finance reports were filed after the primary election, Brantley had stretched his lead over Godbold, $212,188.43 to $164,441.69.

"Raising money was very hard," said Godbold finance chairman Tommy Greene. "Brantley had all the silk-stocking money, all the business community. We were raising it nickel and dimes."

After all the hammering by Godbold, less than two weeks before the runoff election, the JEA approved the Ebasco Services contract to design and project manage the coal-fired plants for $48.4 million, $9 million less than the original contract. The vote was 6-1 and provided Godbold and his campaign a timely lift.

On April 29, the *Times-Union* reported on another poll which had been conducted two days before the newspaper endorsed Brantley. It showed that Godbold would be the likely winner on May 1 with 47 percent of those polled, compared to Brantley's 37 percent. There were 16 percent undecided and when the numbers were adjusted, it was projected that Godbold could receive 56 percent of the vote.

In the poll, the majority of voters said that Godbold was better qualified, more familiar with problems faced by people, more sincere, would work better with the City Council, would provide better leadership, had run the better campaign and would be more successful in holding down JEA rates.

In an editorial, the *Jacksonville Journal* backed Brantley. "We think it has become clear that Lew Brantley is more likely than Jake Godbold to give us responsible leadership in the mayor's chair."

Four months of spending by the candidates topped $400,000, making it the most expensive mayoral campaign in Florida history. Brantley outspent Godbold by $40,000.

Monday night before the Tuesday runoff election, a dog named "Jam's Uncle Jake" was running in the 11th race at the greyhound track on the city's westside. Campaign treasurer Lee Smith, volunteers Frank

Brown and Frank Cosentino, and I loaded up in a motor home and headed to the track to place a bet on the dog, who was favored to win. At the track, just after the dogs began chasing the rabbit around the rail, "Jam's Uncle Jake" stumbled and fell. We took that as a bad sign.

Heading back to the campaign headquarters, Cosentino pulled the motor home into the parking lot of the Bamboo Luau, a bar and restaurant where westside politicians often hung out. It was late at night and the restaurant was empty except for two men sitting at the bar. One of them was local entrepreneur Ron Taylor, a major Brantley supporter. Taylor was a flashy guy who owned a big yacht and an airplane. He was having a drink, so I went over to speak to him.

I noticed that Taylor was fumbling with something in his hands. Taylor said it was his weekly paycheck. It was a little over $10,000. Ron said he would bet the whole check on Brantley to defeat Jake the next day if I could get somebody to cover the bet.

I went immediately to the restaurant's pay phone and called finance chair Tommy Greene. Tommy said for me to tell Ron that he would take the bet. I then shared what was going on with the others and walked back to Taylor at the bar. Smith went with me. I told Ron that Tommy said he'd cover the $10,000, but somebody needed to hold his check. Taylor agreed, endorsed the check and handed it over to Smith. We pulled back out of the parking lot, thinking, "What the hell…"

On the afternoon following the May 1 election, the *Journal* front page headline shouted, "Godbold's Little People Win." He had defeated Brantley 46,874 (54.8 percent) to 38,575 (45.2 percent). Godbold had won, said the *Journal*, with "a mixture of blacks, feminists, Florida Crackers, and old politicians."

When the high-income precincts came in first on election night, they provided Brantley an early lead with 55 percent. But it was short-lived as votes from north and west Jacksonville, along with the black precincts, started rolling in to thrust Godbold in front. Blacks, which made up 22 percent of the city's population, represented 28 percent of the turnout.

Two days after the Godbold victory, Brantley endorsed him in a joint press conference at the Thunderbird Motor Hotel.

With two elections down, there was one more to go: the 1979 general election where Godbold would face former City Council colleague, Republican Don Brewer. Brewer owned a family insurance business and had been on the council eight years representing Arlington. With Democrats outnumbering Republicans 6-1 in Jacksonville, there was every reason for Godbold and his camp to feel good about a victory on May 22.

With such a seemingly comfortable advantage, Godbold continued his aggressive campaigning and his organization remained in high gear. Turnout on Saturdays at the campaign headquarters was just as large and hard working as before, telephone banks were in full operation

As he did against Brantley, Godbold ran as the front-runner and avoided head-to-head debates or confrontations with Brewer. At one point, he cancelled a televised debate for a trip to Washington to meet with federal officials about the troubled Buckman Street Sewage plant.

He also refused to meet with the *Times-Union* editorial board which had endorsed Hester in the first primary and Brantley in the runoff while constantly being very critical of Godbold. It was a "matter of pride," said his campaign.

The campaign let the *Times-Union* know it did not want the paper's endorsement. I had a full- page ad prepared and sent to the paper refusing the endorsement in the event it was given. They had hammered

Jake over and over and we felt if they endorsed him now, it would confuse our supporters and make them wonder what Jake had promised the paper. Plus, we didn't need it. The newspaper endorsed Brewer.

On the night before the Tuesday election, instead of debating Brewer in front of 35 people at Lakewood United Methodist Church, Godbold threw out the first pitch at a Jacksonville Suns baseball game attended by over 2,000.

When the sun came up on Tuesday, May 22, the Godbold campaign apparatus was in full operation. There were 150 vehicles, including taxi cabs, ready to go. The fleet included 25 rental cars and ten rented vans. In a system designed by Tom Poston, volunteers used citizen band radios, walkie talkies and telephones to coordinate rides and new requests. There was a focus on senior citizens. Twenty nine different elderly sites were assigned a Godbold vehicle.

Hemming Plaza in the center of downtown was where city buses delivered black domestic workers and others each afternoon to transfer to other buses that would take them home. The plaza was like Godbold central. Volunteers were wearing Jake Godbold t-shirts and music from loudspeakers on top of a recreational vehicle blared a song about Godbold to the tune of "Davy Crockett."

When a bus arrived to let off riders, a Godbold volunteer would intercept them and ask them if they wanted a free ride to the polls and then a ride home after they voted. It was a busy place. At one point during the afternoon, Godbold visited the plaza to encourage the volunteers and see how they were doing. He watched as Frank Cosentino (Cos) put bus riders in a Godbold vehicle and the vehicle pulled away. He walked over to Consentino, who was a transplant from Chicago, and asked how he knew he wasn't carrying Brewer voters to the polls. "It's easy, Bubba," said Cos. "I ask them who they are going to vote for. If they say, 'Jake,' I hit the roof of the car once. If they say, 'Brewer,' I hit the roof twice and the car just drives them around."

In the end, all the work paid off. Godbold won with 47,760 votes (56.2 percent) to Brewer's 37,165 (43.8 percent). Brewer conceded about one hour after the polls closed.

Once again, Godbold had prevailed heavily with black voters by claiming 94 percent in 29 black precincts. Black voters gave him an edge of 9,900 votes. Godbold beat Brewer by 10,595 votes.

And, once again, he had failed to win a majority of the vote in upper income neighborhoods.

Fittingly, the victory party that night was held downstairs at Independent Life where the campaign had all started. It was wall to wall people with supporters flowing out onto the sidewalk as the Dude Taylor Band played, "Happy Days Are Here Again."

Godbold only spoke for five minutes, telling the crowd, "They told me I would have the establishment against us, that we would have the newspaper against us…but they forgot we had the people with us."

Sending a signal to the business community which had opposed him, the newly elected mayor said, "Everything is in the past. I'm not a vindictive person. We are starting a new day tomorrow. Together we can build a new Jacksonville—a better Jacksonville. Now, the real work starts. Now, we've got to perform."

When Godbold was officially sworn in as the second elected mayor of Consolidated Jacksonville, 19 newly elected members of the City Council were sworn in with him. Old Jaycee friend, County Court Judge John Southwood, gave Godbold the oath of office. The ceremony was held at the Civic Auditorium in front of 500 people.

In his twenty-minute address, he once again took a shot at the JEA. "We've got to get off our dependency on oil," he said, but warned that the JEA should not rush into approving a contract for design of the coal fired plant "at any cost."

"We move forward, but we make sure we're right at every step," he said. Godbold said Jacksonville must attract industry to trigger economic development, but the city should "pick and choose" the right industry.

Looking at the 19 new councilmembers, he implored for harmony with his administration. "I know your goals and my goals for the City of Jacksonville are the same. We may differ on how to get there, but our goals are the same. We all want a better quality of life."

Chapter 13

KEEP YOUR ENEMIES CLOSE

WITHIN A WEEK of being sworn in as mayor, Godbold began his drive to attract business and good jobs to Jacksonville. One of his mantras was, "If your daddy ain't got a job, then you can't have a quality of life." That was something he wanted to flip on its head.

The leadership of the Chamber of Commerce that had opposed him reached out early to mend fences.

It sent Albert Ernest, chairman of Barnett Bank and the chamber's Central Jacksonville, Inc., and developer Preston Haskell to meet with the new mayor to propose a peace agreement and try to forge a partnership.

For Godbold, if there was any wound as a result of the business community's effort to defeat him, the meeting with Ernest and Haskell was the balm that healed it. What Ernest and Haskell said that day inspired him to take full advantage of the chamber's support, and in many ways, it shaped how Godbold would conduct himself as mayor.

But Mayor Godbold also had his own ideas about how to grow Jacksonville's economy and broaden the tax base. He intended to be hands-on when it came to luring new companies to move to Jacksonville and bringing new jobs. Proof of that is Jay Stein, chairman of Stein Mart, Inc., a national retailer, who moved his company headquarters to Jacksonville because of Godbold's personal persuasion.

"I told him we were considering moving to Jacksonville," Stein recalled. "He said, 'Dammit, you move here and I'm going to take care of you.' You tell me what would be more inviting than that. He said he wanted to be my patron saint. 'I'll take you under my wings.' He said that I could be part of his political family as mayor." The mayor kept his commitment, Stein said. "Jake brought me into everything.

"Whenever there was an event in town that he thought I should attend he picked up the phone and called me. He went out of his way, in an extraordinary fashion, to make someone very new to Jacksonville feel at home."

Godbold created the Mayor's Economic Development Council. "I think everything we want to do in Jacksonville is based on attracting new industry," said the mayor. The council would not duplicate what the chamber does, he said. However, some close to Godbold believed he wanted to have his own economic booster team just in case the chamber failed to follow through on its partnership promise.

In a move that surprised most everyone, he named his election opponent, Lew Brantley, as chair of the new council. Brantley, who had been president of the Florida Senate from 1976-1978, took his election loss to Godbold hard, according to friends.

Godbold chose Brantley because, "He knows business and business people and also has the political savvy to work with government. The future of our economic growth is now in the hands of Lew Brantley," the mayor said when announcing Brantley's appointment on July 10.

Brantley said he accepted the appointment because, "I care about Jacksonville."

"Jake gave him his humanity back," said former Godbold aide Martha Barrett, "and he sent a message to the business community, 'You guys supported him and now I'm giving him to you.'"

Before speaking to Brantley, Godbold reached out to Jacksonville business and philanthropic titan W.W. (Bill) Gay. Gay was Brantley's close friend and had been his biggest campaign donor. The mayor wanted Gay's opinion, and he asked Gay to feel out Brantley.

"Jake phoned me about 6:30 in the morning," Gay recalled. "He said, 'Bill, I know you didn't support me, but I don't blame you and I didn't expect you to because I know you've been a big help to Lew.' He said he wanted me to talk to Lew about being his economic development guy. He said, 'I want Lew to be the chairman of my committee.'"

Gay was unsure. "I said, 'How the hell can you expect him to do that after you just beat him?'" According to Gay, the mayor responded, "Well, he's interested in Jacksonville and I believe he will do what you tell him if both of you agree." Gay said he would call Brantley, but he was skeptical that he would accept the appointment.

Early the next morning, Gay and Brantley met at the Holiday Inn across the street from Gay's office on Stockton Street. Gay told his friend what Godbold wanted. "Lew said, 'What should I do, Boss Man?'" said Gay.

Gay replied, "If you feel inclined, I know you'll do a good job." Brantley still wasn't convinced. "Should I do it?"

"If you do, you will be the biggest man in Jacksonville," said Gay. "You will turn from being the mayor's opponent to being in the biggest job he's got as mayor. We need to get some business in this town."

"Well, I'm willing to do it if you don't think it will hurt us," said Brantley.

"I won't get hurt," replied Gay. "What's good for Jacksonville is good for me. I think Jake's going to do that. I think he's going to push Jacksonville. He's going to want folks who didn't support him working for him."

Godbold didn't wait to hear back from Gay. He called Brantley.

Afterwards, Gay called Mayor Godbold and said, "Son, you are my friend from now on. That took a lot of courage and a lot of guts. I didn't ask you to do it and Lew didn't ask you to do it. I think you did it because it was the right person."

Chapter 14

———— ❧ ————

"WE WANT THE COLTS!"

AUGUST 1979 WAS a turning point for Godbold, and the events that happened that fateful month set Jacksonville on an historic new path.

Doug Peeples, a funeral home director and President of the Northside Businessmen's Club, had heard that the NFL's Baltimore Colts owner Robert Irsay was threatening to move his legendary team out of its long-time home, Baltimore, Maryland because Mayor Donald Schaefer would not build the team a new football stadium. Irsay had been shopping cities like Los Angeles, more as a way to motivate Schaefer to build a stadium than to actually find a new home for the Colts.

Perhaps on a lark, Peeples reached out to Irsay on his own and invited him to come to Jacksonville and inspect the Gator Bowl, a large stadium that hosted two football games a year—the annual Gator Bowl during the Christmas holidays, and the Florida-Georgia game played around Halloween each year.

Godbold and members of the Jacksonville Chamber of Commerce

were caught by surprise when they heard of the invitation and learned that Irsay had accepted. The city was in the position of the dog that finally catches the speeding car. Now what?

Godbold knew right away that receiving and entertaining the Colts owner was bigger than something Peeples could handle, and that the local media would be all over Irsay's visit. The mayor decided to take over. He reached out to Peeples, who accepted Godbold's offer.

The mayor quickly formed a team comprised of members of his staff and the leadership of the chamber.

During 1979, Jacksonville, like the rest of America, was going through a wrenching energy crisis. Shortly after his election, Godbold named me to be the city's energy czar. It was a job I didn't want.

In the meantime, Godbold and his team began meeting and planning what they wanted to do when Irsay was in town. Godbold asked me to attend the first three team meetings, but I declined, saying I was busy "getting everyone's attention" about the energy crisis.

As the day of the visit, Wednesday, August 17, drew near, Godbold called me to attend the final team meeting in his office at 12 noon on Friday, August 12. The mayor said I would be fired if I didn't show up.

When the meeting started in the mayor's office, Godbold asked a chamber representative to tell me what was being planned to host and entertain Irsay. They were going to take him out on a yacht on the St. Johns River, visit ritzy Ponte Vedra Beach, host a luncheon at the toney River Club atop the city's tallest building, and tour swank neighborhoods in Ortega, I was told. To conclude the NFL owner's two-day visit, Godbold friend and confidant Tommy Greene was hosting a who's who reception for Irsay and his family at Greene's palatial home on the St. Johns River in Mandarin.

"What have we left out?" Godbold asked.

With a touch of sarcasm, I responded, "Only the people who just elected you mayor." "He's right," Godbold told the chamber group. "What should we do?" he asked me.

"Well, if it was me," I said, standing in front of Godbold with my back to the chamber guys, "I'd open up the Gator Bowl Wednesday night and invite the whole town to come down and tell this guy that we want the Baltimore Colts."

There were moans. "Nobody will show up and it will ruin everything," said the group leader. "What if nobody shows up?" Godbold asked.

"So, what? If we get an NFL team it is going to be the Joe Six Packs who support the team and buy tickets. Why leave them out now? If they don't show up wouldn't you rather know now they don't want a team?" I said.

"He's right," Godbold quickly responded. "Let's do it."

At about that time, I was feeling like I had a runaway train. It was now around 1 p.m. Friday, five days from Irsay's scheduled visit. The city had no money to advertise and promote, much less support such an event. There were no plans for what would happen once Irsay and Jacksonville football enthusiasts got to the Gator Bowl, if indeed anyone showed up.

"Hold on. Give me a few minutes," I said, leaving the mayor's office to use the phone in a nearby office where I called a couple of important members of the Jacksonville sports media. I told them what was being planned at that very moment in the mayor's office as part of Irsay's itinerary. After hanging up I went back into the mayor's office where everyone but Godbold was hoping I would return and say the scheme would not work. "The chamber thought it was a terrible idea," Godbold said afterwards. "They thought we'd embarrass the city."

"It'll work. Those guys think we are nuts and they don't think anybody will show up. They are going to write about this for the next five days. The television stations won't talk about much else. I think we'll be covered up with media which will help us get out the word," I said.

Godbold had made up his mind. His passion and enthusiasm had kicked in and there was no turning back.

Then I said that to make the 6 p.m. television news that Friday night the mayor needed to hold a news conference at 3 p.m., standing on the 50-yard line of the Gator Bowl, holding a football in one hand and a live young colt in the other. His message was to invite the entire town to the Gator Bowl on Wednesday night to tell Robert Irsay of the Baltimore Colts that they wanted his team to move to Jacksonville.

At 3 p.m., holding a football and the lead rope for a colt, Godbold raised the ball high, looked around at the empty stadium and told Jacksonville through the gathered press, "If you want Bob Irsay to move his Baltimore Colts to Jacksonville, then come out here Wednesday night and tell him we want the Colts."

Then, Godbold concluded his remarks with a surprise announcement. "We're going to have free hotdogs, free Cokes and free beer." I was in shock. After the media had all left, I walked up to the mayor and asked, "Where are we going to get free hotdogs, free Cokes and free beer?"

"I don't know. That's your job," Godbold responded as he walked away.

All of a sudden, auditing city gasoline credit cards, turning up thermostats in government buildings, and replacing 8-cylinder city cars with compacts wasn't on my agenda for the next five days. My small team of four and I had to drop everything and figure out what to do just five days away inside the Gator Bowl. Then we had to make it happen, realizing all the while there was no funding dedicated to such a whimsical event. We weren't sure that anyone would even attend.

The media were relentless in their blanket coverage of every little piece of information coming out of the planning of the event. It started that Friday night and continued morning, noon and night, right up through the 6 p.m. news on the night of "Colt Fever."

Godbold's highly effective campaign volunteer team went to work. Just as in a political campaign, the sign shop was activated. Signs with the Baltimore Colts logo and proclaiming "Colt Fever" were printed by the hundreds. Then, after the signs were assembled, volunteers, headed by Jacksonville firefighters, put up the signs along side roadways throughout the county.

On Monday, Tuesday and Wednesday, as commuters drove to and from work, volunteers stood on street corners and on top of bridges, waving signs and urging people to show up Wednesday night.

I appeared on local television and radio shows and was interviewed over and over.

Most members of the media believed Godbold would fail in getting people to show up at the Gator Bowl on Wednesday, and they were cynical that Jacksonville would ever get an NFL team.

"Irsay is just using you," a newspaper sports editor said. "We're using him, too," both Godbold and I thought. "We realized Irsay was playing games. We knew he was threatening Mayor Schaefer and was using Jacksonville as leverage," said Godbold.

AM radio station WAPE dominated the airways in Jacksonville, primarily because of the station's number one morning disc jockey, the Greaseman. I had worked with the Greaseman and the station in the past to help promote city events. I quickly turned to the disc jockey for help.

The Greaseman had a massive following. Nobody knew what he looked like, but his distinctive voice and outsized radio personality were unmistakable. He was the biggest show in town. The Greaseman agreed to help me and he immediately began talking about the upcoming event.

WAPE also signed on to promote "Colt Fever Night," and began a banner campaign with prizes for the best banners brought to the stadium Wednesday night.

I asked the Greaseman to be the master of ceremonies for the night.

Godbold was nervous about Wednesday night. He knew a lousy turn-out would cause the event to be judged a colossal political blunder, committed in just his second month as mayor. Worse, it would set back the mayor's number one goal of changing negative attitudes and getting the people of Jacksonville to become excited about their town.

But, on the other hand, he also knew if it worked it could be the catalyst for changing the city. Godbold was hoping for a crowd of 20,000.

Meanwhile, my team and I were putting together the agenda for the night.

1. Three skydivers would parachute into the Gator Bowl, a first ever happening.
2. Bands would be positioned throughout the stadium to entertain guests.

3. A cowboy on a horse would race from underneath the stadium to the 50-yard line where the cowboy would fire his rifle several times into the sky.
4. Irsay would be flown into the stadium in a helicopter that would land on the 50-yard line where Irsay would exit and be greeted by Godbold and the crowd.
5. Young cheerleaders would be recruited to be on the sidelines and lead fans in a chant of "We want the Colts."
6. Thousands of matches would be distributed as people entered the stadium. At the end of the event, everyone there would light a match and hold it in the air as fireworks followed.

And, then, there was still the matter of securing "free hotdogs, free Cokes, and free beer."

We called on every source we could think of to collect donated materials. Hotdogs came from different grocery stores, distributors and restaurants, as did buns, mustard and ketchup. The Coca-Cola distributor supplied Coke products.

But we were unable to find a source willing to donate beer. So, on Tuesday I distributed a press release stating the mayor had reconsidered giving away free beer. The release said since Wednesday night was church night in Jacksonville, out of respect there would be no free beer.

The Gator Bowl concession vendor refused to help in any way, which meant that members of Godbold's vast campaign organization were recruited to work the concession stands, making hotdogs and giving out the food and drinks.

Then, federal permission was needed to land three parachutists and a helicopter inside the Gator Bowl. On Monday morning, with the clock ticking, I reached out to the Federal Aviation Authority (FAA) about getting needed federal permits to make both happen. I was told that even if I could get FAA permission it would take at least two weeks and maybe longer to get permits approved.

That's when I remembered that Florida's U.S. Senator Richard Stone and his chief aide had come to see Godbold recently to convince the mayor to join Stone's re-election campaign. Godbold was non-committal. I had been in the meeting.

I called the Senator's chief aide, told him what Godbold was planning to do Wednesday night, and offered a deal: get FAA permits for the helicopter and the parachutists and I would get Godbold's backing for Stone. It worked.

To get donated matches, I phoned Bob Davis, senior vice president of Jacksonville-based Winn-Dixie Stores. I asked Davis if Winn-Dixie would consider "donating some matches that you can light on concrete for the mayor's event Wednesday night?"

"How many matches?" Davis asked. "70,000."

Finally, there were the fireworks. In the past, I had worked with a fireworks company in nearby Bunnell, FL. I contacted them about shooting off a $5,000 show Wednesday night, just three days away. Never mind that I didn't know how we would pay for the fireworks.

On the afternoon of the event, the owner of the pyrotechnics company showed up at the Gator Bowl. I told him to begin shooting off bombs at 5 p.m., over the nearby bridges that carried downtown workers home at the end of the day. I wanted to remind them to come back later for Colt Fever Night.

At about 4 o'clock that afternoon, Walter Butler, the city fire marshal, approached me on the Gator Bowl field and said we would not be able to shoot any fireworks that night because I had failed to get the necessary permit which had to be signed by several city officials, including the Sheriff.

I had hardly slept in the last five days. I said, "Those aren't my fireworks. They're the mayor's fireworks and he intends to start shooting them off at 5 o'clock. Walter, I was in the room when the mayor decided to appoint you fire marshal and one of his biggest reasons was because you can get things done in a hurry." I then turned and walked away to another task.

Just before 5 p.m., fire marshal Butler returned with the signed permit. At 5 p.m., as downtown workers headed over two automobile-packed bridges, bombs started going off, sometimes rattling the bridges themselves.

While all of the preparation for Colt Fever was going on at a furious pace, Godbold and members of the Chamber of Commerce were busy entertaining Irsay and showing him the best of Jacksonville. "Irsay was a very delightful guy, a colorful guy," said Godbold. "He was like a big old teddy bear. He always laughed."

During an inspection of the Gator Bowl, which badly needed renovation, Godbold knew getting the Colts in Jacksonville was not going to happen. "He was very frank in what he wanted and he made it very clear to me. He put his arm around me and he said the first thing Jacksonville needs to get an NFL team—his or anybody else's—was a new stadium. 'You've got to tear this son-of-a-bitch down and start over again.' I knew we weren't ready for that."

A nervous Godbold arrived at the Gator Bowl around 6 p.m., one hour before the evening's activities were to start. "I was never as nervous as I was that night, sitting at that stadium waiting to see if anybody was going to show up."

He was met by aide Rick Catlett, who had been working closely with me in putting the event together. "We were standing on the field and only a couple thousand people were there. He was saying, 'Nobody is going to show up, nobody is going to show up,'" said Catlett.

Catlett stood over 6-feet tall, towering over the 5-7 mayor. With his height, Catlett could see just over the top of the stadium to the Mathews Bridge that emptied into Arlington. He took the mayor up ten or 12 steps. "I said, 'Look at that bridge. There's your answer about people coming.'"

"All I could see was cars coming over that bridge toward the Gator Bowl," Godbold said. Catlett then showed him the Hart Bridge into south Jacksonville followed by the Main Street Bridge into downtown. "There was nothing but cars coming with their horns blowing. It looked like a revolution was going on," Godbold recalled years later.

By the time Colt Fever got underway, over 50,000 people were inside the stadium. Police estimated as many as another 10,000 were outside trying to get in. "The sheriff didn't think there would be much to it and didn't put many officers out there," said the mayor.

"All those people sitting outside in their cars didn't get a hot dog or a cold drink. They just got to say they were at Colt Fever," Godbold said afterwards.

Volunteers stood at the stadium entrances and handed out the matches, telling people not to strike them until the mayor said so.

The Greaseman came into the press box and was put in a private room where no one could see him. He sat on floor so that when he spoke to the crowd, his identity was protected.

There was a definite electricity running through the crowd. Rich people sat next to poor people. Blacks and whites together. Young and old. All of Jacksonville was there that night. "There was— and still is—an awful lot of pride that they played a part in it," said the mayor.

Led by the invisible Greaseman, the crowd shouted "We want the Colts," over and over and over. It made the stadium shake.

After the cowboy on the horse fired his rifle into the night air at midfield; after the three skydivers landed perfectly on the 50-yard line, and when the helicopter swooped into the stadium and Baltimore Colts owner Bob Irsay got out to be greeted by the mayor, the frenzied crowd was still shouting, "We want the Colts!"

Godbold then instructed everyone to get the match given at the entrance. The lights in the stadium went dark. "If you want the Colts to come to Jacksonville," Godbold said, "then show Mr. Irsay the light."

"When those lights went down and those matches went up it looked like a big birthday cake there in the Gator Bowl," the mayor said. "I don't think there was a throat that wasn't tight and an eye that didn't drop tears."

It was a night that turned around a town. Jacksonville, he said, "needed some cheerleaders. Jacksonville needed some pride."

News of the event spread nationwide.

On the following Monday night, world-renowned sportscaster Howard Cosell was broadcasting a Baltimore Orioles baseball game on national television. He used the opportunity to call Baltimore "a city under siege" because of Irsay's threats to move his football team, and the fact that famed lawyer Edward Bennett Williams had purchased the Orioles and there were rumors he was going to move his team to Washington.

In his book, *I Never Played the Game*, Cosell wrote, "At the same time I pointed out, Irsay had recently visited Jacksonville and fifty thousand people in the Gator Bowl had chanted, 'WE WANT THE COLTS!' It seemed to me a sickening thing that was happening to this city on the rebound.

"Can you imagine my feelings when I got the following letter from Jake Godbold, the Mayor of Jacksonville, who quite apparently had misunderstood the tenor of my comments."

Mr. Howard Cosell
American Broadcasting Company 1330 Avenue of the Americas
New York, N.Y. 1009

Dear Mr. Cosell:
   You did a great thing for Jacksonville on Monday night when you chronicled our glorious night of delirium in the Gator Bowl last Wednesday night.
   I believe the citizens of Jacksonville shouted "WE WANT THE COLTS! loud enough for the entire world to hear, especially those 28 individuals who own teams in the National Football League. We know we may not get the Colts to move from Baltimore to Jacksonville, but we also know that this city moved itself closer to the big-time and NFL football. We know that owners other than Mr. Irsay are looking for new homes, and I am not hesitating to move in their directions, also.
   I have named a successful local businessman and sports promoter, Mr. Ted Johnson, to coordinate the entire effort for me, working with the Mayor's Office and the Chamber of Commerce. We intend to meet Mr. Irsay's demand of a "Bankable commitment" of $8 million a year in ticket sales. In fact, we are gearing up now for our sales effort. But, even before we could begin, Prudential Insurance notified us it wanted

1,000 season tickets a year for 10 years. That will be announced
Sunday and should set off a chain reaction since Jacksonville is
an insurance and banking center.

We intend to fix the Gator Bowl up to Mr. Irsay's standards, whether the Colts move here or not, and will probably
use Cleveland's stadium as a model.

Our people are ready and we are proud that individuals like
you on the national level recognize what we have accomplished
and what we plan to do in the future.

"Amazing, isn't it," Cosell wrote.

What the sportscaster didn't understand was Godbold intended to
jump onto any and every opportunity to boost Jacksonville and pump
spirit into his city. The fact that Cosell mentioned Jacksonville on national television provided the mayor a chance to strike.

On the Friday after Colt Fever, Jacksonville businessman Norm
Harrison told the *Florida Times-Union* he was on a business trip to
San Francisco where the NFL was coincidentally having a meeting. On
changing planes in Dallas, Harrison found himself in the company of
several NFL officials. On the plane, he said that Leonard Tosh, owner
of the Philadelphia Eagles, sat behind him, and Bill Walsh of the San
Francisco 49ers sat across the aisle. He mentioned to them that he was
from Jacksonville.

Tosh said that Colt Fever was the talk of the NFL meeting. "He said we
may not have gotten a team, but we made a helluva impression. 'It may
not mean anything to you, but if we were giving out a franchise right
now, Jacksonville would be the number one candidate,'" said Tosh.

A couple of weeks later, Godbold had a meeting in Washington D.C.
with President Jimmy Carter's chief of staff, Hamilton Jordan, to discuss funding for the Automated Skyway Express (ASE) the city wanted

to build in downtown. "When Jordan came into the meeting, he didn't want to talk about anything until I told him how we got 50,000 people to come down to the Gator Bowl for a hot dog and a soft drink."

When the NASL Washington Diplomats soccer team committed to Godbold and the Sports Commission to train in Jacksonville and play an exhibition game in the city in 1980, the Diplomats general manager Andy Dolich said, "The 50,000 at the Gator Bowl pep rally was really impressive. Washington is close to Baltimore and up there, that was big news."

Godbold was right. Irsay was using Jacksonville as leverage to get a new stadium built in Baltimore. He did eventually move the Colts to Indianapolis which constructed a brand new modern facility.

But, with Irsay, Jacksonville's quest to capture an NFL team was just getting started, and Jacksonville's new mayor had taken a mighty leap in getting his top goal: changing negative attitudes in his city. "We got more out of him than he got out of us. We got a great deal of publicity for Jacksonville and that was the first big step in changing the spirit. I knew that night if we could hold that spirit we could accomplish anything."

A season ticket drive followed quickly on the heels of Colt Fever that netted $12 million in season ticket pledges.

Chapter 15

———❧———

RESTORING A REGAL QUEEN

WHEN JAKE GODBOLD was a poor kid growing up in a federal housing project on Jacksonville's northside, the closest he got to the arts and humanities was when the city recreation department played music and showed movies in the gazebo at Brentwood Park. The arts were not something he thought about as a boy or even as a young adult. That all changed when Godbold became Jacksonville's mayor.

"When I was a kid I didn't have the privilege of knowing about the humanities, the arts. I learned when I got into the mayor's office that if it's important to business, important to industry and important to our citizens, then it needed to be important to me," Godbold said.

Early in his first term, the mayor traveled to Washington D.C. to lobby the federal government on Jacksonville's behalf. While there, he made his first trip to the John F. Kennedy Center for the Performing Arts. Just being inside the landmark building proved to be a moving and transforming moment. On the walls of the River Terrace outside the Grand Foyer, Godbold began reading quotes by President Kennedy inscribed there. One in particular caught his attention. He wrote it down, and when he returned to Jacksonville, the quote was framed and put on his desk. To this day he still quotes it often, and when he is laid to rest, the words will be on his headstone.

"I am certain that after the dust of centuries has passed over our cities, we, too, will be remembered not for the victories or defeats in battle or in politics, but for our contribution to the human spirit."

Mayor Godbold prepares for a press conference with aide Martha Barrett

As he embraced Jacksonville's arts and philanthropic community and supported its symphony, museums, theater groups, visual artists and dance companies, he always kept Kennedy's quote at the top of his mind. It was perfect. After all, his chief aim as mayor was to change the attitudes and lift the spirit of his town. The arts, like sports, were perfect agents of change and great partner making that happen.

His strong backing of the arts pleased, but surprised, a lot of Jacksonville's establishment. Trinita Logue (Petersen) was executive director of the Jacksonville Arts Assembly when Godbold was elected in 1979.

I.M. Sulzbacher, who had served on the first consolidated City Council with Godbold, was chair of the Arts Assembly, which was the lead non-profit in town that received city funding and other grants to promote the arts. "I.M. took me to see Jake early on, maybe after he got elected," Logue said. "He said that if we could get Jake to support the arts a lot more people would support the arts."

Logue remembers that Sulzbacher thought the new mayor would hear them out and maybe even help. "He said we need to make friends with him and we need to make friends with the people he represents."

The meeting was a success. "I was just completely blown away by his complete openness, interest in me and what I was doing. It was his enthusiasm," said Logue. "I remember coming out of there thinking, wow, I think he is going to support us."

Jay Stein, chairman of Stein Mart, moved his company headquarters to Jacksonville, he said because of Godbold. Stein became a big Godbold fan and the two men quickly became close friends. "I thought Jake knew what a great city needed and he was ready to move heaven and earth to make it happen, whether it interested him or not," said Stein. "He knew we had to have a good symphony. He knew we had to have great museums. He knew there was more to this city than just the river and athletics. He saw to it that all of those people who wanted the arts and needed the arts got it."

Support the arts Godbold did. Usually, it was a struggle each year for the arts to get even close to the funding it wanted and the money the Arts Assembly thought it needed. Godbold increased the Arts Assembly's funding to $1 million a year. "That was a big amount of money," said

Logue. "We actually broadened the number of organizations that money went to." Traditionally, big hitters like the Jacksonville Symphony, Cummer Art Museum and Jacksonville Art Museum ate up most of the city funds. "We were able to get money out to small theater and dance companies and other companies," she said.

With the increased funding, Logue was also able to bring in various arts groups and have them perform in communities all over the city. "We went to parks on the northside and we put on free concerts and performances."

Godbold knew, she said, what was happening. "Even though I didn't know he was watching, I'd see him and he'd say, 'I like what you did on this, or something like that.' And, I would say, wow, he knows."

Godbold's support went beyond increased funding for the Arts Assembly. Among other things, he held a pair of events, including a black-tie gala, to raise funds for the money-strapped Jacksonville Symphony Orchestra.

In 1981 Godbold hosted a Mayor's dinner that attracted 200 people. A year later, Godbold attended a White House dinner. "It was the most elegant dinner I ever attended," he said. "When I came back I said, 'Let's copy what they did.'"

Godbold threw the Symphony Spring Spectacular. "Last year," Godbold told the newspaper, "We were lucky to get 200. This year we had to cut it off at 400." The Spectacular was planned to raise $50,000 for the symphony so it would not have to lay off any musicians. Prior to the event, the Jessie Ball DuPont Foundation gave the symphony a sizable contribution, eliminating the need for Godbold's money raising party. He held it anyway and reduced the ticket price to $100 each. $10,000 was raised.

After the event, Wini Rider, women's editor of the *Times-Union*, wrote that the Symphony Spring Spectacular was "one of the most spectacular dinner parties this city has ever seen."

When the symphony's long-time maestro Willis Page resigned in 1983 over an internal disagreement and started the River City Band, Godbold adopted it as the official city band and made sure it received financial help from the city. During the remaining five years he was in office, it was normal for the River City Band to be present at city functions to perform.

The crown jewel of Godbold's partnership with Jacksonville's arts community would become the historic Florida Theatre, a grand movie house that first opened in April 1927. The theater offered an escape from stress with two hours of great entertainment in a setting of opulence, and for only a dime. It was where many people had their first date.

During Godbold's days as a kid growing up, he recalled, "The Florida Theatre was a very special place for people in the forties and fifties. I can remember going there on the weekend and it was always a special thing. Living in Brentwood you didn't do that every day. It was a special event and you went with friends and dates." Like so many who grew up in Jacksonville, Godbold maintained a long-time love affair with the old theater. "They had this guy play a big organ. When it was time for him he would come up in an elevator in a tuxedo or suit. He'd also play the piano and they'd have words on the screen and the whole audience would get into it and be singing. "

In its hey-day, the Florida Theatre was open from 11 a.m. until 11 p.m. and was home to first-run movies, news reels, and occasional stage presentations. In 1956, Elvis Presley performed two shows at the Florida Theatre under threat of an arrest warrant from Judge Marion Gooding if Presley shook his famous hips. Gooding was present for both concerts and Presley obeyed the judge's orders. Jake Godbold and his girlfriend Jean Jenkins were also in the audience.

But over time the grand theater, which was designed in the Mediterranean Revival architecture style, had been allowed to decline. Its beautiful high ceiling interiors were in decay when the theater was officially closed in May 1980.

In many ways, the historic theater at the corner of North Newnan and East Forsyth Streets, just a couple of blocks from City Hall, was the symbol of a downtown that had run out of steam and was on life support when Godbold became mayor in 1979.

Several influential Jacksonville citizens, who had grown up enjoying the Florida Theatre, started thinking of ways to save and restore it before it fell victim to the wrecking ball and the bulldozer. They were led by architect Ted Pappas and attorney Doug Milne. "We talked about it all of the time in the arts community," said Logue. "One day Doug and Ted came to me and said they wanted to go to Tampa and see what they've done with their theater, the Tampa Theatre, because it's just like ours."

The Tampa Theatre had opened in October 1926, and like Jacksonville's show palace, the theater in Tampa was designed in the Mediterranean Revival style. Tampa residents, like people in Jacksonville, started moving to the suburbs in the late sixties and early seventies. The downtown theater was also abandoned and allowed to deteriorate. In 1973, Tampa citizens who loved the theater banded together, got city officials involved and started a rescue effort. The city assumed the theater's leases and the county's Arts Council started programming and managing it with concerts, special events and movies.

Milne, Pappas and Logue made an appointment and the trio drove to west central Florida to meet with Tampa Theatre officials on a Saturday.

"We got very excited about what could happen. And, then, of course, Jake and I had a love fest over restoring the Florida Theatre."

The seven story Florida Theatre was owned by Plitt Southern Theaters, Inc. Logue enlisted Jacksonville lawyer Howard Dale to research Plitt and begin conversations about the feasibility of the Arts Assembly purchasing the boarded-up facility. "We started talking about it on the Arts Assembly board and we decided we were going to try it."

With $500,000 from the state, $350,000 from the city, and $100,000 from other sources, the Arts Assembly purchased the Florida Theatre in October 1981 from Plitt Southern Theaters.

With the theater in hand, Logue and members of the Arts Assembly board turned to Godbold. He toured the theater. "They opened it all up. There was a dusty and muggy smell inside, but when the lights went on you could still see the beauty of the handwork and painting over the stage. The masonry was cracked and falling down. Those beautiful curtains were down. I was very excited about how we could do this," said Godbold.

Godbold agreed to lead a $4 million fundraising campaign to pay for the theater's grand restoration to the splendor of days gone by. Jacksonville lawyer and business leader Charles Towers suggested to Godbold that he enlist William Nash, president of Prudential Insurance Southern Central Operations, who had recently moved back to Jacksonville. Shortly before Towers made his recommendation to the mayor, Godbold attended a meeting of the U.S. Conference of Mayors in Houston. On the return trip home, Nash and his wife were on Godbold's plane. "I happened to say, 'Mr. Nash, I hope you aren't disappointed about leaving a big town like Houston and coming to Jacksonville.' He said, 'Hell no. Fran and I are tickled to death to be coming home. This was our home and its going to be our home for good.'"

In his meeting with Towers, Godbold asked, "Do you really think Nash would do that?" Towers said, "Only if you ask him." Godbold immediately called Nash and asked him to meet. "He was excited and tickled to death that I asked him to take that on." From that moment on, the two men worked closely together.

On August 26, 1982, the Arts Assembly and the city, with Bill Nash as chairman, kicked off the Florida Theatre Restoration project with a Dancing in the Streets party on Forsyth Street in front of the theater. Tickets were $30 each and the street was packed with people having fun as they danced to music from 1930-1980. There were also performances inside the theater.

At the time of the fundraising campaign launch, the Arts Assembly had raised $1,825,000 from government sources, $832,400 from private sources, and it needed another $2.3 million to meet the goal of $4 million.

The *Florida Times-Union* editorialized the day after the kickoff that while the Florida Theatre project was off to a good start, more people and businesses needed to step up. "Mayor Jake Godbold pointed out the enlightened self interest that should help motivate Jacksonville to mount a successful campaign when he said that, 'The role of the arts in a successful downtown redevelopment has been proven in city after city, and the Florida Theatre is a historic and cultural resource which will make a unique contribution to Jacksonville's next decade of unprecedented growth.'"

During the theater's renovation, the mayor would go once or twice a week at lunch time to see the construction. Aide Rick Catlett usually joined him. "We'd get a hot dog and a bag of popcorn at a little place next door and I'd go inside, halfway down in the theater, sit there, eat lunch and watch this artist on scaffolding hand doing those little pieces of art work. It almost got addictive. I remember when it was finished how beautiful it was. I wished everybody had a chance to see how it was and how it became."

At the time of the Florida Theatre campaign, Jacksonville was well underway with construction of its coal fired power plants to replace the city utility's reliance on high priced imported oil and replace it with coal. Shearson American Express senior vice president Arnold Greenfield was the city's financial advisor. Godbold had recently returned from Shearson's headquarters in New York City where he spent two days signing $1.6 billion in municipal bonds to finance the coal fired plants. It was the largest single municipal bond financing project in U.S. history.

"One day, Martha (Barrett, the mayor's press aide) came in my office and she had a *New York Times*. She read where Shearson was having a nationwide campaign to pick out city art projects to contribute to and invited proposals. It had the name of the lady in charge of Shearson's philanthropy and said her staff would select the winning cities and how much money they would receive," said the mayor.

Godbold's staff and the Arts Assembly submitted a proposal for the Florida Theatre. "Martha came in and said they chose the groups and we aren't on the list." The mayor was not pleased. He phoned Shearson's Greenfield. "I told him I was disappointed and he was happy to come and see me to talk about it." Greenfield told the mayor the decisions had been made. "I said I wanted a shot at her. I want to talk to her and make another presentation. Greenfield had made Shearson a lot of money handling that bond deal."

Greenfield made an appointment for the mayor and his team.

After they arrived at the Shearson headquarters they were led into a large conference room. "We waited a pretty good while," said Godbold aide Catlett. "You felt like the conference room table was 100 yards long. There were three services of orange juice, coffee and a continental breakfast on one end and three on the other end. You almost had to raise your voice for the people on the other end to hear you."

When the meeting finally began, Godbold and his team made their presentation. "She didn't look like she was jumping up and down," said the mayor. "I didn't think it was going our way."

"He asked her for $1 million," said Catlett. "Well," said the woman, "that would be the largest single contribution in the history of our company to one project."

Godbold responded, "I want to explain something to you. Do you have any idea what is the largest single municipal bond issue ever signed on Wall Street here in New York just a few months ago?" She replied, "No." "It was for Jacksonville. $1.6 billion," said the mayor. "And, do you have any idea who handled that bond issue? Your company. Now, I think that you and Shearson should reconsider adding us to that list of cities you are donating money to the arts. This is a wonderful project and your company has made an awful lot of money off this city. Now, I'm asking you to come back and help the city and its arts programs." There was an unconfirmed report that the mayor also hinted that if Shearson didn't help Jacksonville it might be excluded from doing any more business with the city.

"He got his point across," said Catlett. "He may only have a high school education but he was not afraid to be in meetings with those people."

On October 1, 1983, the newly renovated, glorious and historic Florida Theatre had a grand re-opening fit for a regal queen. The next morning, the *Times-Union* said, "more ruffled shirts, boiled shirts, stuffed shirts, limousines, sequined dresses, black bow ties and gowns were at North Newman and East Forsyth Streets last night than in the past 60 years."

All 1,978 of the $50 seats in the theater were filled with the Who's Who of Jacksonville. There were speeches and thank yous *ad nauseum.* And, there was entertainment for everyone, from a Cole Porter Review to a medley of electronic organ music backed by old film clips, a performance by the London String Quintet and a night-ending concert by Vassar Clements, who played blue grass, country and jazz.

Fittingly, Clements closed out the evening playing the mayor's very favorite song, "Orange Blossom Special."

In mid-December, a little more than two months after the grand re-opening, Godbold received word that Shearson American Express had agreed to donate $500,000 to the Florida Theatre restoration. The terms were $100,000 a year for five years. At the time, it was the largest single philanthropic gift the company had made to a city project.

"The support of Jake made all the difference in the world," said Logue. "Just knowing he was behind us. Knowing he was so positive in every way. There wasn't anything he didn't want to try. There wasn't anything he didn't want to do. He would always get mad when anybody said anything negative about Jacksonville. He wouldn't allow it. Jake was special and you knew it the minute you were with him."

On November 4, 1982, the Florida Theatre was added to the U.S. National Register of Historic Places. On April 18, 2012, the AIA's Florida Chapter placed the theater on its list *of Florida Architecture: 100 Years, 100 Places.*

In 2018, 134,053 people attended concerts and events in the Florida Theatre, ranking it sixth in attendance for U.S. theaters with fewer than 2,000 seats, according to Pollstar, a concert industry publication.

Chapter 16

BUILDING A FOUNDATION
FOR THE NFL

THE LONG MARCH to land an NFL team for Jacksonville started on that hot August 17, 1979 evening in the Gator Bowl. It continued for the next 14 years and finally concluded on November 30, 1993 when National Football League Commissioner Paul Tagliabue announced Jacksonville was one of two cities getting an expansion franchise that would begin play in 1995.

The next mayor after Godbold—Tommy Hazouri—kept the quest alive until 1989 when a prospective ownership group, "Touchdown Jacksonville!," organized by Jacksonville insurance executive and developer Tom Petway, stepped in to provide private leadership and funding to continue the community effort. Petway was joined by eventual Florida Governor Jeb Bush, insurance executive Ron Weaver and later his brother, shoe magnet Wayne Weaver, and others. Wayne Weaver would eventually become the lead partner of the group. When Jacksonville secured the team, Weaver became chairman and the principal owner.

On the afternoon of the NFL announcement, former Mayor Godbold was sitting in the green room at television station WJXT Channel 4. So far as anyone in Jacksonville knew, nobody had a clue if the city would be one of two cities chosen from five finalists. The entire community was on edge. In March 1992, the city and "Touchdown Jacksonville!" had survived the first round of cuts at the NFL's annual winter meeting, from 11 to 7, then made it again when the list was reduced to five competing cities: Jacksonville, Baltimore, St. Louis, Charlotte and Memphis. While everyone was hopeful, Jacksonville was considered a long shot.

Godbold was nervous as he watched the monitor in the green room. He did not know WJXT had a live camera focused on him. The instant Tagliabue announced "Jacksonville," the former mayor dropped his face in his hands. "I said, 'Oh shit. We got it.' I cried."

"I thought we would someday get a team, but not under me. We came close two or three times and I knew what we were doing wouldn't be in vain," Godbold said. "I was so positive it was like a mission. We had to do all of this work so that somebody after me would be able to secure a team for Jacksonville."

What happened during the eight years Godbold was mayor laid the ground work for that historic and long-awaited moment. Some of it was very public as Jacksonville blatantly courted other NFL owners who flirted with moving their teams. Sometimes it seemed like the city was a revolving door, with teams from St. Louis, Atlanta, New Orleans and Houston making calls on Godbold and Jacksonville.

Godbold aide Rick Catlett was in the middle of it all and often took the role of lead NFL dog for Godbold. The courtships were intense and frustrating. "When it was over and they didn't move here, we'd get a little depressed." However, said Catlett, "We learned so much by going through it. Every time it made us better at the end. We always learned something, plus we made friends."

Those friends would come to really matter. Owners like Bud Adams in Houston, Lamar Hunt in Kansas City, Rankin Smith in Atlanta, Bill Bidwell in St. Louis, Joe Robby in Miami, and of course, Irsay who had moved the Colts to Indianapolis. The best friend Godbold and Jacksonville had, however, was Hugh Culverhouse, a Jacksonville lawyer who owned the Tampa Bay Buccaneers.

Godbold recalled that even before the Irsay visit, watching an Oilers home game on television was what first ignited the notion of going after an NFL team. "At the time, the city of Houston wasn't doing good. Oil was depressed and the economy was slow. But, there was so much excitement that Sunday in that stadium. They stood up and sang, 'We're the Houston Oilers.' There was all that blue and white color, all the flags and pomp. When the camera moved around to all those people, there were so many different kinds of people there. Hispanic, blacks, whites, young and old. There was so much pride in that stadium."

That, said Godbold, is what Jacksonville needs. "We need something this big that we can all support." He told his wife Jean, "I want to do this. I want to seek a football team for Jacksonville."

Catlett says he always thought using a football team to create enthusiasm in the city was Godbold's focus. "His focus was making people feel good about Jacksonville. He used to say, 'We aren't going to have anybody move here if the people who live here don't like it.'"

Catlett had been a member of my special events team when Godbold pulled him up to his staff. "Rick really grew up on our staff. His real assignment was working with the Sports Commission and he got to know all of those people in the NFL," said Godbold. "He knew every owner, he went to every meeting, every reception. Anything that had to do with sports, Rick did it. They liked him, they communicated with him. They knew when they communicated to him, they were communicating to me."

Legendary coach Bum Phillips of the Oilers was first to approach Jacksonville after Irsay's visit. Phillips called Godbold. "He had a horse farm and raised horses in Ocala and he made it known he'd love to be coaching the Oilers in Jacksonville," said Godbold.

Of all the teams that called on Jacksonville, Godbold said, "We came closer to getting the Oilers than any other team." There were several private meetings with Godbold and with a group of Jacksonville business leaders who were interested in owning an NFL team, including heart surgeon Dr. Roy Baker, developer Jack Demetree, and developer Steve Wilson. Phillips attended some of the meetings, as did the Oilers general manager. "They wanted to move the team and said they were going to make a decision soon."

The meetings, Godbold said, "were very secret. They didn't want the people in Houston to know."

At one point, Godbold started believing the Oilers were going to relocate to Jacksonville. "It got so close I could feel the excitement of being able to say we had signed a team. We got very close and had the contract." But, then, owner Bud Adams threw in a ringer. The Oilers owner wrote into the contract that he wanted the new Jacksonville owners to also purchase some of his properties in Houston. Godbold said the city couldn't participate in that. Demetree and Wilson decided to visit Houston and take a look at Adams' properties. "It was condos and office buildings with very few tenants in them. The real estate market in Houston was terrible," said Godbold. The prospective owners returned to Jacksonville and told Adams they couldn't agree with his demand.

"It was a real disappointment, but it didn't slow us down," said Godbold. Afterwards, Adams moved the Oilers to Nashville.

Over time, making NFL friends worked for Jacksonville. When Falcons owner Smith was thinking of relocating his team from Atlanta, Jacksonville was right there. "We knew we weren't going to get the Falcons, we just did that to help Rankin Smith," said Catlett. Smith returned the favor when he gave Godbold's team the NFL owner's manual that described and analyzed what every city seeking a team was doing. "He also said, 'Rick, the numbers you are telling me aren't the numbers the league is giving me.'" Armed with that information and the manual, Godbold and his team called on the NFL. "We told them, 'These numbers aren't right. You aren't referencing the same documents we're referencing.' We laid the documents out on the table. As a result, they let their accounting firm, Price-Waterhouse, go."

Chiefs owner Lamar Hunt, who started the American Football League, turned his general manager over to Catlett and the team. He helped them understand how to put together a deal from the NFL perspective.

"Culverhouse was the leader for us. He talked to Jake all the time. We pretty much listened to what he told us to do," said Catlett.

Culverhouse made sure Jacksonville was invited to each NFL owners' quarterly meeting, the only non- NFL city in attendance. Godbold made sure Jacksonville was always there, with the mayor at the lead. "We went to every meeting and we always had a hospitality room for the owners with the plan to get to know as many of them as possible," said Catlett. Catlett, along with Godbold's chief administrative officer Don McClure, C.P.A. Larry Jaffe, bank president Hugh Jones, and others lobbied the owners, team executives, and senior members of the NFL staff. "We were there to make friends and get information on what we needed to do to get a team."

Two key friendships that Catlett and the others made were with Don Weis, the NFL's executive director, and Jim Steig who ran the NFL's special events. Weis ran the Super Bowls and he was in charge of NFL expansion. "His job was to get as many cities prepared for NFL franchises so the league had options. That was our goal." Steig put together the owners' meetings.

"They called us the 'Rug Rats' because we'd stand in the hall waiting on an owner to come out of the meeting to go to the bathroom and we could speak to them," said Catlett. At breakfast each morning, Catlett and the team would go to the cafeteria, "because they all came."

During the owners' meeting in Hawaii in 1981, Tex Schramm of the Dallas Cowboys wanted a vote to move the annual Pro Bowl game. Culverhouse immediately phoned Godbold to see if the mayor was interested in going after the game. "Heck yea," Godbold replied. The mayor and others then fired off telegrams to the owners urging them to move the game to Jacksonville. The next day, the vote was tabled until the summer meeting. That didn't stop Godbold. He had his Sports and Entertainment Commission put together a full-blown presentation, fly to New York, and meet with commissioner Rozelle for two hours. Afterwards, Godbold told the *Times-Union*, "Very frankly, those people were absolutely shocked at what the Gator Bowl was going to be."

In 1982, Jacksonville was one of ten cities invited to make a 15-minute presentation to the owners to host a Super Bowl in 1985 or 1986. Only Jacksonville and Pasadena were not in the NFL. Pasadena, home of the Rose Bowl, had been the site of a previous Super Bowl. Other cities making presentations included Anaheim, California, Houston, Miami, New Orleans, Pontiac, Michigan, San Francisco, Seattle and Tampa.

If Godbold wanted to put Jacksonville along side some of the country's top cities, and put the city's NFL quest on the minds of NFL owners, this was a big opportunity. The meeting was held in early June inside the Grand Hyatt Hotel in New York City. Godbold and the 12-member Super Bowl Task Force went ninth.

Weeks had gone into preparation. The Task Force knew it had to stress Jacksonville's positives: an expanded Gator Bowl to 80,000 seats, mild weather, the convenience of I-95, and the St. John's River which ran through the middle of town, just across the street and south of the Gator Bowl.

The city also had to try and answer how it would deal with some obvious shortcomings, especially a lack of the needed 25,000 hotel rooms for out of town fans. The Task Force pointed out that Jacksonville was in very close proximity to Daytona Beach and St. Augustine and had upscale resorts nearby at Amelia Island and Ponte Vedra Beach. But the Task Force didn't stop there.

Calling its presentation, "Super Bowl in the Super City Aboard the Super Ship," the Task Force told the owners that it had an agreement with the Norwegian Cruise Lines to bring the S.S. Norway, the world's largest cruise ship, to downtown Jacksonville to provide plenty of rooms and offer a post-Super Bowl cruise.

Southern Bell executive John Bell, who was chair of the Sports and Entertainment Commission's football committee, led the presentation. He was followed by Ginny Archer of the Norwegian Cruise Lines, Albert Ernest, president of the Chamber of Commerce, and Godbold. A six-minute video was also part of the presentation. In his remarks, the mayor invited the owners to visit Jacksonville before making their decision. "We are truly ready for a Super Bowl," he told the owners. "We asked Mr. Bob Irsay, owner of the Baltimore Colts, what we needed to do to get into the NFL. He told me, 'Son, you've got to build a new stadium.' We did."

Godbold concluded by saying, "If there is room in this country for the NFL to grow up, then the NFL needs to spread its joy around to the non-NFL cities."

Afterwards, the mayor told the media, "I don't know what any of this means, but the smile on Mr. Rozelle's face seemed to say, 'We're pleased with your presentation.'"

For the mayor, there was only one way to chase the NFL, and it was the same way he met most every challenge and opportunity. "You approach it in three ways—interest, preparedness and commitment. We're all three."

After Godbold left office in 1987, Catlett continued to be in the forefront of Jacksonville's NFL effort, joining "Touchdown Jacksonville!" as a staff member. Catlett says that he and "Touchdown Jacksonville!" members Weaver, Petway and the others knew prior to Tagliabue's announcement on November 30, 1993, that Jacksonville was being selected as an expansion city. "We knew we were getting the team before the announcement. They called and said, 'The meeting is in Chicago and you're going to get the team.'"

Chapter 17

Bringing Back the Spirit, One Event at a Time

As Mayor, Jake Godbold often said, "All I do is bang these damn drums, every day." It was his way of saying that he believed his number one job was making the people of Jacksonville feel good about living in their city and selling Jacksonville to the outside world.

"I was trying to change the damn image of that first poll that said Jacksonville people don't like their own city. They're negative. They don't like downtown. They don't like the mayor," said Godbold. "There wasn't any pride here. I felt like the best way to change those attitudes was to have a good time downtown and make it a fun place to come, make it clean and make it safe."

Godbold permanently removed me as energy czar and put me in charge of creating and producing special events.

Bringing people together to celebrate and have fun began with Colt

Fever. From that moment on, there was something happening in Jacksonville all of the time, gatherings of hundreds and often many thousands of people.

Any excuse to do something was seized upon. If a Broadway play came to the Civic Auditorium, it was celebrated. When the U.S. hostages were taken in Iran, Godbold held a noontime "Stand Up for America" hard hat rally at the Daniel State Office Building, complete with the Marine Color Guard, hundreds of American flags, patriotic music and the street in front of the building painted a red, white and blue to read: "Iran, Let Our People Go." That was followed by a "Candlelight Vigil" on the river in downtown.

When French auto maker Citroen wanted to film a car commercial in downtown, Godbold's team rounded up 200 horses to race down the north side of the Main Street Bridge. And, when author and actress Gloria Vanderbilt came to Jacksonville to promote her line of jeans at May Cohens department store in downtown, Godbold teamed with May Cohens special events director Jonelle Mulrain to bring Vanderbilt into town with a police escort and receive red carpet treatment. On weekends, for fun, a barge was docked at the new Southbank Riverwalk and concerts were performed by the Jacksonville Symphony.

Coastline Drive, just west of City Hall and in front of the state-owned Daniel Office Building, became a favorite site for celebrations like "River Day" and "Dancing in the Street." Hemming Plaza in the heart of downtown came to life with events and concerts.

Because there was little to do for students from the University of Florida and the University of Georgia each fall on the weekend of their big football game in Jacksonville, Godbold and his team opened the old, boarded up Jacksonville Terminal and threw the "World's Largest Fraternity Party" there. It drew thousands of celebrants. On St. Patrick's

Day Jacksonville celebrated with an "Everybody's Irish Festival," complete with green beer.

There was so much going on that the media started calling Godbold and me, "Barnum and Bailey."

"We wanted people to love Jacksonville and love living here. These events helped make people feel a part, it was their city. We were in this together," said Godbold.

While there were some Godbold critics who complained that the festivals and special events were little more than "bread and circuses," Godbold and his team truly believed that without a drastic reversal of negative attitudes that permeated the city, they would accomplish very little. That included raising revenues to invest in badly needed infrastructure, economic development and job growth.

The biggest event following Colt Fever was Mayport and All That Jazz, a music and seafood festival in the Jacksonville fishing village of Mayport at the mouth of the St. Johns River. In addition to having fun and getting folks excited about Jacksonville, Godbold wanted to promote the fish houses and restaurants there.

"Fernandina Beach, just up the road, had a shrimp festival every spring that drew thousands and thousands of people. I wanted to do something like that at Mayport," said Godbold. He told me to figure out what to do. The mayor was thinking that perhaps Mayport would be a great site for a big fishing tournament with a seafood component.

I believed that music had to be an important part of any special event. One day I took a tape player and tapes of country-western, rock and roll, and jazz music out to the Mayport ferry which carries cars and passengers back and forth across the St. Johns River from Mayport on the south to Heckscher Drive on the north. I listened to the music to see what would work best in that environment while shrimp boats glided in and out of the village docks and large tankers passed by in the river channel.

I returned to Godbold and recommended the city hold a jazz festival that featured food booths sponsored by Mayport seafood restaurants and the community's non-profit organizations. He wanted to give the people of Mayport some ownership in the event.

The first jazz festival was held at Mayport in October 1980 and featured artists Della Reese, legendary drummer Art Blakey and his Jazz Messengers that included 17-year-old trumpeter, Wynton Marsalis, trombonist Urbie Green and Buddy DeFranco, who was known as Mr. Jazz Clarinet. More than 70,000 people jammed into the tiny coastal community to hear 13 performances in 13 hours. The one-day festival was dubbed "The world's largest free jazz festival."

In October 1981, the second Mayport and All That Jazz Festival was held. Dizzy Gillespie was one of the headliners. Other performers included Della Reese, drummer Buddy Rich and sax player Phil Woods.

PBS produced an hour-long special that featured Gillespie, Woods and pianist newcomer Marcus Roberts. It was shown internationally. Police estimated attendance was 100,000.

Because it had far outgrown the tiny fishing village of Mayport and the U.S. Navy refused to continue letting the festival park automobiles at the adjacent naval base, in 1982 the festival was moved to an open piece of ground downtown on the St. Johns River across from the Gator Bowl. Once again, the third year was a huge success with 100,000 festival goers. The next year, 1983, the jazz festival opened the brand new $3.4 million Metropolitan Park on that same ground. PBS began its fall season with an eight-hour live production from the festival with comedian/pianist Steve Allen and pianist Dr. Billy Taylor as co-hosts.

Today, 39 years after its beginning, the Jacksonville Jazz Festival continues as a signature event in downtown Jacksonville.

Once Metropolitan Park opened, Godbold used it to host the Spring Music Festival and the Country Music Festival, drawing tens of thousands to enjoy the riverfront while dancing to outstanding music acts like the Beach Boys, Four Tops, the Association, Platters, Ronnie Milsap, Earl Thomas Conley, and the Temptations. In 1985, over 150,000 lapped it all up at the Spring Music Festival.

In stirring up good feelings about Jacksonville, Godbold wanted everyone included, especially blacks and senior citizens. The mayor wanted to make sure both groups participated in and benefited from what he called Jacksonville's "quality of life."

For seniors, he created the Mayor's Older Buddies (M.O.B.) and held fishing tournaments, dances and numerous social events. He also always made sure that when he had a special event, seniors were well represented. Godbold built seven community centers around Jacksonville so that seniors would have a close, convenient place to go eat, have activities and socialize with others. "I didn't want them to be lonely. I wanted them to enjoy their lives."

When Michael Jackson's Victory Tour came to Jacksonville in 1984 for three sold out concerts in the Gator Bowl, Jake persuaded Jackson to give him 300 tickets for seniors for each performance. "He didn't blink an eye. He was all for it. His people didn't think seniors would want to go to a concert that would last until midnight," said Godbold. "I told them these were very active seniors. We had buses and a good organization that will get them there." Godbold personally joined his team to put the seniors on the buses, escort them to the concerts and provide food and drinks. "To see the joy of those 300 seniors each night was overwhelming," said Godbold. "They had a wonderful time."

In 1979, a judge granted an order that the original Lone Ranger, Clayton Moore, could no longer wear his famed mask. The owner of the character anticipated making a new film version of the Lone Ranger's story and he wanted a younger actor to play the Lone Ranger in the movie. The 65-year-old Moore had to give up his mask, something that had been part of Moore's identity all his adult life. I seized on the judge's ruling to invite Moore to Jacksonville for "Lone Ranger Day," a large public protest with the M.O.B. Hundreds of the city's seniors paraded through downtown wearing their own Lone Ranger masks. The seniors were led by Moore on a large white horse. He was wearing Foster Grant wraparound sunglasses.

Godbold was aggressive about ensuring minority participation in everything, especially when it came to special events. If, for instance, the city was going to throw "The World's Largest Fraternity Party" the night before the Florida-Georgia football game, then it would throw a party the night before the Bold City Classic, a football game between Florida A&M University and Bethune Cookman College. It was called, "Dancing in the Streets" and was held on Coastline Drive behind City Hall and in front of the Daniel State Office Building on the riverfront.

I called on city employee Gordon Boyer, who was nicknamed "Rembrandt," to get his team of firefighters and other volunteers together and paint the A&M Rattler logo on Coastline Drive in front of the Daniel building. While we were painting the street, I saw a young black man standing on the steps of the Daniel Building watching us. He had tears in his eyes. I approached him and asked, "Are we doing something that offends you? Because if we are, we'll stop." The man replied, "No. I just never thought I would see my school's logo painted on a street in downtown Jacksonville."

The next night the party was a huge success. Twenty different black non-profit organizations and churches lined food booths along the riverfront and the smells of frying fish and chicken, barbecue and other foods wafted over the crowd. At 6 p.m., timed for live coverage on local news shows, the world- famous Florida A&M band, the "Marching 100," performed on top of the Rattler logo painted on the street the night before. To top off the entertaining, two R&B bands performed from a stage at one end of the festival. Over 20,000 people attended.

"I had a great time," said Godbold. "Everybody was so happy, no sadness. Jacksonville had been like 'We don't have laughter here,' (from "Annie"). There was a lot of happiness," he said.

"That's when it felt as mayor that it's happening. You're bringing that spirit back one inch at a time, one event at a time and it's beginning to grow."

Chapter 18

Doing Okay When They Call You 'Jake'

Like so many of Godbold's friends, Glen English was a Jacksonville product who went to work for the city's public works department after he got out of school. When Jake ran for mayor in 1979, English came out of retirement to campaign for Godbold. The campaign paid him to be Godbold's traveling aide and be at his side all of the time. It was a perfect fit for the affable and fun-loving English. When Jake was late for an event, English could smooth it over, usually with humor. When it was time for Godbold to leave so he could get to the next stop, English knew how to extricate him without ruffling any feathers.

"He was very pleasant for me to be around," Godbold recalled. "He always made you feel good. You couldn't be around Glen without having a good attitude. He could take the most horrible things that happened that day and he'd turn them into very funny stories. He turned the whole nightmare around to a funny story."

Once Godbold took office July 1, 1979, English went back to work in City Hall and was at the mayor's side as one of the people assigned to Godbold as a traveling aide to get the bustling mayor from place to place. While Jake enjoyed his company, he had another idea for what he wanted English to do.

As president of the City Council in the summer of 1978, Godbold proposed creating a system and naming a single person to handle all the citizen complaints that were flooding council offices. Mayor Tanzler was opposed to the idea because he didn't want council members to get credit for resolving problems. He said council members should just refer any complaint they receive directly to the mayor's office. Godbold responded, "You don't get re-elected like that. That ain't nothing but good political sense."

During his visit to Baltimore with the Chamber of Commerce in his first year as the elected mayor, Godbold heard from Baltimore Mayor Donald Schaefer about the importance of paying attention to little details to change attitudes so you can rebuild your city. Schaefer, who was not married, loved being mayor, just like Jake. He rode the city's streets, always with a legal pad, looking for problems like pot holes and uncollected trash, then he made sure the problems were corrected right away. Schaefer set up an internal process to handle citizen complaints, making sure fixes were made to what was reported broken.

When Godbold replaced Mayor Tanzler for the first six months of 1979, he discovered the Mayor's Office had no process for handling complaints. If a complaint was called in by a citizen, it might be written down on a sticky note, but then again, it might just be ignored. "Guys in the rich section of town could call the mayor's office and they get somebody they know. Their complaints get taken care of," Godbold said. "But, the poor guy out there with a stopped-up pipe flooding his yard, or a tree that has fallen onto his property, he doesn't know how in the heck to get help," said Godbold

It was such an unruly and disorganized process, English said, "Sometimes people would forget what they were originally complaining about the time they got to someone who could do something."

Godbold created a "Complaint Department," set it up just down from his office, and he put English in charge. English was provided a computer, secretary, staff assistant and a senior citizen volunteer. Cards were printed and distributed throughout the community that said people should call English at 633-3715 if they have a complaint.

Godbold commissioned a study to determine what kind of complaints were coming in, where they were coming from and what departments were getting the complaints. A system was installed so that when a complaint was received it was routed to English. If a complaint went directly to a city department, it was sent to English. If he wasn't available at the time, English always called the citizen back to discuss the problem. The complaint was recorded in the computer and a copy was sent to the department head responsible. The citizen who complained was sent a post card confirming the complaint had been logged by the city. The department head had ten days to act. After five days, if the complaint wasn't handled, the department head would receive a second copy with a question: Why wasn't this handled? If there was no action after 15 days, English sent the complaint to the mayor. Once the complaint was handled, the citizen received a letter telling what action was taken.

There were times when Godbold would phone English at home after midnight to direct him to take emergency action on a complaint.

"Glen would go out on complaints where a person would be cursing and raising hell, and by the time he left, I'd get a call saying, 'I sure enjoyed Mr. English.' They would say Glen explained why something couldn't be handled by the city, and he'd tell them funny stories." If the problem was not something the city should do, English would say, "You don't want to be embarrassed and you don't want the mayor to be embarrassed because this is something we can't do."

"Whey they are unreasonable," English told the *Times-Union*, "our approach is to let them get it out of their system. Some of them start off and they will burn your ear right off."

Sometimes, a complaining citizen wanted to do more than "burn your ear right off." Take the lady who called all the time, saying she was blind and making complaints about city-owned University Hospital. One day, English decided to go see the woman. "She came after me with a butcher knife. She can be violent," he told the mayor. "Glen said, 'If she ever calls you don't let her come to see you.'" Later, the woman showed up in the mayor's office wanting to see Godbold. Naomi Glover, the long-time receptionist for the mayor under both Tanzler and Godbold, wouldn't let her see the mayor.

"Naomi came running in my office. 'Mr. Mayor, Mr. Mayor, no matter what you hear in the lobby don't come out here.' Then, she slammed my door and locked it." That was followed by loud noises outside Godbold's door. "I hear bang, bang, bang. I went up to the door and opened it and there was this lady rolling around on the floor." She was wrestling with the mayor's security guard, policeman Tommy Reeves. "Tommy was yelling, 'Get somebody. She's killing me.' She was beating him to death with her walking stick."

Reeves was trying not to injure the woman as she was biting him on his shirt. "He was bloody all over." Another police officer, Glen Brown, rushed in and got the woman off Reeves. She was taken to the hospital for an examination. Reeves, too, was taken to the hospital and had to have shots for the bites.

All complaints were not the same, but each one got attention. Once, a man came into the complaint office and told English he needed an artificial leg but didn't have any money. English used his sources to get the man an artificial limb.

English was the court jester on Godbold's staff and often contributed laughter to an intense and busy work environment. Godbold aide Rick Catlett, who also drove Godbold as well as being the mayor's liaison with the NFL, was often late for work. It was not usual for Catlett to phone the mayor's office receptionist with an excuse. He was either sick, overslept, had car problems, or forgot about a meeting. Naomi would then pass along Catlett's message to chief administrative officer Don McClure. Catlett also had to call English so English could pinch-hit if Godbold needed to be driven somewhere. Catlett's frequent tardiness became an in-house joke in the mayor's office.

One day, during a meeting of the mayor's staff, English volunteered that he had devised a way to save time and reduce the expense of dealing with Catlett's phoning in an excuse. "I've made up this list of excuses and given each one a number. This way when Rick calls in he can save time by just giving Naomi a number and then she can pass the number along. For instance, if he's overslept, he can just say #5." Even Catlett thought it was a funny suggestion. Catlett, of course, often had to drive Godbold late into the night, drive home, and then early the next morning pick up the mayor at his house. He felt like he had a good reason to be a little tardy sometimes.

Taking a page out of Schaefer's play book, Godbold always had his legal pad. "I would always carry a legal pad with me, always. I never went out of that office without a legal pad in my car. Every damn thing I saw out there I'd write down, whether it was a tree, a ditch or pot hole and I'd turn it over to Glen when I got back." Often, Godbold would stop where he found a downed tree or pot hole, give the citizen English's card and say, "If it isn't handled in five days, you call me." Godbold's complaint department became a great public relations tool. "It was very important to these little people."

Once a week Godbold and English rode the city's streets and through its neighborhoods together, looking for problems the city needed to fix. The drive around normally happened on Monday morning for two hours.

The trips were unannounced. Godbold would speak to people he saw along the drives, but these were not for glad-handing. They were looking for potholes, trash, abandoned vehicles, checking the status of city parks and making sure incoming complaints had been resolved.

"It's important to let people know you're interested and involved," he told *The Florida Times-Union*. It was something that had to be done every week. "It helps the employees to let them know you care and what they're doing is important."

It was also a way to make sure city employees were doing their jobs. The last thing they wanted was to be goofing off and Godbold drive up. That happened early in his first term and word spread quickly around city government about the mayor's ass-chewing of slacking city workers.

Hank Moore was Godbold's director of public works. He and English were good friends. Moore was a tall, big-jawed retired Army colonel. When he spoke to his public works employees, they listened.

When he told them what needed to be done, they did it. One day, the mayor was headed to a meeting at the port when he spotted a large pothole on Talleyrand Avenue at Bliss Street. Godbold called it in to English, who contacted Moore. "Hank called his guy and said the mayor's out there and he saw this big pot hole near Talleyrand

and Bliss." A short time later, the public works employee called Moore back. "Colonel, I've been up and down this street and I can't find that pot hole the mayor's talking about."

Moore said, "Well, you go back down that street until you find it and don't come back in here until you find it." Once again, the employee phoned Moore. "I've been up and down all these streets and I can't find that pot hole." Moore let him have it. "Goddammit to my soul," he shot back. "If the mayor said there's a pot hole out there, there's a pot hole out there. You find it. And, if you can't find it, you dig a pot hole and then cover it up."

The Florida Times-Union once had a reporter ride with the mayor and English during one of their morning inspections. The reporter later wrote that the mayor's car drove by the Gator Bowl parking lot that was an eye sore before Godbold became mayor. He had it paved and landscaped. There was a city worker there. The car stopped and the newspaper reported, "Jake said, 'Looking good, man.'" When the worker saw it was the mayor, he shouted, "Hey Jake." Godbold said, "That's when you can tell you're doing okay. When they call you Jake."

Chapter 19

IF AT FIRST YOU DON'T
SUCCEED...

METROPOLITAN PARK, A reborn 23-acre dirt parking lot across the street from the Gator Bowl, opened as a new $3.5 million riverfront people's park in grand style on Saturday October 15, 1983 with the worldwide telecast of the fourth annual Jacksonville and All That Jazz Festival.

At 10 a.m. the gates opened and 2,000 early visitors were led inside by the Excelsior Brass Band, the best of New Orleans Mardi Gras. Over the course of the day, more than 120,000 people were introduced to this new jewel a little east of the downtown skyline. They were entertained by renowned jazz artists like trumpeters Dizzy Gillespie, Freddie Hubbard and Wynton Marsalis, drummers Buddy Rich and Art Blakey and pianist Billy Taylor. Gillespie was declared "King" of the festival and sported a huge crown during his performance.

Taylor and pianist/comedian Steve Allen were hosts of an eight hour live telecast produced by PBS that opened the network's fall season.

Incredible smells wafted across the crowd, coming from food booths that were serving seafood, barbecue, shish kabob, Mexican, Italian, and Chinese dishes. A small navy of pleasure boats anchored in the river just off the park's bulkhead. Fireworks exploded over the St. John's River during the finale of a one-hour jam session featuring Gillespie, Hubbard, Marsalis, Rich, Blakey, Taylor and Allen.

The night before, the festival's sold-out black-tie patrons party was held in WJCT's 8,000 square foot sound stage that starred Buddy Rich and the Buddy Rich Band, along with jazz bands from Orlando and Kansas City.

Friday afternoon, the festival weekend kicked off with the first Great American Jazz Piano Competition, won by future Grammy winner 20-year old Marcus Roberts of Jacksonville. Harry Connick Jr. of New Orleans finished second.

John Wilson, jazz critic for the *New York Times*, who had served as one of three judges for the piano competition, wrote in the *Times*, "Jacksonville and All That Jazz has been so successful, in fact, that it helped turn a parking lot into Metropolitan Park, a $4 million, 23-acre entertainment facility, and eight hours of this year's festival were broadcast live by public television."

It was a grand ending to what had been a grueling journey with twists, turns and roadblocks that began three years earlier when Mayor Godbold first unveiled his vision to create the St. Johns Esplanade on downtown's city-owned northbank waterfront which had been concrete parking lots for decades. The esplanade would be the mayor's crown jewel of downtown revitalization, a magnet to attract a new hotel, convention center and other buildings. He saw it as a place for music concerts, outdoor dances, picnic areas, boat mooring, and where visiting future Presidents would address the public. It would include pedestrian malls along Hogan and Laura Streets.

Godbold's plan to open up river access to the public also included two more parks; one at the Metropolitan Park site and another at Charter Point on Arlington's north shore, which had 1,400 feet of waterfront.

The esplanade project got off to a good start when the Florida Cabinet approved $1 million to help fund it. The cabinet also authorized the Florida Department of Natural Resources to apply for another $500,000 from the U.S. Department of the Interior. The esplanade was to cost $4.5 million with $2.25 million from the city and the balance in other state and federal funds.

"Carter (Jimmy) was President and the Interior Department wanted to prove that urban parks, where families could congregate and play, would cut down on crime," said Godbold.

Godbold was counting on a 400-room hotel to be constructed adjacent to the esplanade. The Jacksonville-based Charter Co. was negotiating with the Hyatt Corporation of Chicago to build the hotel, provided the esplanade became a reality.

But there was a problem to solve that would eventually derail the esplanade dream. Coastline Drive was a road along the river's edge that ran from Pearl Street and the Seaboard Coastline (CSX) headquarters on the west and wound eastward to the Jacksonville Shipyards at Liberty Street. For the esplanade to become reality, Coastline Drive would have to be closed.

Prominent Jacksonville surgeon Dr. Samuel Day, a member of the chamber who said he favored downtown development and was not opposed to a downtown park, launched a petition drive against closing the road. On August 19, 1980 Day delivered a stack of petitions to the City Council meeting and was accompanied by a large group of citizens opposed to closing Coastline Drive.

"We spent millions of dollars building the road and we have enjoyed it," he said. "It is the only way you can get through downtown rather rapidly without stoplights. It is a very ideal route that gives you a scenic route as well as an efficient one."

As a compromise, Godbold proposed re-routing Coastline Drive through the park. "This is not the absolute solution, he said, but we have so many players involved in this thing that we're trying to balance them on a tight rope." Charles Kelly, vice president of real estate for the Charter Co., said the compromise violated "the concept of a downtown civic complex for people, not cars, and makes the project less desirable."

In March of 1981, facing growing public opposition, City Council held up approval of the esplanade plans. Some council members were opposed to closing the drive. To make matters worse, the state said it wouldn't accept a park that had a road running through it.

In the summer of 1981, Gov. Graham wanted back the $1 million that had been approved for the esplanade. Frustrated by the delays but not giving up, Godbold pleaded with Graham. "I told the Governor to please not do that. That's the heart of my downtown development plan." Graham gave the mayor two weeks to get the road closed or give up the funds. "I said that I hadn't been able to get it done in a year, so I don't think I can get it done in two weeks."

The council voted 16-2 in late August 1981 to approve $200,000 for an esplanade study and design of the downtown waterfront park. That gave Godbold the opening to file a formal application with the state for its funding. The state said construction on the park had to begin by January 27, 1982. Shortly after, the cabinet reaffirmed state funds for the esplanade.

The opposition to closing Coastline Drive remained relentless. Helen

Lane, a prominent Jacksonville philanthropist, took on a high-profile leadership role. In mid-October, she wrote a letter to the *Times-Union* attacking any disruption of the road. "It would be a needless expenditure of millions of dollars. Also, it would create one of the greatest traffic jams in Jacksonville."

Godbold was more than agitated. A consultant's report said the site adjacent to the esplanade for a convention center was not large enough and lacked room to expand. That study, along with all of the public opposition, prompted Godbold to put the brakes on the esplanade just before Thanksgiving in 1981. A week before his decision, the City Council chambers were overrun by 200 opponents to closing the road.

"I guess the general public will think because of 50 people showing up last night I've decided to back off," he told the press, showing his frustration. "I'm not going to roll over and play dead because of 50 people. If the council wants a petition with 5,000 names on it for the esplanade, we can do that, too."

The clock was ticking. The state said construction of the esplanade had to start in two months, late January. Council president Joe Forshee said he was thinking of withdrawing the esplanade legislation. The *Times-Union* and *Jacksonville Journal* both editorialized their opposition.

The pressure was wearing on the mayor. He appealed to business leaders for support and said he wanted to have a meeting with all the different parties involved to try and reach a consensus. "When we come out of there we'll come out with one plan, one commitment, and we'll all be on one road together. Somewhere, somehow, this city has to get together and decide where in the heck we want to go," he said. Once again, Godbold lashed out at using valuable downtown riverfront property for parking lots.

On December 16, the governor said he was willing to extend a decision on the esplanade until January 20, 1982.

Nothing happened in January to give Godbold a boost of optimism. After two years of trying, on February 12 he threw in the towel. He was worn out. The dream of an esplanade on the river in downtown to be the magnet for downtown revitalization was dead. "There's no way we're going to close the road," he said. "There's been opposition to closing the road and I don't want to go against a majority opinion in the community." In addition, he said, the city should scale back its plan for a 210,000 square foot convention center that was projected to cost $32 million.

"I'm very disappointed in not being able to fulfill my plans." He also said that he hoped to get together downtown anchor companies Independent Life, the Charter Co., Seaboard Coastline, Florida Publishing Co., and real estate company Stockton, Whatley, Davin, "and do something about that area."

Godbold put a 30-day deadline on himself to come up with an alternative plan or he would tell the governor to spend the state's money somewhere else.

The frustration was almost overwhelming. To ease the stress, the mayor fell back on something he enjoyed more than just about anything else. He retreated to a senior citizens nutritional site to revive his spirits. "When I feel bad, I just need to take a ride to a nutritional site," he said. "Senior citizens are my favorite people. They aren't mean. They aren't sarcastic."

Noting that the U.S. Interior Department selected Jacksonville as one of ten cities for federally funded waterfront recreational beautification in June 1980, the day after Godbold's announcement of capitulation, the *Times Union* editorialized: "We think Jacksonville citizens have just witnessed a healthy example of democracy at work. A great number of citizens saw aspects of the riverfront project that they found objectionable and they expressed themselves. And, the mayor responded."

Godbold was desperate. The last thing he wanted to do was lose the state funding, which was also key to receiving federal money from the Interior Department. Even if he couldn't close the road, the mayor wanted Jacksonville to try and keep the money. He called a meeting of some of Jacksonville's top business leaders and proposed they try and convince the governor to let them move the funds to the empty 23 acres at Metropolitan Park.

"Sometimes the game plan doesn't work. Do you compromise and get something, or go full speed ahead and get nothing? I'm not proud of that position, but I'm being honest with you," he said.

Then, as he often did, the mayor gave his business advisors an opportunity to fully discuss the proposal and come to a decision. "Everybody was talking and talking," Godbold recalled. "I just wanted to get out of the room, so I told them I had to take a long-distance telephone call. I told them to keep talking and when they made a decision, if I wasn't back to come and get me."

At one point, Godbold's chief aide Don McClure told the mayor that the group was not going to be able to make a decision. "I went back in the room and said, 'I need your decision on this. I've got to have an answer. Do we want to go in two weeks and get a final vote on closing the road and they turn it down? That's a signal to the governor and there won't be any if, ands, and buts. He's going to take the money.'"

Or, asked the mayor, "Do we go to the governor's office and convince them to let us move the money to Metropolitan Park?"

One of those in the room that day was Prime Osborn, the retired chairman of Seaboard Coastline Railroad and perhaps the most influential person in Jacksonville. Osborn spoke up. "I think we ought to see if the mayor can convince the governor to okay moving the money to Metropolitan Park and not take a chance on the council."

The others agreed.

"It's better to keep the money in Jacksonville rather than arguing," said Godbold, noting that the state received $72 million in federal park funds over the past seven years and Jacksonville had only received $1 million of the money.

Graham was unavailable when Mayor Godbold and a team of business leaders traveled to Tallahassee, so they met with Lt. Gov. Wayne Mixon. Mixon approved the new plan for Metropolitan Park and the governor ordered the $1 million put back on the Florida Cabinet's agenda.

While Gov. Graham was okay with moving the funds to Metropolitan Park, the feds weren't so eager. Broadcast Park, home of the city's public television station, WJCT Channel 7, anchored Metropolitan Park. The new plan included using funds from WJCT as a local match to federal dollars. WJCT, which had envisioned a festival and arts center on the property, said it would raise $2.25 million to match state and federal funds.

Interior and Park officials said there was no precedent for using private development like WJCT as a local match. The city's proposal, said the feds, had numerous problems.

Godbold was in for another fight, and he was wondering how all of this would affect his upcoming 1983 re-election campaign.

Unwilling to accept the first federal reaction to the Metropolitan Park plan, Godbold appealed to President Carter. The President told Interior Secretary James Watt to meet with Jacksonville's mayor.

With Metropolitan Park plans in hand, Godbold and members of his staff flew to New York City and met with Watt over lunch at the Plaza Hotel. "We had this drawing about Metropolitan Park and we showed him what we wanted to do," said Godbold. Watt was receptive. "He didn't have any doubts that this would be a great project, but he had a lot of doubts about Channel 7." Watt was concerned that WJCT would try to capitalize on the park to make money. He told the mayor, "We're not going to let them use this for their purposes. We want it to be a public park and if they want that I'm willing to work with you."

Jake Shows Metropolitan Park plan to the media.

Watt wrote a note on a napkin and told Godbold to take it to his assistant secretary. The note told Watt's assistant to look at Jacksonville's plan and "see if we can't help this."

"He told us where to go and gave us a private number to call," said

Godbold. The mayor took his note on the napkin, along with the Metropolitan Park plan, to Washington. "They agreed to move the money," said Godbold.

Another hurdle was cleared, but it wasn't the last. Now, Godbold found himself in another battle with WJCT president Fred Rebman. "When we got into negotiations with Rebman, it was a bastard," said Godbold. "It was drug out for months. Here we had the state and federal money sitting there."

One day, the mayor went into chief aide McClure's office where McClure and recreation director Julian Barrs were on the speaker phone trying to negotiate an issue with Rebman. Godbold was hot under the collar and he interrupted the call. "I'm going to tell you something, Rebman. You and Julian are going to fuck around until we lose the $4 million. And, I can tell you now, ass hole, you are going to take the blame for it. People in the community will never help Channel 7 again. If you screw me up on this money you'll never get my help and I will make sure the chamber and business community know you personally fucked this up. That's it. I'm not arguing about this anymore."

In late March 1982, Rebman said the station was $750,000 short of its pledge to contribute $2,250,000 and he called on the city to fill the gap. The Interior Department had ruled that the WJCT land could not be used as a $2 million match because it was owned by the city.

Godbold said he didn't want the money to come from City Hall. But, a couple of weeks later the *Jacksonville Journal* editorialized that the City Council should consider funding for the park, a suggestion that several council members rejected out of hand.

By mid-April, Godbold reversed course and sent a proposal to the council calling on the city to share in the cost with Channel 7 by providing $1,024,000. It was approved. One month later, the state's Department of Natural Resources approved $2.25 million for the park, more than two years after the application was made in July 1980. On May 18, the Florida Cabinet unanimously approved the expenditure without discussion.

Just when Godbold thought he could breathe easier, in July 1982 the feds slashed $500,000 from the project because they felt the park was too elaborate. If the plan wasn't changed, the feds also threated to pull the rest of the matching funds. Citing the fact that the park would become home to the jazz festival, and the amphitheater would be used by other professional groups, it was not eligible for federal funding.

After some intense negotiations that placed a cap on how many events with professional entertainment could be held in the park each year and directed WJCT funds, not the city's, to pay for construction of the stage, ground was finally broken on December 8, 1982. Joining the mayor with a shovel was Gov. Graham, council president Clarence Suggs, and Ira Koger, a Jacksonville developer and patron of the arts who was chairman of WJCT's board.

"Metropolitan Park…is an example of the best which can be accomplished in Jacksonville," said a *Times-Union* editorial. "When completed the park will be dedicated to improving the quality of life of our citizens by utilizing this city's unique resources and environment."

At the end, $1.75 million was contributed by the state and federal governments, $1 million from Channel 7 and $750,000 from the city. The park would include a riverfront pavilion, reconstructed bulkheads and docks, an amphitheater, and an exhibit mall area.

The park had to be completed in ten months, by the first week of October, and a week before the fourth annual Jacksonville Jazz Festival was to be staged there in mid-October.

Mayor Godbold at ground breaking for Metropolitan Park.

Chapter 20

—————∼∼∼—————

"You Are My Bastards"

ON THE OCCASION of the fiftieth anniversary of Jacksonville's highly recognized emergency rescue service in late 2017, the Jacksonville Association of Firefighters asked former mayor Jake Godbold to speak at a dinner and celebration attended by over 500 firefighters and guests.

"Some people call you bastards," Godbold said. "I tell them you may be bastards, but you are my bastards." The crowd roared its approval.

Godbold and Jacksonville's first responders have enjoyed a strong mutual admiration for five decades. It was city councilman Godbold who introduced legislation in 1967 that took ambulance service away from warring private operators and turned it over to the city's fire department. In his two campaigns for mayor, the firefighters' union endorsed Jake and turned out an army of volunteers to build and distribute yard signs, knock on doors and donate money. In many ways, they were the backbone of his considerable political organization.

As a show of their admiration, after Godbold left office the firefighters named a new fireboat after him, and the Police & Fire Pension Fund named is new headquarters building, the City Hall Annex, The Jake M. Godbold building.

"You've got to remember that these were young, enthusiastic hard-working guys. I always thought the police officers belonged to the sheriff and those firefighters belonged to me," said Godbold. "I needed to keep them in line and help them at the same time."

His favorite was Gary Keys, a brash ball of fire who would bluntly say whatever was on his mind, often to the mayor. Keys was a born leader. "Keys was a man's man who the others would follow," said Godbold. As mayor, Godbold appointed the former union president the fire department's chief of operations.

But Keys was also more than a little mischievous, like the fictional Peck's Bad Boy. He was a brilliant fireman but he definitely annoyed the mayor at times. One day, Godbold's chief aide Don McClure told the mayor it had been reported that Keys took an ambulance, loaded a goat into it and then drove the ambulance and goat to a nearby farm. Godbold told McClure to handle it, "but I don't know how."

McClure spoke with Keys and then reported back to the mayor. "I asked him to tell me the truth," McClure said. "Did he haul a goat in a city ambulance?" McClure told the mayor that Keys responded, "If I carried a goat in a city ambulance it was a sick goat." Godbold laughed and said, "Just work around that."

Keys was often criticized for failing to adequately file reports. In 1984 a grand jury cited the fire department for poor management and a lack of communication. While Godbold was irritated, his faith in Keys was unmoved.

On the weekend of Saturday August 18 and Sunday August 19, 1984,

Godbold's belief in Keys was rewarded when a lightning bolt struck a 60-foot tall gasoline tank containing 1.4 million gallons of premium unleaded gasoline at the Triangle Refinery, a tank farm in the highly industrial area on Talleyrand Avenue.

The three-alarm fire required all off-duty firefighters to respond. In addition, first responders from Atlantic Beach, the Coast Guard, Florida National Guard and all three Jacksonville Naval bases were called into help.

Lightning struck the tank around 4:15 Saturday afternoon, shooting fire balls as high as 200 feet and eventually pushing a black pillar of smoke 1,000 feet into the sky. To complicate fighting the fire, the tall tank sprang a leak at its base, pouring about 200 gallons of fuel an hour into the surrounding area. That caused additional fires to ignite, distracting the firefighters. Some fuel also leaked into the nearby St. Johns River.

Because of a shortage of fire retardant, the tank fire burned for about 14 hours before it ruptured at 6:15 a.m. Sunday, causing the earth to shake and creating a flaming inferno. Some firefighters said it was like a "river of fire." Others compared it to being in a napalm attack in Vietnam.

"When that tank ruptured, if anybody tells you he wasn't afraid is either crazy or he's telling you a damned lie," a firefighter told the newspaper.

It was like a war, said Godbold, who was there with his firefighters, dressed in a chief's coat and boots and wearing a Jacksonville Suns baseball cap.

"Those firemen were right up against the tank," said the mayor. Weary firefighters were getting some needed rest by lying on blankets on the ground. "I told Keys he needed to send the guys home to get some rest." Keys told Godbold that when he sent them home, they washed up and came right back. "They want to be here. The best I can do is give them a blanket."

"I saw the way they worked together and would be up in that fire," said Godbold.

Without needed foam retardant, the fire would continue to burn with a mighty force. Some firefighters went to closed businesses where they knew there was foam. They broke in and took it. Foam was brought in from Jacksonville International Airport, the Coast Guard, Mayport Naval Station and the Kings Bay Naval Submarine Base in St. Mary's, Georgia. A truck carried 40 five-gallon containers of foam from Hunter Army Airfield in Savannah, and the Coast Guard used a C-130 transport plane to bring foam from Elgin and Tysdall Air Force bases in west Florida.

Twenty hours after it began, the blaze was over. The area looked like a war zone. Exhausted first responders and their chief, Gary Keys, started going home.

Afterwards, Godbold heaped praise on Keys and the firefighters for containing the blaze under such precarious and dangerous conditions, preventing it from burning out of control, destroying more property and taking lives.

And, Mayor Godbold told the media, "Chief Keys may not be able to fill out forms, but as long as he can fight a fire like this, I'll hire a secretary and let her fill out forms for him."

Chapter 21

JUMPING ON GYMNASTICS

IF THERE WAS any doubt when Mayor Godbold took office that he would hit the road running, it was certainly being erased quickly.

In early 1980, Godbold and his sports team started courting the United States Gymnastics Federation to become the host site of the 1980 Olympic Gymnastic Trials. Never mind that Jacksonville was not known as a gymnastics town. In fact, at the time there was only a single facility in town that coached gymnastics for kids.

On March 4, Godbold and U.S. Gymnastics Federation executive director Frank Bare announced the trials would be staged in the Jacksonville Veterans Memorial Coliseum, Thursday May 26, Friday May 27 and Saturday May 28. At the time of Godbold's announcement, it was becoming evident that President Jimmy Carter was not going to permit U.S. athletes to travel to Moscow for the 1980 Olympics because American hostages were being held in Iran. So, for Jacksonville and the nation's very best gymnasts, the trials would be THE event.

NBC also announced that for the first time it would produce a two-hour live prime time gymnastic trials telecast during Friday night's compulsories.

For a new mayor trying to kindle his town's spirit, grabbing the trials was a big opportunity to fan the flames. Drawing record crowds, especially when national television was involved, was the goal.

Historically, Olympic Gymnastic Trials had not been heavily attended. Godbold wanted Jacksonville to be different. Once again, it was time for him to "beat those damn drums."

Over the next two and one-half months, nothing was left undone to sell tickets. The mayor called on Jacksonville businesses to buy blocks of tickets and a strong free media campaign was launched.

Jacksonville's two daily newspapers and three television stations gave the upcoming trials exceptional attention.

"We're walking the line to see whether we truly want to be a big-league city, or if we want to stay bush league," Godbold said at the time. "This is the type of thing we've been trying to do to bring national attention to the city. It took an awful lot of hard work by a lot of people."

Federation executive director Bare credited Godbold's salesmanship in large part for landing the trials, along with the city's enthusiasm. Godbold, he said, "is a guy who can sell ice to the eskimos."

While Godbold's main focus was selling as many tickets as possible, he made sure the city paid attention to other important details. The coliseum, site of many rock concerts, had to be completely steam cleaned and 2,000 seats were replaced. Paying special attention to the athletes and coaches was also a priority. They would be in Jacksonville for a week and Godbold wanted them to enjoy their stay and want to return.

The gymnasts were housed in the newly renovated Holiday Inn City Center in the heart of downtown. Every detail was handled and every athlete's wish was granted. Whether it was the jazz festival or the gymnastics trials, Godbold's attitude was that when anybody visited Jacksonville to perform for a city-sponsored event, he wanted them to leave town afterwards telling their friends and peers how great they were treated. Jake realized that these people traveled from town to town to perform and often where they had visited was a blur. They were treated like a commodity. That was not going to happen in Jacksonville.

In the weeks prior to the event, Jacksonville's local television stations had gone overboard helping the city promote the events. It was really unprecedented. The local NBC affiliate, WTLV-Channel 12, had launched a promotional blitz, all free to the city.

The night of the national telecast, all of the local stations wanted to be inside the coliseum so they could air their 6 p.m. news shows live. The NBC telecast of the finals wasn't to begin until 8 p.m. Out of the blue, NBC officials said that none of the local stations would be permitted into the coliseum for their live news telecasts, not even the NBC affiliate. The station managers weren't happy. NBC affiliate WTLV general manager Howard Kelly went ballistic. I attempted to get Gymnastics Federation executive director Bare to intercede with NBC. But, Bare had no luck.

Kelly decided to take legal action as a way to resolve the issue. I persuaded him to hold up until I could visit with the NBC officials, who were headquartered outside the coliseum in a trailer complete with the NBC peacock plastered to the outside, just to the right of the front door. When I got to the coliseum, I found Bare and explained to him that the mayor was very upset that NBC was not going to let the local stations come inside to do their telecasts. I told Bare the mayor was coming over for a walk through at 4 o'clock and if NBC had not changed its mind by then, he was going to turn out the lights in the coliseum and there would be no live telecast.

Because Bare had worked with Godbold, he believed what I said and he took me out to the NBC trailer. Bare knocked on the front door and an NBC vice president opened it. Bare told the executive, "We have a problem." Then he introduced me.

I said, "The mayor sent me over here to ask you once again to allow his local television stations to do their live news telecasts inside the coliseum tonight. These are his stations and they have promoted the hell out of this event and that's why it's sold out." The NBC executive told me there was no way they would let the local stations inside.

"Well, that's too bad," I said. "The mayor wants you to know that he will be here at 4 o'clock and if you haven't decided to let them in, he is going to cut out the lights in the coliseum tonight and there won't be a telecast. You guys better have a movie to show."

The NBC executive smirked and said, "He wouldn't do that. We're NBC."

"Oh, he'll do it," I said. "This is his town and these are his stations. And, he's smart enough to know that if he cuts out the lights on NBC, he'll be on the cover of Sports Illustrated next week." Then I walked away. Bare remained to speak to the NBC executive, assuring him that Godbold would, indeed, turn out the lights.

Just before 4 o'clock, Bare found me and said that NBC had given in. I immediately had the television stations notified.

Around 4 p.m., Mayor Godbold arrived at the Coliseum for a walk through. The coliseum was all decked out in red white and blue. Flags, bunting and banners were everywhere. As soon as Godbold got to me,

Bare came hustling up. "Mayor," he said, "this is an historic occasion." Godbold, unaware of what had happened, looked up at all of the red, white and blue and said, "Yes, it is. This is what America is all about."

"No," said Bare. "I mean I've never seen anybody back down a television network like you did." With a puzzled look on his face, Godbold turned to me. "What the hell did you do now?" Godbold didn't find out what had actually happened until 30 years later.

While some local officials were skeptical that Jacksonville would turn out for gymnastics—after all, Jacksonville was a football, wrestling and NASCAR town—attendance for all three events were record highs. Five thousand attended Thursday and Friday nights' events. For the finals on Saturday night, Jacksonville nailed it with a sold-out crowd of 8,806. NBC's two-hour prime time telecast had an estimated 60 million viewers.

Future Olympic gold medalist Bart Connor, who won the trials men's finals, was in awe of the crowds. "We've never seen this many people for trials before," he said.

Jacksonville Journal sports editor Rex Edmonson wrote afterwards, "Jacksonville scored heavily in playing host to this spectacular. It should make the whole city bust its buttons."

Once again, Godbold had parlayed getting a big event to Jacksonville that would rally its citizens and gain national attention. Godbold didn't let much time pass before he started leveraging what Jacksonville had just accomplished. He wanted Jacksonville to host the 1984 Olympic Gymnastic Trials.

For a town with no gymnastics history, Godbold got Jacksonville into the gymnastics mainstream in a hurry. Other prestigious competitions followed the Olympic trials, including the International Mixed Pairs

Championships which brought the best gymnasts from all over the world to Jacksonville three years in a row. Once again, Jacksonville was seen on national television hosting a very successful sporting event.

The third year, Jacksonville could also brag that it had beat out Philadelphia and Indianapolis to be the host city. In 1984 Godbold got his big wish when Jacksonville was chosen to once again be the site of the U.S. Olympic Gymnastics Trials, which turned out to be a golden year for American champions like Connor, Mary Lou Retton, Julianne MacNamara and others. In May 1986 the city played host to a meet between the U.S. and the Soviet Union.

Chapter 22

⁓

*KILLING NUCLEAR, EMBRACING COAL, LOWERING RATES

JUST BEFORE **6:30** a.m. on Saturday January 16, 2018, former mayor Jake Godbold rolled through the security gates and into the parking lot of the city-owned JEA's St. Johns River Power Park, home to Jacksonville's coal-fired plant. He was being driven by long time friend Al Shafer, a retired JEA employee who, with 50 years of service, is the longest tenured employee in the utility's history.

They were there to watch the implosion of the coal fired plant's two 464-foot tall cooling towers which had operated for 31 years before being decommissioned months earlier because the plant had become inefficient and new federal emission regulations pushed JEA to move to cheaper and cleaner forms of energy.

Sitting on a park-like setting of 1,600 acres on Jacksonville's northside at Eastport, the plant was a joint venture between JEA and Florida Power & Light.

Once the plunger, which was just a few feet in front of Godbold, ignited the explosions at 8 a.m., it took just 12 seconds for the gigantic structures to be reduced to large piles of concrete and steel rubble.

The power park's quick demise on that Saturday morning was in stark contrast to the 18 years of turmoil, controversy and financial stress suffered by the JEA's rate payers before the power park's ground breaking on November 25, 1982 during Godbold's first term as mayor.

For years, Jacksonville's electric power had been provided by oil-fired plants powered by imported oil from the Arab-dominated Organization of Petroleum Exporting Countries (OPEC). In the fall of 1973, OPEC embargoed its oil going to the United States and other nations that aided Israel in the Yom Kippur War of October 1973. The embargo caused an earthquake among the JEA, its customers and city officials, sending electric rates skyward and making Jacksonville's power consumption the most expensive in Florida and among the highest in the nation. Many consumers were having trouble paying their electric bills and everybody in town was outraged. Industries considering relocating to Jacksonville went elsewhere.

Even after the embargo ended the following spring, the damage was done and the flow of oil continued to be reduced so that by 1980 the price of crude oil was ten times what it had been in 1973.

In the middle of it all was then councilman Godbold.

Desperate for a solution, city leaders and members of the business community turned to Westinghouse Electric Co. and its Offshore Power Systems (OPS). OPS was a joint venture between Westinghouse and Newport News Shipbuilding and Drydock, which had merged with Tenneco to build floating nuclear power plants. It was a scheme that grew out of a desperation for lower cost electric power and knowing that siting nuclear power plants was a difficult proposition because of public opposition. OPS would set up a factory to mass produce nuclear power plants, then float them out in the ocean miles from any populated areas where they would be positioned on a man-made island anchored in the Atlantic, reducing public outcry, they thought.

OPS picked Jacksonville's Blount Island as the site of its floating nuclear power plant factory with a promise of 10,000 jobs and millions of dollars added to the local tax base. Jacksonville Mayor Hans Tanzler and local business leaders embraced the proposal enthusiastically and agreed to buy one of the floating facilities at a cost of $200 million, freeing the city from the grip of imported oil.

Opposition against the notion of floating nuclear power plants was strong and vocal, both in Jacksonville and across the nation. Locally, a Mandarin grocer named Joe Cury became the face and very loud voice of opponents of the project in Jacksonville. Cury formed an advocacy group called People Outraged With Electric Rates (P.O.W.E.R.) to challenge the proposal. The organization's treasurer was a young lawyer named Harry Shorstein.

OPS purchased a swampy 850 acres on Blount Island from the Jacksonville Port Authority, removed the muck and built roads, a bridge, and utilities. It was a huge undertaking. A 130-foot crane that spanned 675 feet was constructed. It was the world's largest crane. The platform needed to accommodate the plant was enormous, requiring that the harbor basin had to be over 400 feet square.

As the political opposition in Jacksonville intensified against the city buying one of the plants, members of the Jacksonville City Council were forced to take sides. Councilman Godbold had his doubts about the feasibility of the expensive and untested project. However, it looked as if the stampede in favor of the city contracting to purchase a $200 million floating nuclear power plant was going to win despite the intensive pushback by Cury and others. That's when former P.O.W.E.R treasurer Shorstein, who was appointed the city's general counsel by Tanzler in 1974, stepped in and basically said the whole notion was nuts and could bankrupt the city. His blunt opposition had an impact on members of the council and his warnings demanded attention from the mayor and other city leaders. Shorstein had stopped the stampede to purchase an OPS produced nuclear floating power plant dead in its tracks.

As conservation became a defense against the high cost of the energy crisis, power demand was down nationwide and any desire for a floating nuclear power plant disappeared. When President Jimmy Carter put a moratorium on the construction of nuclear power plants it was pretty much a death sentence for Jacksonville-based OPS. In 1984 OPS folded its tent, and in 1985 its Blount Island property was sold to Herb Peyton's Gate Petroleum Co. for $17 million.

In 1977, JEA completed a study on the feasibility of converting its operations to coal with a consultant's recommendation that the city's utility form a joint venture with Florida Power & Light to build and operate a 2,600-megawatt coal-fired plant. The consultants also recommended that the plant be constructed on one of two sites in Clay County, setting off an intense and bitter fight with a neighboring county that was highly opposed to the recommendation. It got so bad that some council members considered imposing a special tax on people who worked in Jacksonville but lived in a different county.

At the same time, the JEA faced internal turmoil. Three managers were fired and the utility was $12 million behind in its annual payment in lieu of taxes to the city. Royce Lyles was dispatched to the JEA from the city finance department to help put its financial house in order.

In 1978, several Jacksonville engineering firms wanted to design the proposed power plant and the bidding war was intense. One of the most aggressive was Reynolds, Smith & Hills (RS&H), led by its president Bob Alligood. RS&H lost when the JEA negotiated a contract with Ebasco Services of Atlanta for $57.5 million. Behind the political scenes, Alligood and his RS&H associates continued a campaign to torpedo Ebasco, showing me documents indicating that the contract JEA had negotiated with EBASCO was much higher than it should be. I confidentially took the information to my friend, council president Godbold, who would soon become the interim mayor.

Godbold appointed a special committee of the council to examine the contract, which hired a Houston consultant who proclaimed the contract was, indeed, $20 million too high in his opinion. Godbold called the contract a "sweetheart deal" for Ebasco. The JEA was forced to renegotiate the contract which resulted in $9 million in savings and other improvements.

When Godbold was elected mayor in 1979, he knew he had been successful during the campaign in large part because he had gone after the financial mismanagement and mountain of lost trust that Jacksonville voters had in the city's electric utility. Not only were electric rates through the roof, JEA facilities were not being maintained and blackouts outraged customers and scared away prospective industries. He also made sure voters knew that he was the one who had saved rate payers millions of dollars by re-examining the JEA's contract with Ebasco to design the coal-fired plant.

Now that he was officially sitting in the mayor's chair, Godbold owned all of the problems, high prices, oil shortage and angry citizens. After the election, the new mayor was invited to a luncheon at Jacksonville's Naval Air Station. "I thought it was to meet the leadership of the Naval base and in some ways, it was. But, when I came into the room it was full of a lot of admirals and chamber members. The message was, 'What are you going to do about electric rates?'" At that point, Jacksonville's rates were second highest in the nation. "'If you don't get them down, the Navy is going to take a second look at Jacksonville,'" Godbold remembered. "'It's just too much of our budget.'" The new mayor decided then that he had to get deeply involved.

Godbold knew electric rates weren't high because of the JEA's poor management, but he firmly believed that the public's lack of trust was because of "the board's arrogance toward the rates. They didn't communicate with the public. Their attitude was, 'We don't have to listen to this. We're an independent authority.' The public hated them and that had to be changed."

Godbold dispatched his highly qualified finance director Royce Lyles to the JEA. "Royce did a wonderful job," said Godbold. "We worked very close together to make sure we all were going in the same direction." Lyles supported the plan to build the coal-fired plant, but he faced a skeptical community. "He was working himself to death trying to convince the public that coal was the way for us to go. One day he came to me and he said, 'I've gone as far as I can go. I must have you and your office behind me and backing us up.'"

In 1980, the JEA abandoned any plans it had to construct the coal-fired plant in Clay County. Instead, a site was selected on Jacksonville's northside at Eastport, near some of Godbold's favorite fishing spots off Heckscher Drive. Predictably, the decision was met with a public outcry from northsiders, led by their district council member Joe Forshee. Mayor Godbold didn't like the Eastport site either. Northside residents filed a suit to stop the plant from being built in their part of the city.

The JEA kept moving forward. In 1981 it hired Wall Street financial services company Shearson American Express to sell the bonds that would pay for construction of the plant. Jacksonville lawyer Tommy

Greene, a long-time friend, confidant, and Godbold campaign fund raiser, had been hired by Shearson to convince JEA board members to hire the firm.

In January 1982, Mayor Godbold, who had ripped apart the original Ebasco contract and expressed his opposition to the Eastport site, reaffirmed his support for the coal-fired plants, but he said he wanted the JEA to answer some questions. The JEA had estimated the construction cost to be $1.4 billion.

State Rep. John Lewis claimed the plant would cost an additional $400 million. "I've been out front to build the coal plant and I still am," said the mayor. "But as chief executive officer of this city, I have to make sure we can afford it." Godbold said he wanted a report from the JEA on how much plant construction would be, how those costs would be paid, and what the price of electricity would be after the plant opened.

In late March the City Council voted 18-1 to approve a $1.8 billion joint venture between JEA and FP&L to build a 2,600-megawatt coal-fired plant. Northside councilman Forshee was opposed. In the more than two years since the plant's inception, the council passed 15 different pieces of legislation supporting the venture. This bill also said that "whenever possible" local laborers and contractors should be hired. The JEA said 1,800 jobs would be created during construction and another 500 would be needed to run the plant.

The council also approved a resolution authorizing the JEA to issue the bonds for the plant.

Three days later Godbold signed the ordinance authorizing construction of the $1.8 billion coal-fired plant with a first phase scheduled to open in December, 1985. It would be "the most expensive undertaking in Jacksonville history," said the *Times-Union*.

But, even with all of the forward momentum, the JEA and city were about to meet other expensive speed bumps.

In many ways, A.P. McIlwain was a political gadfly in Jacksonville who could mostly be ignored but for one important thing. He was president of Jacksonville Shipyards, Inc. (JSI), owned by the Fruehauf Corp., and in 1977 the shipyards was Jacksonville's largest civilian employer with approximately 3,000 workers. So, on April 28, 1982 when the JSI said it intended to stop construction of the coal-fired plants, JEA and city officials had to take the threat seriously, even though the mayor said the shipyards was "playing games."

Local labor leaders believed the shipyards wanted to stop the plant because McIlwain and others feared the shipyards would lose its labor force once construction started. Others thought the reason was because with a plant powered by coal, the oil tankers that spent time and money at the shipyards would disappear. The shipyards, however, said their opposition was because of concern about the costs, the possibility of electric rate increases, and the cost of repaying the bonds.

Godbold, who frequently clashed with McIlwain, was not happy. "We're paying an awful lot of money so the shipyards can play games with us," he said.

In mid-May 1982, Circuit Court Judge Henry Martin approved the sale of the $1.8 billion in bonds, good news for the JEA and a setback for McIlwain. The big question then became, "Will the shipyards appeal the ruling to the Florida Supreme Court?" If it did, the project would be delayed, adding an additional $350,000 a day to construction costs.

In a letter, Godbold urged McIlwain not to appeal. McIlwain didn't wait long to reply with a letter to the mayor letting him know the shipyards planned to take its appeal to the state supreme court.

Two months after the circuit court ruling, the shipyards, along with an attorney from the state attorney's office, presented written arguments to the supreme court. The shipyards said the bonds should be approved in a public referendum before being sold. The state attorney said the city had indirectly pledged property taxes to pay for the coal-fired plants. The state supreme court agreed with the circuit court judge and approved sale of the bonds.

One final hurdle was cleared in September 1982 when labor unions signed a pact with the JEA agreeing to no work stoppages while the JEA agreed to no lockouts. Managing director Lyles said the agreement would save hundreds of thousands of dollars by avoiding delays and should help the JEA negotiate lower interest rates. In addition, the agreement called for a four-day, 10-hour work week with a fifth day optional at straight time pay to make up for days lost because of rain.

Ebasco Services was also hired as project manager.

Finally, after almost two decades from when the conversation first began and six years after serious talks started, the JEA's board members, Mayor Godbold and other city officials twirled 16 gold painted shovels to break ground on the coal-fired plant. But, even that ceremony was delayed for 45 minutes when a rain storm hit the area.

The mayor said it was "truly a special day for Jacksonville." Construction, which was to begin in early January, would create 1,800 jobs and six million work hours, he told the crowd.

For the northside residents and Councilman Forshee who were so opposed to building the plant at Eastport, the JEA promised the 1,600-acre site would have a park-like atmosphere. The plant also hired many people in the area for good paying jobs.

Mayor Godbold and JEA chairman Walter Williams celebrate long-awaited construction of coal-fired plant.

For Godbold, it was one more major accomplishment to tout in his upcoming 1983 re-election campaign. More important, it was a huge investment that would provide affordable energy to Jacksonville's citizens and make the once hated JEA a selling point to incoming industry for three decades.

Phase 1 opened in 1987 before Godbold left office, and the second phase came on line in 1988.

Chapter 23

———— ∞∞ ————

REBUILDING A 70,000 SEAT SLUM

ON SATURDAY NOVEMBER 11, 1978, the University of Georgia Bulldogs defeated the Florida Gators 24-22 in the 45th meeting of their classic football rivalry in Jacksonville's worn-out Gator Bowl.

When the game was over and the thousands of rival fans had returned either to their schools or hometowns, much of the talk was not about the football clash. Instead, there was heavy criticism from all quarters about the way Jacksonville treated its visitors. People left town unhappy and with a bad taste about their experiences because of hotel price gouging, poor parking and lousy facilities.

With that backdrop, newly installed Mayor Jake Godbold stepped in as host of the 1979 football contest, knowing that a repeat of 1978 would probably doom any chance the two university athletic directors would agree to another contract with the City when the current contract ended in 1980. Godbold was relentless in doing everything possible to avoid a repeat of 1978. It was all hands-on deck for his staff and department heads. No excuses. To lose the annual game, which was the biggest thing happening each year in Jacksonville, would be a huge national embarrassment, and would cripple Godbold's effort to convince Jacksonville citizens to have pride in their hometown and show the NFL that Jacksonville belonged on the big national stage.

After the 1979 game, the *Times-Union* wrote that everything surrounding the game "went off like clockwork," setting an entirely different tone for contract negotiations.

Nearly three months later, on February 4, 1980, Georgia iconic head coach and new athletic director, Vince Dooley, and Florida athletic director, Bob Moore, met in Godbold's City Hall office to sign a new three-year contract. Bill Kastelz, *Times-Union* sports editor, wrote afterwards, "It hasn't even been 18 months since the Georgia-Florida game left a trail of anger and bitterness which threatened for a time to wreck a tradition." That threat was over. Instead, Kastelz wrote, "…when Monday afternoon it came time to sign a new three-year contract between Georgia and Florida, it was strictly a love fest in Mayor Jake Godbold's office."

After the new contract was signed, Godbold said, "We never want to take this game for granted, whether it's a one year, three year or five-year contract." Coach Dooley responded, "What pleases me is your office has lived up to its pledges. Georgia is happy that the problems of the year before have been corrected because this game has been just great for Georgia and Florida."

With the constant talk about moving the annual game from Jacksonville and instead playing it on a home and home basis at the two universities, Godbold knew full well that Jacksonville could not sit on its hands. Georgia was planning to expand its stadium from 60,000 to 77,000 and Florida had plans to increase its stadium capacity from 62,300 to 70,000.

Godbold was tagged "Mayor Jock" by the media because of his push for big-time sports.

Godbold told Dooley and Moore that he was going to ask City Council for a bond issue to upgrade the Gator Bowl's facilities and increase its seating from 72,000 to over 80,000. He had complained from almost the time he became mayor that Jacksonville had been a "slumlord" over its sports and entertainment complex. He told the two athletic directors, "I'm embarrassed…about the dressing rooms at the Gator Bowl. If we're going to be a big-league city we can't have bush league facilities."

In early July, as he started to make his public push for funds to repair and upgrade the Gator Bowl, Veterans Coliseum and Wolfson Baseball

Park, the mayor repeated his charge. "We've been slumlords in this city much too long. We have a Gator Bowl that we want to bring top notch football into, but we don't want to put a dime out to keep it safe and keep it up. As we make money in these facilities, we've got to take money back and put it into these facilities."

A month and a half later, in mid-August, Godbold proposed a $74.5 million revenue bond issue that included $11.5 million targeted to renovate the Gator Bowl. The plan included:

- expanding the seating capacity more than 10,000 seats,
- adding new restrooms, concession stands and an elevator,
- building a new press box and future loges to accommodate box seats above the press box,
- paving the parking lots,
- enclosing the structure with an outer wall of steel.

The proposal called for $65 million for the Gator Bowl, coliseum and the baseball park, public works and recreation projects and neighborhood parks, along with $10.4 million for a downtown riverfront park and convention center. The mayor told the City Council he wanted the entire plan to be completed in three years.

Then, the political roller coaster ride began as 19 members of the City Council, each with a special agenda, started deliberations with confusion, criticisms and a ton of questions. On September 18, a frustrated mayor warned that council inaction might kill the Georgia-Florida and the Gator Bowl games. He said the 1980 games may be the last if the council didn't act. "It scares me to death to have that indecisive City Council down there having to make tough decisions that will carve the future of this city. They're too worried about getting re-elected and scared about a recall election to worry about the future of this city. They better get off it and get on with it or this city is coming to a screeching halt."

Godbold was referring to a petition that had been submitted with 16,757 signatures to recall 17 of the 19 council members who had voted for a 40 percent pay increase which the council later rescinded.

The mayor was truly concerned that the Gator Bowl was structurally unsafe and that Jacksonville would lose the Georgia-Florida game because he would have to close down the stadium. He instructed his chief aide Don McClure to get a report on the stadium from a structural engineer before the upcoming game on November 8.

Four days later, City Council president David Harrell sent a letter to the council members saying the council needed to float a revenue bond issue to handle the projects on Godbold's list, including the Gator Bowl. Harrell also appeared before the council's finance and rules committees to urge council action. The committee members voted narrowly to send the proposal to the full council, where it was rejected, 8-10.

As Godbold had instructed, a structural engineer from Law Engineering Testing, Co. began examining the Gator Bowl for signs of decay, including checking the stadium ramps, metal decking and steel frame. In mid-October Godbold announced that the engineer found that some parts of the 32-year old Gator Bowl were so unsafe he may have to cancel the upcoming game unless major emergency repairs could be made within 25 days. Cancellation, he said, would cost Jacksonville $19 million and probably cause the city to lose hosting the annual football classic. A Florida athletic official confirmed Godbold's statement, telling the *Times-Union*, "If that's the case, Jacksonville would lose the game forever."

Godbold then asked the council to approve an emergency appropriation of $275,000 for a quick fix to the most serious areas of concern. While some council members complained of being pressured by the mayor, the emergency expenditure passed unanimously. On October 16 an editorial in the *Jacksonville Journal* said, "Mayor Jake Godbold took on the whole city council in a game of chicken this month. He won, too."

With employees working 10-11 hours a day, including weekends, North Florida Erection, Co. completed its work two days before the big game.

Following a 1980 successful game, 13 council members stepped up to endorse a $20 million capital outlay and recreational bond issue that included the Gator Bowl, which was approved 13-4 on a December 10 vote. To help gain approval, the bond issue also included $585,907.14 in "lollipops" for each council district, allotments that would increase to $1 million each if the council kicked in $6.4 million set aside for other projects. On March 26, 1981, more than a year after Godbold had told Dooley and Moore that he would ask for a revenue bond issue for Gator Bowl renovation, the council revisited the issue and approved a $24.5 million revenue bond issue, $4.5 million more than the first version, which upped each "lollipop" to $1 million.

In mid-May, Godbold announced that by the 1983 Georgia-Florida game the Gator Bowl's seating capacity would be expanded by 10,000 seats, which would make the stadium among the largest in the nation. Two months later, the mayor said the newly renovated stadium would also include 26 private boxes on the stadium's west side that would be sold for $7,000-$10,000 a year. The Gator Bowl, Godbold also said, is being prepared for Jacksonville to bid on the 1985 Super Bowl.

Minus the 10,000 new seats and the private boxes, the Gator Bowl was declared safe and ready on November 4 for the November 8, 1981 kickoff. Once again, the Georgia-Florida game, with badly needed stadium repairs and a promise of more to come, was a success for Jacksonville.

Seven weeks later, as fans filed out of the December 28 Gator Bowl game between Florida State University and West Virginia University,

Hobbs Development & Construction Co. of Panama City started the $12.8 million six phase renovation of the stadium. It was a job that had to be completed by October 15, 1982. The first phase included:

- 10,000 more seats,
- 16 plush boxes,
- modern press box,
- new electrical system,
- new elevator.

Following phase one, Hobbs' punch list included:

- steel replacement, sand blasting, repainting of the stadium,
- reworked aisle system and another 3,300 seats and ten more boxes,
- four restrooms and four ticket booths,
- second elevator.

The east stands had to be finished by March 15, in time for soccer and summer football.

There was no question that the timeline for completion was a tight one for Hobbs, even under the best of conditions. Godbold said, "I know the importance of the date (October 15, 1982). I will take the blame if its not finished by then. But I will not be alone. I can guarantee that the Hobbs Construction Co., will be dead."

Adding private boxes to the Gator Bowl was an idea borrowed from other newly constructed or renovated stadiums around the country. For the Gator Bowl, there would be 14 boxes seating 12 and 10 boxes seating 16. In addition, there would be a pair of 21-seat boxes for the mayor and his sports commission, as well as city council members. Those two boxes would automatically be turned over to the owner of any NFL team that opened a franchise in Jacksonville.

As with nearly everything else involved in the Gator Bowl's renovation, figuring out how to disperse the private boxes and how much to charge became a political football, as the mayor made one proposal, the council made another and a compromise was finally fashioned that didn't make Godbold happy. The city would offer seven of the 12-seat boxes and five of the 16-seat boxes to the highest bidders, and a lottery would be held for the remaining boxes.

"I don't like the way that does it," said Godbold. He wanted to set a price for the boxes and give everybody an opportunity to purchase one. Interested buyers had to submit an application and include a $2,000 cashiers or certified check.

October 14, 1982 was a big day. It was Gator Bowl inspection day. Hobbs was supposed to be finished, according to its contract with the city, or face $13,013 a day penalty. That afternoon, the private boxes would be auctioned off and sold in a lottery.

George Register, Jr., of Register Engineers and Planners, was hired by the city to be project manager for the Gator Bowl renovation. Register said the work was "not substantially complete," meaning, he said, it was 95 percent done. He primarily blamed more than 135 change orders to the contract and excessive rain, which was 65 percent more than the previous seven years during the same time period. Register recommended Hobbs' deadline be extended to October 29, one week before the November 6 football game.

In the meantime, John Bowden, the rambunctious leader of the Northeast Florida Building & Construction Trades Council, had been flaming rumors that the stadium work had not been done to specification and the stadium was not structurally sound. He called on state attorney Ed Austin to conduct a grand jury investigation.

Godbold ordered stress tests to either confirm the rumors or put them to rest. Three tests were performed over several days, and on October 29, Godbold announced that the stadium was safe.

Bowden's allegations, it turned out, were based on a report by a disgruntled ironworker subcontractor from Miami who had a dispute with Hobbs and left three months early. After four hours of testimony, on the Thursday before Saturday's game, the grand jury said the stadium was safe and found no basis for the allegations of shoddy work. Afterwards, Austin told the media, "That is totally a safe structure. It's magnificent in its beauty. It's a structure every citizen should be proud of."

Bowden, who had called on Austin to take his charges to a grand jury, said afterwards that Austin and members of the grand jury "weren't qualified to determine if the structure is safe."

After touring the new Gator Bowl, Greg Larsen, *Times-Union* sports columnist, wrote, "That piece of property over on Haines, Adams and Duval Streets is no longer an eye sore. For once, the Florida- Georgia game fans will be seated in a real stadium instead of what appeared to be an extension of the Jacksonville Shipyards. That old bucket of bolts and rust is history, replaced by a truly big-league stadium."

On Friday, the day before the game, Hobbs hoisted a large banner in the stadium that read, "Hobbs Construction Co. Welcomes You to the New Gator Bowl." Later, when Godbold inspected the stadium, he ordered it be taken down. It was replaced with a larger banner that said, "Mayor Jake Godbold Welcomes You to the New Gator Bowl."

The new and expanded Gator Bowl was not only a big plus for the Florida-Georgia game. Just a few weeks later, the annual Gator Bowl game had a record crowd of 80,0913 watch Florida State defeat West Virginia, 31-12, despite an inch of rain and 50-degree temperatures. The most successful Gator Bowl ever included 46,000 out of town visitors, generated an estimated $10 million in revenues, and had a $21.5 million economic impact on Jacksonville.

For Mayor Godbold, there was a special cherry on top. He had accomplished what Baltimore Colts owner Bob Irsay told him almost three years earlier he needed to do if Jacksonville wanted an NFL team: build a new Gator Bowl.

Chapter 24

———— ✺ ————

SAVING HISTORY TO BUILD
A CONVENTION CENTER

THE MINUTE 28-YEAR-OLD Steve Wilson stepped foot in Jacksonville in 1973 after relocating from a bank in Atlanta to work for the Charter Co., he started to impress people as a financial wizard and someone who operated with "quiet power," as one of his partners described him.

The Charter Co. was a Jacksonville based conglomerate that included mortgage, banking, land developing, real estate, oil and publishing that was ranked 61st in the *Fortune 500* in 1984 when it filed for bankruptcy protection.

In many ways, Wilson was understated and boyish looking with his shock of ruffled blondish hair. He quickly caught the attention of Charter's CEO, Raymond Mason, and became a rising star in the company. Eventually, Wilson became CFO at Charter and put together a billion-dollar financial package to purchase Carey Energy Co., thrusting Charter deep into the oil business and making it the toast of Wall Street. But, after six years of working for the fast-growing and now much larger company, Wilson realized that the opportunities to do the entrepreneurial deals he enjoyed were fewer. In 1979 he started his own company, Wilson Financial Corp., to perform real estate deals and buy outs.

Wilson also eased his way into civic and social circles in Jacksonville. He especially focused on efforts to preserve and revitalize the historic Riverside/Avondale section of Jacksonville just west of downtown. That's what first brought him into contact with the old boarded up and dilapidated Jacksonville Terminal, a majestic 1919 train station that, prior to being abandoned in 1974, had been a bustling transportation hub jointly owned by railroads Atlantic Coast Line, Florida East Coast, Seaboard Air Line and Georgia Southern & Florida, and Southern. During World War II, Northeast Florida's young men had paraded through Jacksonville Terminal as they went off to war and returned home. After the war, Jacksonville families sent their teenagers off to college from the train station.

When it opened after World War I, Jacksonville Terminal was the largest railroad station in the South with its 14 massive limestone Doric columns out front. The huge concourse had a full-size restaurant along with shops and food stands. As a sign of the times, the station also had a separate waiting area and restrooms for black passengers.

For almost a dozen years, Jacksonville had discussed and debated the pros and cons of building a convention center in downtown. After so many fits and failures, some of the town's business leaders said that Jacksonville had a reputation as a place people drove through but never stopped.

When Godbold became mayor, the convention center discussion was again heating up, especially at the Chamber of Commerce. "When I was a young boy downtown always had a lot of conventions. We had hotels in downtown and they were full," said Godbold. "They had big restaurants, the Rainbow Room, and bands on Friday and Saturday nights. Crowds would come and there was a good time downtown." Mayor Godbold quickly moved to the front of those wanting Jacksonville to build a convention center. "I thought we needed a convention center because I grew up in a town that always had conventions."

Swayed by the chamber and builder-developer Preston Haskell, Godbold tended to favor building a convention center on the site of the old Sears building in downtown off Bay Street. It was known as the Quad Block. Charter Co. owned the old Mayflower Hotel at the Quad Block, so Wilson was very familiar with the site. "It was only six acres and that's not big enough for a convention center," said Wilson.

When Godbold led his annual Chamber of Commerce Leadership trip to San Antonio in 1981, Wilson went along. His hotel room overlooked the San Antonio Convention Center. It was in that San Antonio hotel room overlooking the city's convention center Wilson first had the idea of proposing that a restored and renovated Jacksonville Terminal become the city's new convention center. "I had an option to buy the train station for a small amount of money," said Wilson. "I loved the train station. Everybody loved the train station." Wilson thought about making the station a festival market place or a park and ride center for downtown. "I didn't know what I would do with it when I got the option, but I knew I'd never tear it down." Like so many other young men, Wilson's father came back from war through Jacksonville Terminal. "I came up with the idea of putting the convention center at the train station in San Antonio."

He first proposed the idea to his good friend Charlie Towers, a

Jacksonville business, legal and political icon. Towers was just as connected as he was smart. At one time, he owned several private utility companies, most all of the city's taxi permits, as well as Jacksonville's bus company. He also led one of Jacksonville's most prestigious law firms. In many ways, Towers was omni present. He was well-liked and highly respected. It was Towers who first introduced Wilson to Godbold. "We started working on the train station together."

Towers started hooking Wilson up with some of his influential friends and business associates. The group of two eventually became a powerful partnership of eight. Towers and Wilson were joined by developer Jack Demetree, W.W. Gay, owner of a huge mechanical contracting company, Wesley Paxon, owner of a big electric company, developer-investor Martin Stein, William Nash, CEO of Prudential Insurance, and the Charter Co. Engineering firm Reynolds Smith & Hills joined as an advisor. Each partner was financially strong and all were well-respected in Jacksonville. "I was the youngest guy in the room," Wilson said. "I went to them because they wouldn't let me get started if they thought it was a bad idea."

Towers had been a Naval war hero during World War II and he called Wilson "Skipper." Two or three mornings each week, Towers would pick up Wilson around 6 a.m. and take him to meet with members of the City Council to talk about his convention center idea. "Charlie would say, 'Skipper, the mayor is in charge of this, but where people fail is when they don't talk to the City Council.'" Councilman Joe Forshee represented Jacksonville's blue collar northside. He was about as far away from Wilson's lifestyle as someone could be. "Forshee was great. He said a lot of people love that train station and they don't want anything to happen to it." Towers and Wilson met with each of the 19 council members.

"I got a call from Wilson," said Godbold. "He said he'd not gotten involved in politics until I got elected and he's taken a real interest in downtown. Steve said, 'Mayor, I think you're making a mistake in building a convention center on that spot (Quad Block).' So, I said why don't we sit down and talk about it. He came to the office and gave me all of the reasons we shouldn't build it on the quad block."

Wilson told the mayor he thought the train station would be a great place for a convention center. "You would be saving a great historical building that people love and want to restore, and you'd be building your convention center," Wilson said.

Godbold liked the idea, "but I wasn't convinced." The mayor asked Wilson to put together a proposal to build the convention center at the train station. He asked Preston Haskell to also do the same thing on why the city should pick the Quad Block.

Just as he did with other big decisions, Godbold named a blue-ribbon committee to help him determine whether or not the city's new convention center should be at the Quad Block or Jacksonville Terminal… or neither. Head of the committee was Prime F. Osborn, retired chairman of CSX and perhaps the most respected individual in Jacksonville. He was joined by investor and Chamber president Jim Winston, attorney Frank Surface who represented Central Jax Inc., and Godbold's chief administrative officer Don McClure.

The day of presentations by Wilson and Haskell was highly anticipated. Wilson and his partners were ready, but Wilson was a little nervous. The Mayor's conference room was packed. Osborn sat at the head of the table.

When Wilson addressed the group, he was prepared. He used slides to demonstrate how the train station's 232,000 square feet would be more than adequate for conventions, where and how the convention center could be expanded if necessary, explained how other city convention centers work, and explained how the convention center could be financed. Then, Wilson concluded with a "Wow!" factor. He proposed to the committee that the convention center be connected by the upcoming skyway rail to the proposed festival market area in downtown on the river. Finally, he assured Osborn and the others that his team could meet the city's time table.

Wilson called it "a watershed decision" for Jacksonville. Even Haskell was impressed.

Haskell made his presentation supporting the Quad Block. "He wasn't well prepared, which was so unusual for Preston," said Godbold. Haskell told the committee the terminal site was in an isolated area. The convention center should be able to offer conventioneers retail shopping, bars, restaurants and hotels. Godbold rejected that. McClure said the terminal site would have a "snowball effect" on other downtown businesses and "inspire construction of a new hotel." Jacksonville, McClure said, would compete with Orlando, Tampa, Charlotte and Nashville for conventions.

One of those Wilson invited to the meeting was Michael D. Spear, vice president of the Rouse Co., who was waiting on the location of the convention center site before considering building a festival market place in Jacksonville. Rouse had built Harbor Place in Baltimore and Faneuil Hall in Boston.

Godbold stayed out of the decision publicly. "Jake knew how to take on the chamber that wanted the convention center downtown. He did that by letting us do it. He never talked against us. He gave us quiet encouragement. He was brilliant in how he did that," said Wilson.

Wilson's Jacksonville Terminal proposal was recommended to Godbold by the Osborn committee. At the time, the mayor thought the committee would need only three months to negotiate a contract with Wilson's group.

WRONG.

After several months and negotiations going at what Wilson called "a snail's pace," he pushed for a contract to be ready for the City Council by January 1983, ahead of the city's spring elections. Wilson was hoping for contract approval before the politicking started. But, in November 1982, council finance chairman Bill Carter announced that once the contract reached the council, his committee would need six to eight months of review before any action could be taken. City Council president Henry Cook introduced a resolution into council naming the Civic Auditorium as a "backup" site for a convention center. It was an idea that had been floated and dismissed three years earlier.

Nine months after negotiations began, Wilson's goal of getting a contract passed before the spring elections was dead. Little progress was being made and he was frustrated. There were big arguments over costs and the scope of the project. Wilson told the committee, "We still don't know what you want." Another of Wilson's partners complained, "They've done one week in nine months." The committee wanted to hire another consultant, frustrating Wilson even more. "They're decisioning this thing to death," he said.

Arnold Greenfield, senior vice president of Shearson American Express, had been hired by the Osborn committee as a financial consultant. In April 1982, Greenfield recommended that city and state revenues be used to back bonds for the convention center.

On June 1, the Osborn committee said that new cost projections had increased to $70-$75 million, up from the earlier estimates of $25-$50 million. Buying the building and the 20 acres of land, along with building construction renovations, would cost $30 million. It would cost another $40-$45 million to buy an additional seven acres of land, construct an automated skyway system, and make improvements to streets and utilities. The committee said the city could expect $34 million in state and federal funds to help pay for the project.

The Jacksonville Journal weighed in with a positive editorial on June 3. "Thousands of rank and file citizens of Jacksonville support the project because they have a profound love of the 'old depot' and want to recycle it for useful work in today's society in order to preserve the city's most historical landmark."

Godbold often said that a number of large projects he initiated faced significant public push back, including the Dames Point Bridge, J. Turner Butler Boulevard, and the Southbank Riverwalk. "But there was no opposition to saving the train station. Everybody wanted it saved."

One year after the council had designated Jacksonville Terminal as the proposed site for the convention center, Godbold asked the council to consider a $25 million revenue bond issue, along with an annual city subsidy of $750,000. Council President Henry Cook told Godbold the council was sold on the train station site, but wary of the financing.

Finally, on June 20 Osborn delivered the committee's report to the mayor. It recommended that the city immediately purchase the 20-acre site and contract with Wilson's group, Jacksonville Convention Center, Inc., for development of the convention center. The committee also recommended that bonds be retired by revenues from the city's operation of the convention center.

After nearly two years, the contract was finally before the council, and once again Wilson hoped for prompt approval. But, in late October Council President Clarence Suggs delayed a vote on the contract after Councilman Forrest Boone insinuated Wilson and his partners were hoodwinking the council. That triggered Wilson and he threatened to pull back his convention center plans. "We're not going to be accused of ripping the city off, and if that's a consensus of the council, we'd rather not do the deal. We'll take our piece of real estate and you can go somewhere else."

Godbold jumped into the middle. "If there's any hanky-panky going on I'd be the first guy to stand up and blow the whistle." Years later, Godbold would say that Boone "was a pimple on an elephant's ass."

The Florida Times-Union also spoke up editorially. "An economic disaster looms for Jacksonville if efforts to convert the Jacksonville Terminal site into a convention center collapses from 11th hour insinuations that people of Jacksonville are being ripped off. Actually, they are being offered a tremendous bargain. That bargain is being endangered by City Councilman Forrest Boone."

On November 22, 1984 the City Council agreed to buy the property for $5.58 million and pay the fees and guarantees the Wilson group was seeking from the city. It was $6.56 per square foot, compared to property in the area that was selling for $8-$10 a square foot. Wilson and his partners had $4,425,087 invested in the deal. When it was all over they had made only $1,154,913. More important for Wilson was knowing he had helped save one of the city's most precious historical buildings.

On April 23, 1986, the mayor and Florida Lt. Governor Wayne Mixon opened a new Water Street, reconfigured and completely landscaped to provide a wide open and direct link from the convention center to downtown, the newly constructed Enterprise Center and Omni Hotel, the Jacksonville Landing which would open a year later, and the soon to be built Barnett Plaza. Mixon also brought a state contract for $2 million to rebuild the Park Street viaduct at the convention center.

"This is another part of the puzzle," Godbold said at the Water Street ribbon cutting. "Now, we're seeing our dreams come true."

Two years after Osborn and Godbold broke ground, the Prime F. Osborn Convention Center was ready for a grand opening befitting the queen of a great city. All of Jacksonville was proud and excited. On October 17, the *Times-Union* wrote, "Jacksonville has a unique convention center, probably one of the most distinctive in the nation. Its appearance, location and potential economic benefits alone make the public party tonight marking the opening of the Prime Osborn Convention Center well worth attending."

Mayor chats with Mayor's Older Buddy Mrs. Leota Davis at Convention Center opening.

And attend they did. The people of Jacksonville came by the thousands. A public grand opening celebration with whistles, balloons, music and fireworks greeted the crowds as they surged inside. Godbold was full of emotion. "This is part of our heritage," he said. "We've not only built a convention center, we have saved a landmark. This train station has been a great part of our past, and this convention center will be a great part of our future."

Unfortunately, Osborn, the Jacksonville heavyweight who handled the negotiations that brought the convention center from over 12 years of wishful thinking to reality, passed away ten months earlier, in January, at age 70.

In the earliest days of construction, Godbold hired convention center veteran Tom Mobley away from Denver. Mobley said he took the job because he wanted to be involved in building a convention center from the ground up. Mobley announced that when it opened, the convention center was already booked 50 percent for the next two years. Seventy percent, he said, was considered full booking.

First up, on November 17, the highly sought exhibit "Ramses II: The Pharaoh and his Time," opened. It was a gargantuan collection of the artifacts and treasures that belonged to the pharaoh who ruled Egypt for 67 years, 1290-1224 B.C. Prior to coming to Jacksonville's brand-new convention center, the exhibit had been in Montreal and Vancouver. In Jacksonville it was presented by the Jacksonville Art Museum. Over 100,000 tickets were sold in advance and attendance was expected to exceed 500,000. The exhibit remained at the Osborn for four months, until mid-March 1987.

Chapter 25

MICHAEL JACKSON-A VICTORY FOR JACKSONVILLE

ATTENDING NFL MEETING after NFL meeting where he pitched Jacksonville's new spirit and an eagerness to do big things paid off in a way totally unexpected for Mayor Godbold.

Godbold and his team were in Washington D.C. in the spring of 1983 to make a presentation to host a Super Bowl at the NFL owners meeting. "I often wondered why we'd be the only city there to make a presentation that didn't have an NFL team," said Godbold. "I was naïve enough to think they were going to give us a game when the fact was, they weren't going to give us a Super Bowl game." It was difficult for cities which had an NFL team to land the big game. "But, I went into the meeting thinking we had as good a chance as anybody."

Jacksonville's bid for a Super Bowl was engineered by Tampa Bay Buccaneers owner Hugh Culverhouse, who had been a Jacksonville attorney. He wanted Jacksonville to have a team for several reasons.

Culverhouse loved the city and thought having an NFL team would give it a real boost. He also believed if Jacksonville had a team there could develop a great rivalry between his Buccaneers and the new Jacksonville squad. Just as important, he really liked Godbold and admired his enthusiasm for Jacksonville.

"He (Culverhouse) told us he wanted us to get known by the other owners and know that Jacksonville was a great football town even though we were from a small market," said Godbold. "He also wanted playoff games to be held at neutral sites and he thought with our big stadium, it would make a great place for a playoff game."

Ironically, the presentation made by Godbold to secure a Super Bowl game contained many of the elements used years later by Jacksonville to be chosen to host a Super Bowl in 2005. For example, using cruise ships on the St. Johns River in downtown as hotels.

Unbeknownst to Godbold, Michael Jackson, the "King of Pop," and his brothers were working with promotor Don King to put together a nationwide tour featuring the Jacksons that would be called the Victory Tour.

Earlier, Chuck Sullivan, son of New England Patriots owner Billy Sullivan, had traveled to Los Angeles to see if he could get the Jacksons to choose the Patriot's home, Sullivan Stadium, to host the Jacksons' Boston area concerts. During his meeting, Sullivan learned that the group's talks with its original promoter had ended and the Jacksons were looking for a replacement. Sullivan returned to Boston and put together a financing plan to promote the entire Victory Tour. At the time, the Jacksons were only going to perform in ten U.S. cities, with three performances at each city.

In April 1983, Sullivan learned that he would be the promoter, despite the fact that his company had never handled a concert tour. It was a big victory for Sullivan, who had guaranteed the Jacksons concert revenues and made financial commitments that would later become a huge stretch to achieve. It eventually caused the Sullivans to lose ownership of the Patriots.

In May, a month after Sullivan was named tour promoter, the NFL owners' May meeting was held at the L'Enfant Plaza Hotel in Washington. During the meeting, Sullivan lobbied other owners to host the Victory Tour and agree to financial concessions that would make the tour more profitable.

After his Super Bowl presentation, Godbold and the others were in the hotel lobby discussing how they had done. Sam Kauvoris, the sports anchor for WJXT Channel 4, was also there. "A guy came over to me and said that Chuck Sullivan, the owner of the Patriots, wanted to see me in his hotel suite at 3 o'clock," said Godbold. Kavouris wanted to know if he could attend the meeting. "I told him he could go, but I wasn't going to tell Sullivan that he was with the press. If Sullivan only wanted to speak with me, then he'd have to leave."

At the time, there were rumors floating around that the Sullivans wanted to sell or move their team. Godbold assumed that was what Sullivan wanted to discuss.

At 3 p.m., the Jacksonville mayor knocked on Sullivan's hotel suite door with Kouvaris behind him.

They went in and sat down. "Sullivan said, 'I can't give you an NFL team or a Super Bowl game, but what I can do is offer you something equal to three Super Bowl games.'"

Godbold said, "I didn't know whether to get excited or laugh or what." The mayor was suspicious. "I didn't know what he was using us for."

Godbold asked Sullivan, "What could be larger than a Super Bowl game that you can deliver to us?"

Sullivan said, "Mayor, you can't go out and talk about it. We're still in negotiations, but we're ready to sign a contract with Michael Jackson to bring what we call the Victory Tour to ten cities in the U.S. It will be three nights in ten cities."

Godbold was hooked. "I got excited. My thoughts were if you were going to bring Michael Jackson to only ten cities, I would sure like to have Jacksonville mentioned as one of those ten cities. 'Hell yes, we want it,'" he said.

Sullivan told Godbold that he selected Jacksonville because of the large capacity of the Gator Bowl. The stage for the concerts, said Sullivan, was going to be enormous, which meant that a lot of the seating would be lost. Jackson had designed the stage, which weighed 365 tons and was over 19,000 square feet. With the stage installed, the Gator Bowl would probably still hold an estimated 50,000.

"From that day on we had it," said the mayor.

After the meeting with Sullivan, Kauvoris found a pay phone and he called WJXT news anchor Tom Wills. He said, "Listen, we're not getting the Super Bowl, but Michael Jackson is going to open his tour next year in Jacksonville with three shows." Wills, Kauvoris said, "was speechless."

The Jacksons announced the Victory Tour in November 1983. The first set of concerts would be in Arrowhead Stadium in Kansas City in early July. Dallas would be second and Jacksonville would be the third stop, July 21, 22 and 23. That gave Godbold and the city only seven months to prepare for what would probably become the biggest happening in the city's history since the fire of 1901 that burned down the town. *Florida Times-Union* reporter Franklin Young wrote, "Michael Jackson is coming to town in a way that makes Colt Fever look like a minor head cold."

There was much to be done. For one thing, the mayor had to get the City Council to approve $445,000 in financial concessions for the Jacksons, including free use of the Gator Bowl for the three concerts.

Most all of Jacksonville was excited and, as the concert dates grew closer, the excitement and anticipation only grew stronger. But there was a very vocal, though small, opposition, primarily against the city providing financial concessions to get the Jacksons to Jacksonville. The face of that opposition was a former television news reporter and anchor named Ernie Mastrionni. Because of his longtime high profile in the community, he attracted more news attention than most others could. By then I had opened my own public relations and promotion firm and I took on the role of speaking in favor of the concerts and the financial concessions.

A very conservative group of mostly white men belonged to an organization called the Bull Snort Forum. The group met monthly for lunch, usually to hear from elected officials and discuss political issues. The club scheduled a debate between Mastrionni and me for one of their lunch meetings in the ball room of the Hilton Hotel.

I hired some help, a Michael Jackson impersonator named David James whose performances made him a hot ticket around the south. The night before the debate, my team and I went to the hotel ballroom where we installed a sound system and stage lighting. The next day, when it came time for us to debate, I told the club that I had brought some help for my opening statement.

That's when the Jackson song "Billy Jean" started blaring, the ballroom doors flew open and the Jackson impersonator entered the room, singing, dancing and moon walking among the tables of the astonished club members. Complete with Jackson's celebrated sequined white glove on one hand, the impersonator came up on the dais to the microphone. He looked over at Mastrionni and said, in that whispery Michael Jackson-like voice, "Mr. Mastrionni, I wanted to give you my glove.... but Mr. Tolbert said to just give you my finger." The crowd was a little shocked, but amused. The debate was on.

The City Council approved the contract with Sullivan's company, 18-1, one month before the concerts began. The city would spend $320,000 from the city treasury, and another $125,000 from the tourist development bed tax.

When the time for the concerts finally arrived, Jackson and his brothers were in town for a few days. That gave Godbold opportunities to visit with him. Jackson was donating all of his money from the Victory Tour to charity. He told Godbold he wanted to help children. "He wanted to give 1,000 tickets to underprivileged kids," said Godbold. The mayor's office helped coordinate the transportation to carry the children to the concerts.

Then, there was Malanda Cooper, a young girl with a short time to live because of sickle cell anemia. Her big wish was to meet Michael Jackson. She wrote a letter to the mayor. Malanda got her wish when Jackson met her back stage prior to one of the concerts.

Later, Malanda attempted to have Jackson visit other sick children in University Hospital, but it could not be arranged. Upon learning that Jackson was unable to visit the hospital, Godbold's team enlisted David James, the Jackson impersonator, to entertain the children. "I went to the hospital and I enjoyed him as much as Michael," said Godbold. "Those kids had big smiles on their faces. He brought them a lot of joy."

While in Jacksonville, Jackson also created a $100,000 music scholarship endowment that continues to provide three $3,000 scholarships annually to college bound music students, based on merit and need.

Another $32,150 was donated to Jacksonville charities, and $24,988 was paid to the city for administrative expenses.

Jackson gave Godbold 300 tickets for each concert for his beloved senior citizens.

When all the receipts were totaled after the Victory Tour had left town, the city made $89,000 from sales and tourist development bed taxes. An economist at the University of North Florida said the three concerts had a $10 million economic impact on Jacksonville.

The Jacksons collected more than $4 million in Jacksonville.

After saying the Victory Tour would only visit ten cities and Jacksonville would be the lone site in the southeast, promoters later increased the number to 55 cities with the final three concerts being held in early December in Los Angeles at Dodger Stadium. Jacksonville attendance for the three sold out concerts was 135,000, more than many of the other cities, including Dallas, East Rutherford (New York), Buffalo, Philadelphia, Denver, Montreal, Chicago, Cleveland, Atlanta, Miami, Houston and Vancouver.

For Jacksonville and the 135,000 who were able to get tickets to at least one of the concerts, the Victory Tour was a great success. It made for a frenzied and exciting summer. It was as if all of Jacksonville had Michael Mania.

The one hour and 45-minute concerts blew the roof off Jacksonville and rocked the nights away in the Gator Bowl. To call the concerts extravaganzas is akin to saying the Atlantic Ocean is wet. They were elaborate and featured well-choreographed dance routines. There were red and green lasers, dry ice fog, fireworks, video images and what was described in the media as "Star Wars-styled theatrics."

The 25-year old Jackson and his brothers performed a 15-song set.

And, for three straight nights, the Gator Bowl was alive with 45,000 screaming, swaying and dancing fans.

For Godbold, the Victory Tour was all he had for hoped from the first time Chuck Sullivan said he wanted the Tour to visit Jacksonville. It brought tremendous attention to Jacksonville and put the city in the same sentences as some of the country's top cities. Thousands of the concert goers were from cities and towns across the southeast. It also brought together the city's citizens, rich and poor, black and white, young and old, all dancing and singing Jackson songs in unison inside Jacksonville's Gator Bowl.

Just as important, Jacksonville's Victory Tour sent a message to the NFL that Jacksonville was a city that could play in the big leagues.

The Tour lasted six months and there were multiple stories about controversy, confusion and missteps caused by promoters Chuck Sullivan and Don King.

The Jacksons made money from the Tour, but it was the last time the brothers would perform together, primarily as a result of tensions that developed during the Tour. As an example, Michael flew from city to city on his private jet, while his brothers flew commercial. By the time the Tour was half over, the brothers were taking separate vehicles to concerts. When Michael got word near the end that Sullivan and King were planning a European tour, he let them know he was not interested.

Chuck Sullivan did not make money from the Victory Tour. He had negotiated bad deals and by the time the Tour turned west, shows weren't selling out. Some shows were cancelled. At one point, money was so short that Sullivan stopped payment on a $1.9 million check to the Jacksons. In the later stages of the Tour, Sullivan said he had losses of $5-$6 million. When it ended in Los Angeles, he said he had only made half a million dollars.

Because of their losses, Sullivan and his father started quietly letting the NFL know that the Patriots and Sullivan Stadium were for sale. They were asking $100 million for both. The Patriots went to the Super Bowl the next year, but even that didn't pay the debt piled on as a result of the Victory Tour. At one point, reports said that Sullivan wrote to Michael Jackson asking for money to bail the team out.

Michael never responded.

In 1988, after nearly four years of a financial blood-letting, Sullivan went bankrupt and sold the stadium to Robert Kraft for $25 million. Sullivan sold the team to Victor Kiam in 1988 who sold to James Orthwein who thought of moving the team to St. Louis or selling it, but Kraft had negotiating rights which forced any prospective buyers to go through him. In 1994, Orthwein sold the Patriots to Kraft. Since then, Kraft's Patriots have been to nine Super Bowls and won six.

Chapter 26

———∿∿∿———

SMASHING WIN BUILT
ON PARTNERSHIPS

WITH NINE MONTHS remaining before the 1983 spring mayoral election, Mayor Godbold seemed in public to be undecided if he was going to seek re-election. But in private with his friends and supporters there was zero doubt that he would run again and campaign hard.

"One day I'm all jacked up and I feel like I still have some things I'd like to accomplish," he told the newspaper. "I see things that have been done and I say, 'Gee, I helped to do that.' That helps make it all worthwhile."

Later, he said the bad outweighs the good as mayor. "I start getting disgusted with it. Sometimes people start questioning your integrity and things like that." Being re-elected, he said, meant being away from his family and business another four years. "I probably will run, but I still have to give it a lot of thought."

His record during his first term certainly merited another four years. He had impacted every constituency in Jacksonville, including the establishment and business community which aggressively opposed him in 1979. By 1982, led by the Chamber of Commerce, Jacksonville's business and social elite were on the Godbold train. Working in partnership, the mayor and business community had racked up win after win to alter attitudes and begin changing the face and future of Jacksonville.

Surprising to much of the establishment was Godbold's support for the arts in Jacksonville, helping raise money for the Jacksonville Symphony Orchestra and the city's art museums. Trinita Petersen, executive director of the Arts Assembly, echoed what most felt when she told the *Florida Times-Union*, "He's done a remarkable job for us." In his first year, he gave the Arts Assembly a 21 percent increase in funding and allocated another $200,000 to Jacksonville arts groups. "And, he has been the most influential citizen for the Florida Theatre restoration project."

Jake and Gov. Graham at ground breaking for Prudential Insurance southeast headquarters, part of the $10 billion decade.

JAKE!

Jacksonville Bank president Jack Uible and developer Henry Faison show mayor model of bank, Omni Hotel development.

Godbold had not only managed to capture the loyalty and support of Jacksonville's business leaders, he had also won over the affection of many of their wives. Among his strongest allies were the members of the Jacksonville Junior League, women like Courtney Wilson, Julia Taylor, Annabelle Hudmon and Kay Zambetti. He embraced the Junior League's causes, even serving as host to boost attendance for the League sponsored annual Women's Tennis Association championship at Amelia Island resort, featuring such female tennis greats as Chrissie Everett and Martina Navratilova. Two of his most vocal supporters became Helen Lane, a Jacksonville philanthropist who had publicly opposed Godbold's efforts to close Coastline Drive to build his esplanade, and civic leader Pam Paul, also a philanthropist.

In many ways, the mayor was ahead of his time. Godbold placed a high premium on women and put many into important positions in his government, appointing women to boards and supporting issues important to them. His staff and other top leadership posts included Betty Holzendorf, Martha Barrett, press aide, Linda Sullivan, Director of Senior Programs, Ruth Waters, Fleury Yelvington, Gwen Yates, Ethel Masters, Madelyn Levin, Dale Eldridge, Dr. Pat Cowdry, and Harriet Harrell, to name just a few.

"He really made women important in his administration and he listened to them as well. They knew that we had important decision-making jobs in his administration and not just fluff," said Barrett, his press aide and the staffer who controlled the mayor's calendar.

For senior citizens, an important voting group, Godbold had a special love affair. He had created the Mayor's Older Buddies (M.O.B.) and organized and promoted seniors throughout the community. He had convinced 200 different businesses to cut prices for seniors, secured funds from the federal government to purchase two buses and three vans to transport seniors, built community centers where seniors could gather to eat and socialize, created numerous social events like fishing tournaments and holiday dances, established a senior citizens forum, and often he would make mid-day stops at senior activities and provide everyone with a free lunch.

For blacks, who had supported him overwhelmingly in the 1979 campaign and provided Godbold's margin of victory, the mayor had delivered. He brought blacks into high level positions of the government in unprecedented numbers, including on his staff, as division chiefs and appointed positions on Jacksonville's independent authorities. Godbold had fought vigorously for a minority set-aside program to give black businesses opportunities when government contracts were awarded, and he championed affirmative action. The mayor had also created a summer employment program for underprivileged black youth, provided funds for Edward Waters College, an Historic Black College, and supported Dr. Martin Luther King, Jr. Day as a paid holiday.

"Jake Godbold gave black folks hope," said E. Denise Lee, who first joined Godbold's 1979 campaign as a young field worker and later served 26 years on the Jacksonville City Council, as well as two terms in the Florida Legislature. "He brought the kind of hope and support I'd never seen anybody do."

Like most all elected officials, Godbold was not immune to criticism, which often got under his skin. In August 1982, the mayor told the *Times-Union*, "People don't criticize you for doing nothing, but there's always public opinion for or against something if there's something happening. And, since I've been in office there's been something happening everywhere: on the northbank, on the southbank, in the arts, with the river, renovating the Gator Bowl, sports. You name me an area and, boy, we're making things happen."

By September 1982, any doubt that Godbold would seek re-election was erased when his supporters announced a major fundraiser to launch his 1983 campaign. It would be a $1,000-a-couple gala reception at St. Johns Place and was being led by 14 major Jacksonville players, both Republicans and Democrats, as well as representatives from business, labor, and the black community. The host committee included Chamber president-elect Jim Winston, Chamber president Albert Ernest, Committee of 100 president Republican Earl Hadlow, Republican insurance executive Ash Verlander, black businessman Willard Payne, black University of North Florida executive Dr. Andrew Robinson, Florida Board of Regents member Cecelia Bryant, philanthropist and civic leader Pam Paul, labor leader Randall Gardner, lawyer and community leader Bill Birchfield, and business and civic icon W.W. Gay.

The early fundraiser was suggested by Republican Verlander. It netted $265,000, a Florida record for a single fund-raising event. One $1,000 ticket buyer was former Jacksonville Mayor Hans Tanzler, who said the gala was attended by the "Who's Who of Jacksonville."

It was so very different from four years earlier when Godbold had almost zero support and financial backing from Jacksonville's establishment. Lawyer Tommy Greene was Godbold's finance chair and major fund raiser in both of his campaigns. "The second campaign was easy," he said. "I raised money a different way. Rather than go out and get nickels and dimes, I raised it a thousand dollars at a time. He (Godbold) had a four-year record and that made it easy."

One reason Godbold and his top supporters wanted to raise a lot of money early was to discourage any potential challengers. For the most part, that fact, along with Godbold's intense political roots throughout the political landscape, kept the coast mostly clear.

Sitting district City Councilman Harold Gibson had been making it known for months that he planned to run for mayor. He wanted to become Jacksonville's first black mayor. During the months leading up to the campaign, Gibson often vocally opposed issues Godbold brought before the council. More often than not, he was on the losing side.

Longtime Godbold friend and former council colleague Lynwood Roberts refused to close the door on a 1983 mayoral campaign. Some of his friends thought that if a well-known white candidate like Roberts, now Tax Collector, entered the race, he'd have a chance to win if Godbold and Gibson split the black vote.

Under different circumstances, 53-year-old Gibson might have had a different result than what eventually happened in the April 1983 first primary election. He was considered the first serious black candidate for mayor in city history. Gibson had plenty of high profile government experience. He had been a top aide to Mayor Tanzler for several years as Tanzler's council liaison, been elected to the Civil Service Board, and he was a city council member. Gibson had also been an executive with Westinghouse's Offshore Power Systems, an ill-fated plan to build nuclear power plants that would float off the Atlantic coast. He owned his own business on the city's northside and was a reported millionaire.

In early November 1982, sitting beneath a City Hall portrait of Jacksonville namesake Andrew Jackson, Gibson ended months of saying he wanted to be the next mayor with the official announcement of his campaign. As expected, he came out of the gate criticizing Godbold. "The priorities that have dominated the current administration over the past three years include the champagne and caviar issues: Colt Fever, Gator Bowl sky boxes, painting streets, esplanades and festivals. While these things may add dimension to our city…they are not addressing the real issues, the bread and butter issues that face all of us, including the realities of an overcrowded jail, a deteriorated sewer system."

Meanwhile, Godbold continued to collect campaign funds with a $25 a person fund raiser and other individual donations. By the end of November, the mayor had amassed a record $375,000 and he ended further contributions. When election day came, he had amassed more than $392,000.

In mid-February the *Times-Union* listed the contributions from individuals and businesses to the candidates of $500 or more. Godbold's list filled seven full columns of the page. Gibson had two names, his and one other.

On December 10, Roberts removed himself from the mayoral discussion by saying he planned to run for re-election as Tax Collector.

In February, when Godbold, Gibson and Republican Dean Trieble paid their $2,501 qualifying fee at the Supervisor of Elections office, the mayor was late and kept the press waiting. He had walked the few blocks from city hall rather than drive his city car to a "political event."

Unlike his 1979 campaign, this go around Godbold brought in a pair of nationally known Democrat political consultants from Washington D.C. Bill Hamilton was the pollster hired by the Chamber right after Godbold's first election who told the new mayor that until attitudes changed in Jacksonville, he would get nothing accomplished. Bob Squires was a hot-shot media consultant who had made television commercials for many of the leading Democrats in the country.

Probably because they were from out of town and unfamiliar with the culture and local politics in Jacksonville, Hamilton and Squires both recommended to Godbold that he ignore Gibson and not campaign in the black community. "They said he was a well-liked businessman with a good reputation. Don't make him a hero out there by campaigning against him," Godbold recalled. "They said you can win with just the white vote."

But a few of Godbold's top black aides and I vehemently disagreed. Betty Holzendorf, who was Godbold's highly respected, very aggressive and extremely intelligent council liaison, went ballistic. She, a couple of other black campaign leaders and I met with the mayor and presented him an ultimatum. Holzendorf said, "You've served them well. You've kept your promises. Now, they have to make a choice. If they want to support Gibson let them do that but give them a choice." Then, Holzendorf banged in the nail. "If you're going to take their advice and not campaign in our community, we're going to resign."

Godbold didn't need much convincing. He knew he had strong relationships and deep support in Jacksonville's black community. He enjoyed campaigning with black voters and he was anxious "to take it to Gibson out there."

"I decided they were right. We needed to do everything in the black community we did in the white community," said Godbold.

John Bowden was a rough and tumble labor leader in Northeast Florida. A former boxer who wore expensive pin stripe suits, Bowden was head of the Building & Construction Trades Council. During Godbold's first term, the mayor was aggressive in recruiting new business and new construction to Jacksonville, often stressing that Florida is a right to work state and contractors could pay lower than union wages. During a trip to Washington to lobby for more ship repair projects for Jacksonville companies, the mayor said labor in Jacksonville would be less costly than in Virginia and other states. That enraged Bowden, who maintained a high media presence, always fighting for more jobs and better wages for his union members.

"My remark led him to believe my talk about cheap labor was an insult," Godbold said. "I was only trying to help the construction business for him and his people."

In late 1981, Bowden got everybody's attention when he launched a bumper strip campaign against Godbold. The labor leader printed and distributed 10,000 bumper strips that read, "Jake was a Mistake." It was rare public pushback against the mayor.

A year later, at the union's annual Christmas party, Bowden invited Godbold to speak to his members. Some speculated that the ice was thawing between the two men after Godbold had insisted that the JEA pay union scale wages to construction workers building the authority's billion-dollar coal fired plant.

On March 18, 1983, Bowden and his union endorsed Godbold for re-election. "He'll be a better mayor because of the criticism I've given him," Bowden told the press. The mayor was also endorsed by the North Florida Labor Council (AFL-CIO).

As much as Gibson tried to get traction for his campaign, it appeared more and more obvious that he was in over his head. While he could be aggravating to Godbold and his supporters, his campaign almost became irrelevant.

Gibson's public comments and criticisms of Godbold were like desperate political "Hail Mary" passes, drifting out of bounds or falling short or simply sailing over everybody's heads. For instance, Gibson said Godbold had made Jacksonville look like a "Jerk Town" by trying to get the Baltimore Colts, despite the fact that 50,000 people had jammed the Gator Bowl that night and the town continued to talk feverishly about getting an NFL team.

Three weeks before the April 12 primary election, Gibson threw a fundraising party featuring Count Basie and his orchestra. It lost money. He expected to sell 3,500 tickets but sold only 700. In the March 21 finance reports to the state, Gibson had raised just $40,561 compared to Godbold's $378,956. And, Godbold had stopped seeking donations the prior November.

That same week, Gibson told the media that the mayor was forcing city employees to work in his campaign or be fired and he called on State Attorney Ed Austin to investigate. Gibson also claimed that Godbold staffers were following him around to events and said the mayor was giving jobs to political cronies.

When Godbold announced in the spring that the mayor's summer youth employment program would hire 3,400 disadvantaged youths 14-21, Gibson accused him of politicizing the program.

Godbold generally ignored Gibson and refused to appear with him at public forums and debates. When the political and mostly white Bull Snort Forum held a debate, Jake didn't show. Instead, he was at black Edward Waters College receiving a humanitarian award from the A.M.E. Church of Florida "for bringing the community together."

During his campaign, Gibson argued that he would get 60 percent of the black vote and 30 percent of the white vote, enough to win. But day after day, Godbold stole his thunder. Sen. Arnett Girardeau, the first black to be elected to the Florida Senate in more than 100 years and chair of the Duval County Legislative Delegation, endorsed Godbold, saying he kept his promises to the black community. "You don't kick someone in the teeth who's done so much," Girardeau said.

He was also endorsed by the A.M.E. Ministerial Alliance, which Gibson called "a sellout of the black community."

On the ground, Godbold's vast and experienced campaign organization was blanketing the city, knocking on doors, putting Godbold signs in yards, calling voters, stuffing envelopes, signing postcards and organizing for an all-out Get Out the Vote effort on election day. Flush with campaign cash, the campaign left nothing undone. Under the campaign slogan, "Godbold/Jacksonville: Partnership for the Future," campaign materials were tailored to specific areas of town.

Meanwhile, Gibson complained that Godbold "partners with the wrong people: wealthy businessmen who stand to make big bucks from frivolous projects."

From the mayor's office, every day it seemed something positive was happening. There were ribbon cuttings, ground breakings, road and overpass openings, and a senior citizen fishing tournament.

Godbold was everywhere and constantly in the media.

Godbold's campaign receives big boost with endorsement by Sen. Arnett Giradeau.

Things were going so well for the mayor that even often critical *Times-Union* columnist Robert Blade wrote three weeks before the election, "…he has a record as mayor that he can be proud of. People have the feeling that the city is growing and making progress under his administration. They look at him as an egalitarian kind of leader who plays no favorites and is open to all points of view."

Finally, on April 3, Godbold met Gibson in a televised debate sponsored by the League of Women Voters. For the most part, Godbold refrained from talking about Gibson and instead focused on his record and what he planned to do if re-elected.

Then something really got under the mayor's skin. With the election just a few days away, in a speech to the Northside Businessmen's Club he reversed his strategy and blasted his opponent. Gibson, he said, as a member of the council, had voted against projects that would help those he serves and says the city has ignored. "I'm getting tired of hearing about the pot holes and the ditches when my opponent doesn't even have his phone number listed in the phone book and I'm getting all of his calls to fix the pot holes and the ditches."

The mayor pointed out that Gibson voted against a $33 million bond issue that pumped money into council districts to build sidewalks and fix drainage, all things that Gibson had complained about in the campaign. The bond issue, Godbold said, also had provisions to require that minority contractors be hired for a percentage of the projects.

As a councilman and during the campaign, Gibson said that Jacksonville should build a convention center at one of Jacksonville's beaches, not in downtown as Godbold was proposing. "Holy mackerel," Godbold told the Northside club. "We're trying to rebuild a blighted area in his district and he says, 'build it at the beach.' The people who need jobs don't even have a car. How are they going to get to the beach?"

Gibson responded that Godbold's attack was "a desperate move to save a failing campaign. It's very obvious Jake is losing the campaign and now he's resorting to his usual bluster."

Toward the end of the campaign, the *Times-Union* summed it all up by writing that Gibson says Jacksonville is going down the tubes and Godbold says Jacksonville is on the verge of the greatest economic boom in its history.

In this campaign, Godbold was happy to enjoy the *Times-Union's* backing. On the Sunday before the Tuesday election, the newspaper editorialized, "We believe Godbold has earned voter approval through his role as a unifying force in a city where worthwhile projects have fallen victim to factionalism and division."

As election day approached, Gibson predicted that Godbold would only get 20 percent of the black vote.

After the votes were tallied on Tuesday April 12, Godbold had collected 71.5 percent of the vote citywide. The next morning, the newspaper headline read, "Godbold Thrashes Gibson." The vote total was 60,373 for Godbold, 24,112 for Gibson. Just as impressive, Godbold creamed Gibson in the black community, garnering almost 70 percent. He won most all of the black precincts, including 13 of the 19 precincts in Gibson's council district.

"The black vote Godbold got was absolutely surprising," said Supervisor of Elections Harry Nearing. "I couldn't believe it. I've never seen anything like it."

Gibson refused to call Godbold and congratulate him. He said he would not support the mayor in his general election campaign against Republican Trieble.

Mayor celebrates victory with his wife, Jean Godbold.

Prior to the primary vote, pollster Hamilton predicted Godbold would collect 58 percent of the total vote and said it would be impossible to get more than 62 percent. He had highly underestimated Jake's appeal.

Once the votes were analyzed, it showed that Godbold won in every conceivable category. With 71.5 percent of the total vote, he received 70 percent in the upper income neighborhoods where he had done poorly in 1979, and he collected 80 percent of the white blue-collar vote.

Chapter 27

"Take Your Passion and Make It Happen"

For Jake Godbold, Tuesday July 5, 1983 started early with a 7 a.m. prayer breakfast and finally ended late at night after a public celebration of Godbold's installation earlier that day as a re-elected mayor who had won with huge margins and a strong mandate.

About 130 close friends and several Jacksonville ministers gathered in a room at the Sheraton at St. John's Place to rejoice with prayers for the mayor and praise for his leadership. Almost four hours later in the hotel's grand ballroom, Godbold was sworn in by Circuit Court Judge Virginia Beverly for a second term as Jacksonville's mayor.

It was as if so many people—those who were close to him, the thousands who campaigned and voted for him, and many others who only knew of him through media accounts—had been smiling ever since election day.

At 10:30 that Tuesday morning, over 1,000 gathered for Godbold's installation. It was both a patriotic and an incredibly upbeat occasion, a reflection of Godbold himself.

Just before Godbold was sworn in and spoke to the crowd, Emma Shipp, a former city employee who had wowed the throngs at the Jacksonville Jazz festival the previous October, set the theme for Godbold's remarks when she sang, "Flashdance-Feel the Passion," the Grammy Award winning song from the highly popular 1983 movie, "Flashdance."

Godbold was feeling the moment. He truly believed it was his time. But, mostly, he believed it was Jacksonville's time to capture its dreams. In an impassioned address, he said, "It is time for us to take our passion and make it happen."

"Jacksonville is a city on the move," the mayor told the crowd. Four years earlier, he said, "Instead of building living monuments to progress, we were planting tombstones memorializing our destructive greed."

Jacksonville had been asleep, he said. "The jackhammer was silent," and the "bulldozer was still." Downtown was "a place of shame," he said. "Now the city is wide awake."

The freshly installed mayor touted the partnerships that had been formed between business and government, blacks and whites and the mayor and City Council. As a result, he said the city's economy had mended, downtown was being revitalized and high-tech companies were coming to town. "Warring self-interests have been replaced with working partnerships."

Now, he said, "Jacksonville is no longer a city of lost faith, but a community of believers. We believe in ourselves and we believe in our future. That's because everyone works together. We have a single agenda and a common goal."

Later that Tuesday evening, in the Sheraton's grand ballroom, Godbold's campaign threw a large public celebration. The *Times-Union* pointed out that Godbold's 1979 victory party on the night of the general election had served pretzels and potato chips. But not this night. It was a first-class, "lavish" reception.

Godbold stood outside the ballroom as a receiving line of only one person. His hand was pumped over and over and his face was smeared in lipstick from the kisses and hugs of female supporters.

As always, Godbold and his team made sure that his senior pals, members of the Mayor's Older Buddies, were represented in large numbers. Hattie Floyd, 69, told the newspaper, "I just love the mayor because he's so good to his older buddies. See this pin (M.O.B.)?" she asked the reporter. "I got a list of stores I can go into and get 10 percent off stuff with this pin. I ride the bus from 9 a.m. until 3 p.m. and after 6 p.m. for 15 cents."

On July 7, the *Times-Union* said in an editorial, "It will take, as Godbold pointed out, a dream of the way things may be and the passion to make the dream come true."

A few days following his installation, Godbold delivered his annual budget message to the City Council. Two things he said captured the media.

First, he made real his hint that he was going to call for a property tax increase to pay for badly needed infrastructure improvements, something the council later approved.

But, from a political perspective, he used his speech to the council to end any speculation that he might one day run for another elected office. In remarks that were not part of his prepared speech, the mayor surprised his aides, his supporters and the media. "This is my last four years in politics," he said. "I think I've served my apprenticeship. I want to get back to my business."

For many people, Godbold's surprise announcement signaled that the arthritic pain in his spine was just too much for him to take on everything entailed in running for another office and then serve if elected. Others, however, saw it differently. As Godbold's former aide and campaign sidekick, I was one of those. When asked by the *Times-Union* what I thought, I said, "I think he sees he has a real opportunity to do some things in the next four years and he doesn't want to think about another office hanging over his head. I'm delighted to see, frankly, that he's taking a four-year approach to city programs that have been neglected."

On July 14, the *Journal* said in an editorial, "His well-timed renunciation of further political ambitions frees him to do what he does best: arouse enthusiasm for transforming Jacksonville into a modern, workable urban environment after what he views as a decade of neglect."

Jake sworn in for second term by Judge Beverly.

JAKE!

Chapter 28

———— ❧ ————

STEP LADDER TO THE NFL

IF MAYOR GODBOLD was looking for a gift to keep the excitement and economic momentum going in Jacksonville, he was about to receive an unexpected one when, in 1982, a new professional football league, the United States Football League (USFL), opened play in the spring with eight teams in some of the country's top cities. The business plan of the owners was to compete with the NFL, but not directly against it.

After a successful first season, the USFL brass looked to expand the league into additional cities, and wealthy Clearwater, Florida developer Fred "Bubba" Bullard, who grew up in Jacksonville's Riverside area and graduated from Landon High School, decided he wanted to get into the game with a team in his home town.

"All of this started from a fellow I knew named Billy Cash. He called me up and figured I had enough money to do something like that," said Bullard. To sweeten the pot, Cash told Bullard that he and Ray Graves, former University of Florida legendary coach and athletic director, wanted to come see him and discuss the idea. At the time,

Graves was working for George Steinbrenner, owner of the New York Yankees, in Steinbrenner's hometown of Tampa. After the three men talked about the feasibility of getting a USFL franchise for Jacksonville, Bullard agreed to move forward, provided that Graves would remain on board as an advisor.

The owners of the league's existing eight teams were wealthy men, some whose names were well-known. They believed that the best way for an infant professional league to become viable was to play in the spring, maintain a tight rein on expenses, not pay exorbitant salaries to players, and make the game fun for fans. Way in advance of the NFL, the USFL instituted instant replay and two-point conversions after touchdowns. USFL owners joked that the NFL was the "No Fun League."

The USFL had already added franchises for 1984 in San Diego and Houston. Jacksonville would become the smallest franchise city.

To get a franchise, Bullard had to make a $50,000 deposit to the USFL; then he had to negotiate with John Bassett, owner of the league's Tampa Bay Bandits. Bassett was chair of the league's expansion committee and he owned USFL territorial rights to all of Florida. Bassett gave Bullard permission to start negotiating with Jacksonville, which meant with Mayor Godbold. After the initial meeting with the mayor's chief aide Don McClure and other city officials, Bullard said, "I have received great cooperation from the mayor's office."

For Godbold, having a USFL team in Jacksonville was like getting a stepping stone to his real goal of landing an NFL franchise. The USFL was catching on in its first season, and it had television contracts with ABC and a new cable network called ESPN.

"I just wanted to make that thing happen," Godbold later said. "I wanted to do everything and almost anything I could to accommodate

Bullard on bringing this team. I didn't have to sell him because he was from Jacksonville."

After meeting with Godbold, Bullard said, "He wanted professional sports in Jacksonville. He was an interesting study, from my perspective. He wasn't really satisfied with the USFL…well, he was and he wasn't. He was making Jacksonville well-known primarily through using professional sports."

Jake, always the great believer in building strong relationships, had a new friend in the hopeful football team owner. And, Bullard discovered he had a pal and cheerleader in the sports-driven mayor. "We just hit it off right away," said Godbold. The mayor "was so energetic," said Bullard. "His objective was to put Jacksonville on the map and to get a successful team."

Bullard needed three things if he was going to field a team in Jacksonville in 1984: a lease for the Gator Bowl with the city; approval of himself, personally, by the league's owners; and league approval of the Jacksonville franchise.

Three weeks before the city's May 24 general election, Godbold got his wish when he and Bullard signed a 25-year lease for the 80,913 seat Gator Bowl, which Godbold had just renovated the year prior, adding 18 sky boxes at a cost of $14 million. The lease was signed at a press conference.

"People accuse me of spending too much time on sports," Godbold said. "Really, I don't understand that criticism. A football team in this city is not just a game on a weekend afternoon. It means a lot of jobs and an improved quality of life for our people."

Jacksonville Journal sports columnist Tom Cornelius wrote after the press conference, "Jacksonville's sports minded mayor had a good day. The Jacksonville Sports and Entertainment Commission had a good day. Fred Bullard had a good day. No one is criticizing anyone in this column. Kudos to all."

Next, Bullard needed approval of the lease by the City Council, a process that would normally take a minimum of six weeks. The mayor said he intended to ask Council President Henry Cook to call a special emergency meeting to take up the lease, which would take only three weeks, half the time.

Bullard paid the USFL a $6 million franchise fee, and he met the requirement of showing the league he had $13 million available to operate the franchise.

In the meantime, he negotiated a favorable territorial deal with Tampa Bay's Bassett that included an agreement on sharing players from Florida and Florida State University.

During the entire process, the USFL had remained mum. That silence ended on June 10 when Bullard was notified the league owners had approved his bid and a formal announcement would be made the next week.

USFL Commissioner Chet Simmons made plans to be in Jacksonville on June 14 for a 3 p.m. news conference. The commissioner didn't understand that Jacksonville was Godbold's town. The mayor said he'd make sure the announcement received the maximum amount of news coverage. Godbold scheduled the news conference for 6 p.m. in the press box of the Gator Bowl to accommodate live television coverage by Jacksonville's three television stations, WJXT Channel 4, WTLV Channel 12, and WJKS Channel 17.

The press box was jam packed with city officials, business leaders and sports fans for the USFL's first live television announcement. Just before 6 p.m. the mayor got the crowd's attention. WJXT sports anchor

Sam Kouvaris gave Godbold a countdown and the mayor lifted off, praising Bullard, lauding the USFL and Commissioner Simmons, and talking on the phone with Gov. Bob Graham who had called into the conference. And, the mayor reminded everybody watching the announcement, "If we didn't rebuild the Gator Bowl we wouldn't have a franchise." He also said, "The guy who will make this franchise work will be the beer and hotdog guy."

Mayor Godbold announces Jacksonville's entry into the U.S.F.L. with team owner Fred Bullard (left) and USFL Commissioner Chet Simmons (right).

Godbold spoke for ten minutes, which meant the sportscasters had to cut back to their stations, then return later in the newscasts to pick up the rest of the remarks.

David Lamm, sports columnist for *The Florida Times-Union* wrote the next morning, "Godbold was at his fist-banging, sermonic best. He sounded like a man running for office instead of a man who recently won a landslide re-election."

An unidentified USFL official told one member of the media that Godbold's speech was "an unofficial USFL record for length and impact."

Commissioner Simmons said he hoped Jacksonville's first game would be against Tampa Bay, coached by Florida icon Steve Spurrier, and its second game would be against Donald Trump's New Jersey Generals which included Georgia football great Herschel Walker.

Bullard promised the team would draw an average of 35,000-40,000 per game. "Barring bad weather, we'll put that many in here. I'll bet you."

Through all of the hoopla, Godbold never took his eyes off the NFL, his real target. The city, he told a reporter, "will go full speed ahead to get an NFL team."

Chapter 29

JACKSONVILLE'S FAVORITE
BULLS FAN SPIRITS

NOW THAT FRED "Bubba" Bullard and Jacksonville had an expansion team in the USFL scheduled to open its 1984 season in less than eight months, there was a whole lot to be done if the new team was to meet the promises of Bullard and the expectations of Mayor Godbold.

There was no team name, but that was remedied when Bullard launched a public write-in campaign that climaxed on the late afternoon of July 4th in front of 100,00 celebrants when a large, long banner was unfurled with much fanfare down the side of the Seaboard Coastline Building in downtown on the riverfront. "BULLS," it read, a name that was highly speculated leading up to the unveiling since the team owner's name was BULLard.

There was no head coach, something that Bullard worked hard to reverse in a hurry, always focused on getting what he called the "right guy for Jacksonville." Bullard set his sights high and his first target was

FSU's iconic coach, Bobby Bowden. "I offered Bobby Bowden part of the team. He was sitting there smoking his cigar. I said, 'You can't pass this up.'" Bowden said he wanted to talk to his wife about the offer. "He obviously also talked to some other people," said Bullard. Bowden phoned Bullard and told him, "I can't take the job. But, I want to thank you. You're going to be my best friend." "Why's that?" asked a confused Bullard. "Because I got a helluva pay raise."

Next up on Bullard's coaches short list was Lindy Infante. In the early 1960s, Infante played tailback at the University of Florida under Coach Ray Graves, now an advisor to Bullard. Prior to joining the Bulls, Infante had been the offensive coordinator for the Cincinnati Bengals in the NFL. In 1981, Infante led a high-flying Bengals offense that won the AFC title and played in Super Bowl XVL. Most serious football observers looked at Infante as an "offensive genius" who loved passing the football, something that was very enticing to the Bulls owner. When Bullard offered him the head coaching job, Infante accepted.

While Infante had the reputation of being a good coach, he lacked the kind of strong name recognition and outgoing personality that Bullard coveted to help get Jacksonville football fans really excited. "I looked at our organization and I knew we needed a big-name guy," said Bullard. He and team general manager Billy Cash—who had first encouraged Bullard to buy into the USFL—started talking about just who they could bring in to give the Bulls that "wow" factor. One of the Bulls early hires was Nick Kish, who left a post as assistant coach at FSU to join the Bulls. Bullard and Cash brought Kish into the conversation. "Nick said, 'How about Larry Csonka? I played football with him at Syracuse.'"

Csonka was a football legend. He was an All-American fullback at Syracuse, drafted No. 1 by the Miami Dolphins, played on the Dolphins undefeated season in 1972 and won two Super Bowls. In 1987 he would be inducted in the Pro Football Hall of Fame, and his #39 jersey would be retired by the Dolphins in 2002. He was also named to the Super Bowl Dream Team by NFL Films.

"That's a home run," Bullard told Kish. They called Csonka and Bullard offered him the position of director of player personnel. "He came down and we hit it off," said Bullard.

There were no signed players, but the Bulls needed to start an advertising and marketing campaign to sell tickets. It was kicked off with a promotion called, "This is For Real." Bullard had hired me to handle advertising and marketing. I knew there had been other failed professional football teams in Jacksonville. "That was the water cooler conversation in town. Are the Bulls for real?" I recommended to Bullard that they address that question up front. Having a coach with Infante's pedigree and a legend like Larry Csonka helped the Bulls change the conversation. Both appeared in Bulls television commercials, and Csonka brought in his Dolphin buddy Jim Kiick to do a ticket promotion and appear with Csonka in a television commercial.

With Godbold's aggressive help, season ticket sales soared. When the team topped 30,000, Bulls business manager Charlie Roberts suggested the team create a special section in the end zones called, "Bubba's Buddies," and sell tickets for $4 each. It was a brilliant idea and allowed the beer and hot dog guys Godbold said were vital to success to attend the games. "For the first time, the black community had an opportunity to go to football games in the Gator Bowl," said Bullard.

Bullard also knew that the odds of fielding a winning team in the inaugural season were long. Games, he said, must be fun and family-oriented so if the Bulls are losing, fans will want to return to the next game because it was a good time. "It can't be just about football," he said. Balloon releases, fireworks, bands, and patriotic performances all became the norm at a Bulls game.

The team needed a mascot so a young Brahma bull from the Rockin' R Ranch was recruited. He was a youngster when we started, but I knew it would be fun to watch him grow up with the team. The Brahma was named "Bubba."

Godbold was relentless in promoting the team and selling tickets. "I did make a lot of calls to business to support the Bulls," he said.

"Jake was courting everybody for the NFL, in the meantime he never failed to support the Jacksonville Bulls," said Bullard. "He was all-in 100 percent. He was driving the bus. He would call the office and ask, 'How are our ticket sales going?' Then, he would say, 'Send a couple thousand tickets over here.' He was the greatest rainmaker in the world."

Godbold knew exactly what he was doing and why. "We were trying to build that impression with the NFL owners that Jacksonville was a football town. It became well-known that the two biggest things in getting us to a point where there was a real possibility of an NFL team was Colt Fever and the USFL. If either one of those had been a failure, we wouldn't be in the NFL today," said the former mayor.

"I don't think I've heard of any city in the United States of America where the mayor got that active in making something successful," said Bullard. "There was no twisting of arms," Godbold said. "We'd call business leaders and tell them we had a few more tickets we needed to sell and ask them if they could take some. They always did."

Godbold never lost focus of the dream of NFL football in Jacksonville. "He was over there beating the drums on the other side of the river," said Bullard. "It didn't make me happy because I'd spent millions of dollars. I felt like even though he was a big part of making our team successful, he wasn't satisfied with our love. He wanted even more."

When Godbold was courting the Houston Oilers and coach Bum

Phillips came to Jacksonville for a meeting, Bullard phoned the mayor. "What the hell? You already have a team," Bullard told him. "Well, they contacted me," Godbold said. "Don't give me that bull shit," Bullard replied. "I knew where he was coming from. It was obviously a better franchise if you had one."

If the mayor worked hard for Bulls success, he got it. The opening game on Sunday, February 26 was against the Washington Federals, which the Bulls won, 53-14. Attendance was 49,392, far exceeding what both Bullard and Godbold had hoped. In its second game, the Bulls played Donald Trump's New Jersey Generals with former Georgia great Heisman Trophy winner Herschel Walker at running back. The Bulls lost, but attendance was a whopping 73,227. In their third straight home game, the Bulls lost to Spurrier's Tampa Bay Bandits 28-25 in front of 51,247 fun-loving fans.

The Bulls only won six games in its opening season, losing 12. But, it was an exciting season and attendance remained high despite the team's record. The Bulls led the USFL in attendance, averaging 46,730 per game. (Only seven NFL teams had higher attendance in the 1984 fall season). In the season's final game in late June against the Pittsburgh Maulers, a near tropical storm hit Jacksonville and the Gator Bowl. Despite the downpour, which flooded the field to the point that team benches were floating in the water, more than 30,000 fans waited out the storm for over an hour to see the Bulls win 26-2.

"I ran into a problem," said the mayor. "We had such a fan base and people had so much fun going to these Bulls games that they would get pissed off at me for seeking an NFL team. People were liking them so much it was hindering us going after an NFL team. The public would have been satisfied with the USFL if it had lasted."

After the successful 1984 season, Jacksonville was chosen by the league to host its owners' meeting, which was held at the nearby resort of Amelia Island on the Atlantic Ocean. At the same time USFL owners were meeting, a group of Jacksonville business leaders were gathered at another part of the resort with officials of the NFL New Orleans Saints to talk about buying the team and moving it to Jacksonville.

Godbold aide Rick Catlett, who was the mayor's liaison with all things sports, suggested that as host for the USFL meeting, the mayor should throw a beach party for the owners. Godbold said, "No." He had another idea more fitting his own style. One of the mayor's favorite spots in northeast Florida was just up the road from Amelia Island in Fernandina Beach. The Crab Trap was the opposite of glitzy and beyond being rustic. Its diners sat at wooden tables with holes in the middle where they threw their oyster and crab shells. That's where Godbold wanted to entertain the wealthy owners of the USFL. He took over the entire upstairs of the restaurant.

"I had a limo for each owner with the flags of their team on them," said Catlett.

Trump and his first wife Ivana were attending the meeting. "They were delightful," said Godbold. "We were concerned about this New York Yankee coming to town."

When the Trumps arrived at the Crab Trap, Catlett said, "I'll never forget it. He's got on a thousand- dollar suit and she's dripping in diamonds." Catlett thought they were doomed. But Godbold's gut instinct was spot on.

"Trump takes his coat off and she takes off all her jewelry. They were the last people to leave. We couldn't get them to leave."

In the 1985 season, the Bulls' record improved to 9-9 and attendance once again led the league with an average of 44,325.

When Godbold and Bullard began the USFL journey together in 1983, neither man really believed that the USFL would have a long shelf life. But both also had their reasons for getting so invested in the Bulls' success.

For Godbold, it was proving to the NFL that Jacksonville was worthy of a franchise. Bullard's sights were also on an NFL franchise. He and other owners were hoping the USFL would be strong enough and a big enough threat to the NFL that eventually it could force a merger. Bullard believed that if Jacksonville proved to be a successful USFL franchise, he might end up with a new NFL team.

"I understood as mayor that the league wasn't going to last long. Bullard didn't think it would either," said Godbold. "He thought if they could be in competition and draw some players away from the NFL that sooner or later the NFL would have to make a deal with the USFL for some franchises."

According to the mayor, his NFL mentor Hugh Culverhouse, owner of the Tampa Bay Buccaneers, also thought that might be the eventual outcome. "Hugh convinced me we had to wait, but in between waiting we had to be successful at everything we did."

Prior to the 1985 season, New Jersey owner Trump convinced other owners to move from playing in the spring to playing in the fall of 1986, directly against the NFL. This was despite the fact that in several cities there were competing NFL and USFL teams. Trump also convinced owners to file a $1.6 billion federal anti-trust law suit against the NFL.

The Bulls were one of seven teams that decided to make the move to the fall. The other teams fell by the wayside. But, the Bulls decision included merging with the Denver Gold and taking the Gold's head coach, Mouse Davis.

Bullard supported Trump's scheme for two reasons. "I knew the league was going to fail and there would be few survivors. I feel like if we had a team in the fall we'd be one of the survivors." If the plan failed Bullard said, "We'd stop the bleeding and get out of Dodge real quick. Me and four others were subsidizing the league."

After 31 hours of deliberations over four days in the USFL's $1.6 billion lawsuit, the United States District Court jury of five women and one man found the NFL guilty of two anti-trust violations: using its monopoly power to damage the USFL and maintain control of the professional football market.

That was the good news.

There was also a deflating amount of bad news. The jury only awarded the USFL $1 (damages are tripled in anti-trust cases, upping the award to $3).

Bullard was crushed but still held on to a slither of hope. "I wouldn't call us out until the last piece of dirt is thrown on the casket," he said, adding, "Unless we pull a rabbit out of the hat, it doesn't look good for us playing this season."

Trump's big gamble was a miserable failure.

Charley Steiner had been the radio voice for Trump's Generals and later became the voice of the Los Angeles Dodgers. Steiner had his own take on what happened. "Trump pushed owners to move games to the fall, wanting to incite a merger. It's about him and the brand and on to the next thing if it doesn't work," Steiner said.

Chapter 30

Learning from a 'Ditch'

Shortly after he took office in 1979, newly-elected Mayor Godbold and members of the Chamber of Commerce leadership started planning how they could partner to alter attitudes in Jacksonville, enhance the river city's quality of life and attract economic development and new jobs. One strategy was to visit other American cities which had experienced a "rebirth," especially in their downtowns.

There is a certain irony in that idea when you consider that members of the business community opposed Godbold's election in part because they believed he would not want to travel, would be a poor ambassador, and really wasn't smart enough to learn from the success of others.

They quickly learned that nothing could have been further from the truth.

Because Colt Fever had received national attention in August 1979, there was a certain curiosity among other American city mayors about this young risk-taker who was running Jacksonville. While Godbold and Jacksonville's business leaders would take eight annual Mayor's Leadership Trips to learn from other cities, the mayors of those cities were often hoping they might learn something from Godbold.

Generally, the trips afforded a great opportunity out of the Jacksonville office for Godbold to develop both professional and close personal relationships with some of Jacksonville's most important leaders, people like Preston Haskell, Jim Winston, Albert Ernest, William Nash, Charlie Towers, Jay Stein and others. It also led to the development of some iconic projects in Jacksonville that would alter the city and dramatically change its trajectory.

The first trip was to Baltimore in 1979. The last trip, made shortly before Godbold left office in 1987, was to San Diego. The two trips that are most often remembered were to Baltimore and San Antonio in 1981 because of ideas Godbold brought home as dreams from each city and then worked like hell to turn into reality.

The first vision was to build riverwalks on the south and north banks of the St. Johns River in downtown, an under-appreciated and under-utilized asset that flows right through the middle of the city. Godbold had grown up on Jacksonville's rivers and creeks and he wanted to open up the riverfront to Jacksonville's citizens for recreation. He also believed that public walks on both sides of the river would spur private investment, create jobs and broaden the tax base.

On his 1981 trip to San Antonio, Godbold met Mayor Henry Cisneros who introduced him to San Antonio's famous River Walk, first built as a storm sewer system in the 1920s to prevent flooding. Compared to the vast expanse of the St. Johns River, the San Antonio River Walk is more like a 3.5-mile long, narrow ditch with treated sewer water flowing through it. But, when Godbold looked at that ditch, what he saw were the restaurants, shops and hotels on both of its banks. He saw boats packed with tourists riding up and down. And, he saw lots of people having a good time.

Standing with Cisneros, Godbold told the San Antonio mayor, "I love your river walk." Cisneros replied, "I'll tell you what. You give me your river and I'll give you our river walk."

When Godbold returned to Jacksonville, he said of the so-called waterway that ran beside San Antonio's Riverwalk, "It ain't anything more than a piss-ant ditch." The mayor and his team went to work.

In December 1982, design work on Jacksonville's Southbank Riverwalk was underway. It was a dream that would become a nightmare for Godbold long before it finally opened in late 1985, three years after the construction had started.

In mid-December the City Council approved $525,000 for engineering and design.

The city invited 100 companies to submit proposals to design and engineer the Southbank Riverwalk, a 1.5-mile promenade along the river from the Acosta Bridge on the west to the Duval County School Board on the east. Fifteen firms responded, including nine from Jacksonville. In June 1982, Perkins & Perkins of New Orleans was selected. The firm's principal, Robert "Skip" Perkins, would become the subject of intense press scrutiny and controversy throughout the entire process.

In December 1982 Perkins presented drawings to the DDA. The DDA voted to expand his contract from the original $20,000 for design to $395,895, plus another $77,535 to reimburse him for supplies and services. Perkins then hired three Jacksonville firms: Bessent Hammack & Ruckman (BH&R) for structural engineering, M.V. Cummings for mechanical engineering, and Reynolds Smith & Hills (RS&H) for cost estimating. In addition, he hired a New Orleans firm for landscape and site design. In other words, he jobbed out all of the work. The city was aware of the arrangement.

In its earliest stages, designers wanted the Riverwalk to include a fountain in the river, a boat museum, a high-class flea market and waterside promenades. The walk itself would be a 1.5-mile planked deck.

In its second phase, there were plans for a terraced 3,000 seat amphitheater with a bandstand, four open air pavilions for concessions and restrooms and a café under the Main Street Bridge.

Phase three would add a fresh and salt water aquarium.

Perkins was given one year to complete the final design, from June 2, 1982 until June 2, 1983.

That deadline didn't hold. The DDA needed state approvals because the riverwalk would extend over the state-owned waterway. But permitting was slowed by bureaucratic inertia. "We were ready to go but we had trouble getting permits from the state," said Jim Gilmore, head of the chamber's Central Jax, Inc., who would later become executive director of the Downtown Development Authority. "The mayor used his influence, but we still couldn't get the permit."

In a panic, Gilmore sent his assistant, Jim Catlett, to Tallahassee to see if he could do anything to get the state to turn loose of the needed permit. "He finds the guy who's holding up everything and the guy said he knew how important the permit was to Jacksonville." Then, the bureaucrat pointed to a stack of permit applications and told Catlett that Jacksonville's was near the bottom. "I know this project is so important to Jacksonville because my boss called me and told me my vacation was postponed until I got down to you and got yours done." Catlett had discovered something important and told the bureaucrat, "Give me some time to work on it."

Catlett called Gilmore. "For God's sake," he said, "get a hold of the mayor and have them call over there and get that guy's vacation back… and do it now!" After the mayor's office made the call, Gilmore alerted Catlett it had been done. Catlett went back to see the bureaucrat who said, "I don't know what you guys did, and I don't know who did it, but I got my vacation back. My wife and I are going to be able to take our first vacation in a long time." Then, he reached to the bottom of the stack, pulled out Jacksonville's permit and approved it. "That was a great lesson for all of us," said Gilmore.

When the DDA asked the Florida Cabinet to approve its riverwalk plans in late February 1983, Cabinet aides said the plans were too elaborate and said the café under the Main Street Bridge and the wharf should be eliminated. The state's Department of Natural Resources won't permit anything of commercial value, the aides said.

With the changes made, Godbold told the Governor and Cabinet on March 2, 1983 that the city was anticipating as much as $418 million in new construction as a result of the riverwalk. "I grew up in Jacksonville and as a little boy I played on the river," Godbold said. The riverwalk would include a park and 14 places for public access, the mayor said. It would be funded by $5.5 million in local property taxes. With the Cabinet's unanimous approval, Godbold hoped the first phase of construction would begin in July 1984 and end by the fall of 1985.

Herb Sang, the superintendent of Duval County Schools, reputedly a narcissistic jerk, ran the county's schools with an iron fist. Sang quickly said he did not want the riverwalk to go in front of the school board's riverfront headquarters, where the walk was planned to stop on the eastern end. Godbold was not happy and fired off a letter to School Board chairman Wendell Holmes saying he wanted the riverwalk to go the full distance. Sang, Godbold said, "has a bad attitude."

Stating, incorrectly, that the school board building was the only public property involved, Holmes said, "…we would oppose such a facility as the Riverwalk as it is proposed at this time." The walk would also extend in front of the city's Friendship Park on the western end. Godbold threatened to go forward, regardless of the school board position.

"Sang didn't want his employees being distracted or going outside to walk on the riverwalk," said Godbold.

Waiting on approvals delayed work and the deadline was extended six months, increasing the costs $68,780. The city planned a "river breaking" on March 2 to kick off construction, but the design work fell further behind schedule, delaying construction bids to finally be opened on March 21. Wood- Hopkins Contracting, Co. won the bid and the city signed a contract for $5,955,000 after eliminating the amphitheater, a scenic grove and the marine areas because of excessive costs.

At the urging of engineer Al Hammack of BH&R, the DDA agreed to pay Perkins another $382,900 for contract administration, which required daily reviews of the construction progress. Perkins then hired BH&R to do the work, saying his job was to monitor the work. When Perkins got paid, he sent the money to BH&R.

From the outset, the riverwalk had issues with the design that delayed the project, increased costs and created unwanted controversy about what was supposed to be a gem on the city's riverfront. It started when the contractor discovered he needed twice the amount of steel pilings estimated by Perkins. By March 1985, costs had increased $350,000.

On May 8, Godbold hosted a sneak preview of the unfinished river-walk. Guests dined on the completed foredeck. Godbold said the now $6 million plus project, "...is something that will be a landmark for years. This is something for our kids and for their kids." Perkins was co-host of the event.

In mid-June, the *Times-Union* reported that on four recent applications for city projects, Perkins said he was a member of the American Institute of Architects which had terminated his membership in 1983 for failure to pay local and national dues and bouncing three checks for state dues.

In early July, City Councilman Gifford Grange toured the river-walk. Afterwards, he told council president Bill Basford there were problems, prompting Basford to take his own tour. He found gaps between the planks, planks that were splintered and warped or oozing sap. Godbold promised that the problems would be fixed before the city accepted the riverwalk. Holding Perkins, BH&R and Wood-Hopkins responsible, the mayor said, "It will be done right and it will be done proper." The problems kept pushing back the riverwalk's opening.

Wood-Hopkins said the summer heat was warping the boards. The corners of some of the planks had curled up a third of an inch.

With the project at least six weeks behind schedule, the fingers started pointing. BH&R said Wood- Hopkins should pay to fix the problems and Wood-Hopkins blamed BH&R's design.

City Councilman Eric Smith put the spotlight on other issues, this time the landscaping. Smith enlisted independent landscaper Michael Bryant to inspect the riverwalk. Bryant said that 90 percent of the trees and shrubs planted along the riverwalk were substandard and needed to be replaced. He also said that the plants were unhealthy and smaller than the city's specifications. "The riverwalk should be a thing of beauty—a shining pearl in the town of Jacksonville. The citizens deserve nothing less," said Smith. "If Wood-Hopkins keeps up on this road, I'm going to make sure they never get a job in this city again."

The blame game intensified as Wood-Hopkins said it had warned BH&R a year earlier that the lumber specified in the design was inferior when it forwarded a letter from the South Carolina lumber company that supplied the boards which said the specifications for the decking lumber allowed a variation of up to one-half inch. "This means that the deck floor will not be completely level and even," wrote H.M. Lupold, president of Holy Hill Forest Industries. But, in June 1984 BH&R ignored the warning and approved the lumber.

In addition to warped boards, wooden hand rails were also warped and split, and heavy wooden benches had cracked.

BH&R said there was too much moisture in the boards.

Wood-Hopkins said it was using wood called for in the specifications and was ready to argue its case in court.

Perkins said he had designed the riverwalk to industry specifications.

City public works director Al Kinard threatened to withhold payments for riverwalk work until it met the city's expectations. "This project will be completed to the satisfaction of the city or we simply won't buy it," said Kinard.

As the days ticked off, the controversy continued. In late September, Wood-Hopkins said it had been trying for eight months to have the New Orleans landscape firm solve the problems with plants and trees.

Company vice president Dennis Harrison found that:

- 247 plants specified produce an "extremely poisonous" fruit.
- 64 trees and larger plants had no tolerance to salt spray and were unable to adapt to Northeast Florida winters.
- Planter drains had failed, leaving standing water that damaged plants.
- Undersized plants were purchased because they were all that was available.

In October, an independent lumber inspector reported that the wood used for the decking met the contract specifications, but the nails specified by Perkins were inadequate and partially responsible for the warping boards. That finding prompted the hiring of a second expert to inspect the nails. Later, northside councilman Joe Forshee said, "A damn northside farmer knows you can't put a two-inch piece of plywood down with an inch nail."

Godbold was both frustrated and fuming. He wanted the negative news to go away, and he was anxious for his riverfront vision to open. "I couldn't understand what was happening," he said. "When we started we were told we might have difficulty putting the poles down in the river, and they said it would be hard to lower the walk so it could go under the Main Street Bridge. But, nobody ever mentioned the biggest problem was going to be warped, green wood."

On October 18, the mayor said that a portion of the riverwalk on the eastern end from the school board building to the Hilton Hotel would be open for the upcoming Florida-Georgia football weekend. A celebration was set for November 8.

Frustrated or not, the bad news kept flowing like a river out of control. On November 2, a 225-ton cement structure that juts out into the river just an 'arm's-length from the riverwalk was determined to be unsafe. It had been intended for use as a viewing platform.

Three days later, the second consultant, George Stern, professor from the Virginia Polytechnic Institute Forestry Department, said the architect, contractor and city were all to blame for the problems. "Unfortunately, the riverwalk will give wood construction a black eye, because the design is lacking, the materials are not meeting the specification requirements and the workmanship is not up to par," said the professor.

Godbold's mayor's office was on the 14th floor of City Hall. Its windows looked directly down at the St. Johns River and he could watch construction on the riverwalk across the way. "I got where I didn't even want to look over there, and I would close the curtains," he said. "No good deed goes unpunished."

On November 8, thousands of locals and Florida-Georgia weekend visitors turned out for the party on the St. Johns River and a portion of the Southbank Riverwalk. At 6 p.m., Godbold threw a switch that turned on the lights that lined the riverwalk.

The project costs had increased from $5.9 million to $7.9 million.

When the Mayor's Budget Review Committee (MBRC) recommended that taxpayers pay 68 percent of the costs to fix the riverwalk's issues, Godbold told them to go back to the negotiation table. "I don't think these figures are fair," he said. If the committee can't negotiate it out, the mayor said, "We'll go to court." Then, he let his frustration out. The riverwalk, he said, was a popular project until construction started. "It's a shame that happened. Certainly, a lot of blame can go around to a lot of people, including ourselves. But, every project we've ever been involved in had a certain amount of trouble with it, be it the Gator Bowl or Metropolitan Park, or what have you."

As if the riverwalk problems were not enough for continuous bad press coverage, on December 3 the Florida Publishing Co., owner of the *Times-Union* and *Jacksonville Journal*, asked a Circuit Court judge to order city officials to give it access to all documents "relating to the hiring of design and engineering subcontractors" for the riverwalk. *Times-Union* reporter Dave Roman had been trying to get the documents from public works director Kinard, but Kinard was refusing to turn them over. Ten days after the newspaper's request of Kinard, assistant public works director Stan Nodland asked Perkins for the records. Under the contract, Perkins was supposed to maintain all books, records and documents concerning the riverwalk and produce them for the city upon request.

On December 11, Judge Lawrence Fay ruled that Perkins must give the records to Florida Publishing, including all documents relating to its subcontractors, stating that the documents are public under Florida's Public Records Law. He gave Perkins until 5 p.m. on Friday, December 13 to produce the documents. It had been three months since the original *Times-Union* request. Judge Fay said, "I think Mr. Perkins has thwarted all efforts for those records to be produced."

Even with the judge's order, Perkins, through his attorney Lacy Mahon, refused to turn over the documents, arguing that Perkins was not a part of the suit, was not an agent or employee of the city, and could not be compelled by the city to submit the records. Fay agreed and asked, "Why is Perkins not in this suit?" The judge scheduled another hearing.

On January 2, after hearing that Perkins had delivered about 50 pages of documents to Roman, but nothing pertaining to BH&R, Judge Fay cited Perkins for contempt of court and sentenced him to ten days in jail. Perkins said there was no contract between his firm and BH&R, despite the fact that BH&R had been paid almost $500,000. "I think we're playing games here," said Fay.

Despite all the negative publicity, a bold headline on the front page of the *Jacksonville Journal* heralded the Southbank Riverwalk's early success on January 2: "Riverwalk Off and Running--At Last."

By early 1986, thousands had flocked to Godbold's jewel on the river. While Godbold wanted a promenade where people could walk, jog or sit and watch the river flow by, he wanted much more than a passive park space. He knew that to maximize its value to the community, the Southbank Riverwalk needed to be busy and a place where everyone would want to visit and come back again and again.

"It was beautiful," said Godbold. "When it was all over, I thought it was worth it."

City officials were planning to pack the riverwalk with as many events as possible. "Our objective with the riverwalk is to make it an area facility to attract people, and to attract people, you've got to have activities," said the mayor. Pat Craig, who had been an assistant of mine on events like Colt Fever and the jazz festival, was hired to manage the riverwalk.

For the first time in city history, Jacksonville started aggressively pursuing street entertainers—called "buskers"—that were popular in other cities such as Baltimore, New Orleans, New York and San Francisco. The riverwalk became a favorite for mimes, musicians, magicians and clowns. It attracted street vendors selling shrimp, hot dogs, hamburgers, gumbo, mud pie and ice cream.

Because of the riverwalk's success in drawing large numbers of people, it also increased business at the two hotels which sat directly on the riverwalk east of the Main Street Bridge, the Hilton and Sheraton at St. Johns Place. Sheraton manager Fred Corso used the newly opened riverwalk to promote events at the hotel. He created the Thursday night "River Rally," on the riverwalk in front of his hotel, which was so popular Corso said he made more money on it than he did on room rents. Attendance also increased at the Museum of Arts and Science adjacent to Friendship Park.

Six months into full time operation, the Southbank Riverwalk continued to get high marks. The *Times- Union* said it was "like a magnet, attracting tourists and locals alike," and called it a "center of community events, market for artists, even a chapel for couples making wedding vows." Referencing all of the design and construction problems, the newspaper said, "Visitors don't notice and don't care about any flaws."

In July, the Southbank Riverwalk hosted a water sports festival that featured water ski shows, parasailing, crew races and boat shows. Thousands attended. Forty thousand attended an International Food Festival, and 10,000 jammed the riverwalk for a Jacksonville Symphony Pops Concert. There were juried arts and crafts shows with entrants from as far away as Texas and New Jersey.

Sheraton manager Corso said, "If you just come down to the riverwalk on a Saturday, Sunday or any evening, you'll see an increase in traffic which is unbelievable. With events there, you can't move."

"I think it's to the point where if you hear anybody say anything negative about the riverwalk, they haven't been to the riverwalk," said Craig.

While the Southbank Riverwalk was in business, big time disputes between the city, designer and contractor continued to play out in public. After Godbold's chief aide, Don McClure, admitted that the city rushed the project and authorized the contractor to correct mistakes, the City Council finance committee approved $271,000 to pay for the city's part of the construction overruns. The full council refused to okay the payment, despite the threat of a lawsuit by Wood-Hopkins. In mid-November, a week after the riverwalk opened, the contractor filed a breach of contract suit against the city for more than $600,000. Godbold wanted to settle the suit and not fight it out in court.

On January 21, 1986, the council finance committee voted to authorize the $271,000 payment for a second time. Meanwhile, Perkins continued to turn over documents regarding his hiring of subcontractors to the Florida Publishing Co.

At the end of January, a tentative agreement was reached between the city and the contractor with the city agreeing to pay an additional $332,392 to the contractor after city attorneys said the contractor would probably win in a court battle.

A City Council review of the project said the DDA and city engineers put the riverwalk project on a "fast track" in 1982. It reported that the city took shortcuts, questions weren't asked, project review times were abbreviated and decisions were made quickly. The mayor disagreed that the project was rushed, but McClure said the city "tried to get that moving along as quickly as possible."

"We had so many layers of people there for protection," said Godbold in frustration and trying to understand how the mistakes happened.

In the end, Perkins' subcontractors got 75 percent of the $1 million he was paid for design and supervision on the riverwalk. Of that amount, BH&R received $500,000, including $120,000 to help with design and another $382,000 to oversee construction.

(AUTHOR'S NOTE: Recognizing the importance the Southbank Riverwalk had become in almost 30 years of existence, in September 2013 the city demolished the original riverwalk and replaced it with a concrete structure that opened in February 2015. The project cost $17 million.

Godbold ran out of time—and the City Council ran out of patience—before the mayor could execute the second half of his dream, a riverwalk on the Northbank. Starting with Mayor Ed Austin in the 1990s and extended by Mayors John Delaney and John Peyton, the Northbank Riverwalk now stretches from the Fuller Warren Bridge on the west past the Acosta Bridge, in front of the Jacksonville Landing, under the Main Street Bridge and down to Berkman Plaza on the east.

It could rightfully be argued that Godbold's Southbank Riverwalk, followed by the Jacksonville Landing, first demonstrated how to open to the public Jacksonville's greatest downtown asset, the St Johns River, and provided inspiration for the projects that followed.)

Chapter 31

———— ❧ ————

"Jake Was Just Stubborn and He Wanted to Live"

As this book is being written, Jake Godbold is about to turn 86-years old. While he does not operate at the pace of the fifty-year-old who was mayor of Jacksonville, Godbold is still very active. He calls on old customers at his Gateway Chemical, Co., advises and raises money for favorite candidates who run for political office, fishes at his favorite spots, speaks out on local issues that interest or concern him and organizes lunches and events to keep his many friends close. In many respects, except for occasional bouts with gout, he's a healthy man.

But then there's his neck and back…

For much of his adult life, Godbold has been forced to turn his whole body if he wants to turn his head. That's because of the excruciating pain caused by a serious arthritic condition. It's a large part of his identity and his life's story.

"To look at an x-ray of Jake's spine is a very abnormal site. It's just loaded with spurs and calcium. It's not the way God intended it to be," said Dr. Scott Baker. "He's not able to twirl his head around and that extends all of the way down," said Dr. Baker, a Jacksonville cardiologist. Despite being highly respected heart specialists, Dr. Baker and his father before him, Dr. Roy Baker, have pretty much acted also as Godbold's primary physicians for more than forty years. "There's not much he's going to do medically without running it by me," said Dr. Scott Baker.

The pain began in his neck and moved to his back in the 1970s. When he ran for mayor in 1979 Godbold wore an elastic band around his waist, hoping to get some relief. During the days running up to the 1983 re-election campaign, he was spending six hours a day with ice on his back, having laser beam treatments and taking a powerful drug to minimize the swelling. "It was like someone stuck an ice pick in my back," he told the *Florida Times-Union*. His back was especially painful during the re-election campaign because he had to be on his feet for long periods of time.

The pain is centered in his spinal column and in discs that cushion the vertebrae of the spine. Spurs developed in his neck and lower back and then passed from one disc to another. The spurs press against the nerves. In 1984 Godbold started wearing a Transcutaneous Electrical Nerve Stimulator, an electronic device that was intended to block pain impulses to the brain. He pretty much abandoned the device in 1986.

In mid-June 1986, 53-year old Godbold checked into the Mayo Clinic in Rochester, Minnesota, for two days of x-rays and tests. Even Mayo's prestigious physicians couldn't recommend a plan for lasting relief.

The neck and back pain, the stiff way he walks, and having to swivel his entire body to turn his head are things Godbold has learned to live with every day. But in 2007 Godbold's family, his doctors and a few of his closest friends were trying to adjust to the fact that the energetic and ebullient former mayor was not expected to live.

"Jake is the epitome of a southern boy," said Dr. Baker. "He has southern boy dietary habits, a lot of salt, a lot of sugar and a lot of fried food. There was no vegan in Jake's upbringing." As a result, Godbold developed high blood pressure that was an issue of concern for several years. Eventually, it became an artery issue that required numerous heart angioplasty procedures by Dr. Baker over the years. In the summer of 2007, Dr. Baker and his wife were vacationing in Barcelona. While they were away, Godbold had to have an emergency heart bypass operation. Another Jacksonville heart surgeon, Dr. Ted Wingard, performed the operation. The Bakers flew back into Jacksonville on a Saturday, planning to use the weekend to recover from jet lag before returning to work on Monday.

"We got into Jacksonville about 3 o'clock Saturday morning. About 8:30 I got a call from one of my partners who filled me in on Jake and said there were post operation complications." Baker went to Memorial Hospital to work with doctors assessing Godbold's condition. "Jake had a significant issue. He wasn't doing well." The former mayor "always had issues with anesthetics," said Baker. Godbold was hooked up to a ventilator, something Baker and the others wanted to get him off. "His lungs wouldn't work well enough to take him off the ventilator so he could wake up." He remained in an induced coma and hooked up to the ventilator in the Intensive Care Unit for ten days. Baker's team performed a tracheotomy.

"There were numerous discussions about what the outcome was going to be for Jake. There was a lot of teetering whether there was going to be a positive outcome or not," said Dr. Baker.

On July 4, Baker and his wife had plans to spend the day at the beach. "I got a call that Jake had a cardiac arrest, so we ran to the hospital." Jake was still in Intensive Care. By the time Dr. Baker arrived at Memorial, Godbold had been resuscitated. "Jake was just stubborn and he wanted to live. He couldn't communicate because he was paralyzed."

Baker said that after ten days in the induced coma, "There were people who thought we should back off. That was not the feeling of the family or my personal feeling. We were going to give Jake every opportunity to get well. We persevered and Jake persevered."

"Everybody thought I was going to die," said Godbold. "Most of the doctors didn't think I was going to make it and they had told my family I wasn't going to make it. I really deep in my heart thought that God had intervened. It wasn't time and it wasn't right."

The doctors, along with Jake's wife Jean and his two sisters, Charlene and Fay, blocked outside visitors from seeing Godbold. There was one exception, Dickie Burnett, Godbold's long-time friend and fishing buddy. Burnett visited his pal every day.

Once Godbold was able to leave Memorial Hospital, he went to the adjacent Brooks Rehabilitation for intensive work. "Although Jake is used to being in charge," said Dr. Baker, "he is a very good patient. He worked hard and he did everything he was told to get back."

While he was in the hospital, the popular former mayor received several thousand letters and cards wishing him the best, many from people who sent their church bulletins showing the entire church was praying for his recovery. "I always felt personally that is what saved my life. After all, the medical people put me in a coma and said, 'We've done everything we can do.'"

Chapter 32

———— ✖ ————

THE NIGHTMARE BEGINS

NEW YEARS DAY 1985 rang in for Mayor Jake Godbold with a bold giant headline in *The Florida Times-Union* that read: "Welcome to the Bold New City of Jakesonville." Godbold and his city were on a five-year roll and the article reflected that success. "For the first time in a long while—maybe ever— Jacksonville is not only thinking big, but doing big things," the article below the headline said. It cited such achievements as the new convention center, the Southbank Riverwalk, the festival market on the downtown riverfront, and the continuation of what the Downtown Development Authority was calling a billion-dollar decade.

In downtown, 1984 ended with $277 million in new construction completed and underway, compared to just $6 million when Godbold became mayor in 1979. Another $557 million in new construction was planned, with $217 million in progress in 1985.

Using charm, flattery, persuasion, name calling and dares, the mayor was getting pretty much what he wanted from the City Council.

Councilman Bill Basford told the newspaper that things were happening and Godbold deserved the credit. "I don't think there's any question it's because of the positive attitude of the government here. The credit lies with the mayor, and we are following him."

Jake and his city had become synonymous. He had the wind at his back, and as he looked ahead to 1985, he had big plans. Godbold intended to keep moving forward. "We can never stop and say that's enough. The goals we set two years ago, most of them we have accomplished, but there's no stopping now," he told the *Times-Union*. His list included more work on the Gator Bowl, new drainage projects, convention hotels, a riverfront marina, completing the first leg of the Automated Skyway Express in downtown, a new Acosta Bridge and a second span for J. Turner Butler Boulevard. He also wanted more festivals, parades and events to bring the community together. And, the march to bring NFL football and big-time sports to Jacksonville was always a priority.

"We have to emphasize the importance of setting goals," he said. "We have to know where we're going," he said.

Things were so heady that in the second week of January, westside councilman Clarence Suggs filed a bill to ask the Duval County Legislative Delegation to allow the council to change the city charter so that Godbold could seek a third term. Godbold, while intrigued, pushed back, saying that would interfere with accomplishing his goals for the city. Regardless, Suggs moved forward and in mid-January the council voted 13-5 as an emergency to urge a change in the city charter that would allow the mayor to serve three terms, rather than two.

Members of the legislative delegation didn't exactly embrace the idea, especially considering that two state legislators were planning to run for mayor in 1987, including the delegation chairman Rep. John Lewis.

Meanwhile, Mark Middlebrook and Dave Roman were in 1985 a pair of young, eager investigative reporters for the *Times-Union*. For some time, they had been snooping around City Hall and examining how Jacksonville handled the selection of underwriters and legal counsel for municipal bonds issued by the city.

Dawson McQuaig had been a county court judge before he was appointed the city's general counsel in 1976 by then Mayor Hans Tanzler. When Godbold became mayor in 1979, he kept McQuaig rather than name a replacement. After all, Godbold knew McQuaig when the mayor was on the City Council. That decision to retain McQuaig later became his greatest regret as mayor.

"Dawson's number one job was to protect the city's reputation and he didn't do it," said Godbold.

While general counsel, McQuaig convinced the City Council to change the rules so that, in addition to his city job, he could also do private legal work. When he left the city's employ in July 1984, he set up his office on the 26th floor of the Gulf Life Tower in the office of Greene, Greene, Falck & Coalson, next to the office occupied by Tommy Greene, the mayor's friend, confidant and chief fund raiser.

As a kid, Greene, who was a year older than Jake, had not lived in the Brentwood Projects like Godbold, but two blocks away. The two attended Brentwood Elementary, Kirby Smith Junior High and Andrew Jackson High School, but they didn't hang out together, contrary to the stories that circulated when Godbold was mayor. The two were in high school when Greene first started paying attention to the future mayor.

"My relationship with Tommy as a young person wasn't very close," Godbold said. "He lived in a little house off Golfair Boulevard and I threw their paper. I knew his daddy better than I knew him." Greene, said Godbold, hung out with a different crowd of friends. "They were older with a little more influence and a little more money. We knew each other, but we weren't school buddies."

Jake and Tommy started getting to know each other in the Jacksonville Jaycees. Greene had gotten involved in the organization after finishing law school at the University of Florida. Jake was in the Jaycee leadership, working at Independent Life Insurance, and thinking about beginning his own chemical company. Greene became Godbold's lawyer and his brother, C. Ray Greene, Jr., filed incorporation papers for Gateway Chemical, Co. when Godbold began his own business.

Greene's father, C. Ray Greene, was a pharmacist and owned a drug store just two blocks from Jackson High School. But, Mr. Greene was more than just the proprietor of a neighborhood drug store. He was elected to the Duval County Commission in 1934 and served 28 years, much of the time as commission chairman. He pretty much controlled his northside 13th ward and was a political force in Jacksonville for three decades.

Godbold was new to politics, but not Greene. Politics was in his DNA. As a boy he had worked in numerous campaigns alongside his father. In 1960, Greene started practicing law with his brother, Ray. From 1963-1966 he served in the Florida House and in 1966 he won a seat in the Florida Senate. He served only one term.

"Tommy got close to me when I got involved in politics," Godbold recalled.

In late 1983 and spring 1984, a few people around Godbold began talking among themselves about the obviously close relationship between Greene and McQuaig. One friend privately advised the mayor that it appeared as if McQuaig was acting like Greene's law partner rather than the city's general counsel.

But Godbold found it difficult to believe that his friend Greene or the city's top attorney would do anything improper behind his back.

(Author's note: Former Jacksonville attorney Tommy Greene is my friend and has been for forty years. When I began my public relations firm in 1983 my first office was subleased from Greene's law firm on the 26th floor of the Gulf Life Tower in downtown Jacksonville).

"I constantly warned him about being too close to Tommy," said Godbold. "And, Dawson would always say, 'Tommy would never embarrass you.'"

As general counsel, McQuaig said his office of city lawyers lacked the stature required to advise the city on bond issues with Wall Street, so he outsourced legal work concerning municipal bond issues to private firms.

When he left the city, however, McQuaig began handling some bond issues as a private bond counsel. This set off the delegation chairman Rep. Lewis and gave him an opening to advance his ambitious political agenda. Lewis started questioning the practice. He set up a meeting with McQuaig's replacement, Gerald Schneider, and notified the media. In his meeting with Schneider, Lewis pointed out that every Jacksonville bond issue since 1979 had been handled by Shearson American Express as underwriter or financial advisor. Greene, he said, had served as bond counsel to the city and was also retained by Shearson to represent them.

On February 8, the *Times-Union's* Roman reported that shortly after McQuaig set up his private practice in 1984, Schneider had recommended that the JEA hire McQuaig to work on a $75 million revenue-anticipation note for a fee of $34,000, which was triple what another firm had said it would charge.

John Kelly, of Freeman, Richardson, Watson & Kelly, complained. Lewis asked, "If he's good enough to be selected bond counsel, why didn't he just do it in house (when he was general counsel)?"

To qualify to handle municipal bonds, attorneys and underwriters had to be included in a national registry, Bond Buyers Directory, commonly called the "Red Book."

In 1960, when Ocala lawyer Farris Bryant was elected Florida governor, the only law firm in the state qualified in the "Red Book" was in Dade County in south Florida. As a result, that firm was primary bond counsel for the state, as well as for Florida municipal governments. Bryant wanted to build roads, highways and state colleges. He helped a Jacksonville law firm, Freeman, Richardson & Watson, become qualified in the "Red Book," giving it an opportunity to make millions of dollars in bond counsel legal work. The Jacksonville firm became the go-to bond counsel in Jacksonville and handled the vast majority of the city's bond work for many years.

When Bryant left the governor's office in 1964, he moved to Jacksonville and became a partner in the firm of Freeman, Richardson, Watson & Bryant. Being nudged out of some business by McQuaig and Greene was a very big irritant to the old, staid, blue blood law firm which was accustomed to having the whole pie. Prior to the JEA hiring McQuaig, the Freeman firm had advised the JEA on eight bond issues in the last four years.

Once the JEA bond counsel controversy started, the media almost daily carried one disturbing report after another. By Valentine's Day, 1985, the *Times-Union* had reported that in three years Greene had profited from $2 billion worth of bonds issued by the city and its independent authorities. Since November 1982, he had handled 19 of 23 issues, usually at the recommendation of then general counsel McQuaig. It was reported that he had been paid $2 million in fees. Greene told the newspaper he wanted all the business he could get, adding that the only reason he was being asked about it was because, "I am the mayor's buddy."

The mayor was quickly becoming unnerved. During his political career—and his entire life—he had avoided any hint of scandal. It was his biggest fear. He had taken great pains to make sure his integrity and his motives were always above question. Now this was happening to threaten his agenda for Jacksonville and the momentum he was enjoying.

In a February 15 news conference, Godbold, who a month earlier had been flying high, said he was "shell-shocked" by the reports, adding that he was "embarrassed as hell about this whole thing." Aide Rick Catlett said that, before the news conference, members of the mayor's staff had "advised him not to say that. He (Greene) did nothing wrong."

Godbold also announced that he was naming an eight-person committee to review the city's selection process for bond attorneys and recommend improvements. It included three high profile business leaders and eight top-ranking city employees.

The mayor punctuated his remarks by saying that Greene would do no more bond work for the city during his administration.

If Godbold thought his news conference would turn off the spigot of bad news, he was very wrong. A torrent would follow for the next two years. Middleton and Roman had their teeth into the investigation with the full backing of the newspaper. On February 22 the Duval County Grand Jury began investigating allegations that the city and its independent agencies show favoritism in handling municipal bonds. Then, in March the F.B.I. started its own investigation.

During the 1979 campaign, Greene was Godbold's chief fundraiser, collecting over $320,000 for the candidate, which was a lot for someone like Jake who was not favored by Jacksonville's business community. When Godbold became mayor, Greene, his wife Elaine and their two children were living in a brick mansion on ten acres that fronted the St. Johns River in historic Mandarin. When Baltimore Colts owner Bob Irsay came to town to talk about moving his team to Jacksonville in August 1979, a Who's Who reception was hosted by Greene in his home.

While he drove a Porsche and worked out of his firm's 26th floor offices in the Gulf Life Tower with vast views of the river and downtown below, Tommy Greene's finances were a mess prior to 1979. He was under intense pressure and financial strain. The real estate lawyer had been named individually in 38 lawsuits by banks and other creditors for failure to pay a total of $2.8 million. The Internal Revenue Service had filed seven liens, and courts in four different counties had awarded 27 judgments against him. He was heavily invested in shopping centers, apartment complexes and motels when interest rates spiked in 1976. He was facing bankruptcy. With the help of his older brother, Ray, Greene was able to settle most of the judgments against him.

The targets of the grand jury investigation were the mayor, his chief aide McClure, Greene and McQuaig. All four voluntarily testified before the grand jury. Godbold found himself in an interesting dichotomy. Here he was talking to a grand jury about alleged wrongdoing in the city, when two weeks earlier the *Times-Union* had released a poll the newspaper had conducted showing the mayor had a whopping, unbelievable 74 percent approval rating among Jacksonville voters after six years in office.

Godbold was willing to appear before the grand jury, but he wasn't very happy about it. When he answered questions from the state prosecutor, it was said that he was truthful, entertaining and riveting. Afterwards, some of the jurors asked for his autograph and wanted pictures taken with him.

In August 1985, the Duval County Grand Jury completed six months of investigation. On August 4th the state attorney turned over a sealed report to Chief Circuit Court Judge John Santora. Godbold said, "I'm glad there's a conclusion. Whatever recommendations are made we will immediately start implementing them."

When the report was unsealed two days later, there were no criminal charges. But the grand jury said that JEA members and other city officials "engaged in political favors" and "abuse of discretion" in handling city business. The grand jury cleared Godbold, but it was very critical of JEA members, former general counsel McQuaig, and McQuaig's replacement Schneider.

The report said that JEA paid three times higher than necessary when it hired McQuaig to provide legal services on a December 1984 JEA financing plan. "We received no proof of either the payment or acceptance of money or other consideration in return for political favors," the grand jury said. The report also said, however, that McQuaig had inappropriately charged JEA $5,000 for work on a 1984 $30 million financing plan that he'd worked on as a private attorney while still the city's general counsel.

McQuaig reimbursed JEA, but said the payment was more than justified for the work he had done.

In September 1981, the JEA board—without consulting its staff—had voted to hire Shearson American Express to serve as the lead underwriter on the $1.6 billion in bonds to finance the coal-fired plant being constructed to extricate the city from its complete dependence on expensive imported oil. Shearson had been represented by Greene. McQuaig had sat in on authority subcommittee meetings held to consider underwriters. He had recommended Shearson and two other firms. The grand jury said that McQuaig's participation had gone way beyond just furnishing legal advice. It was "improper, politically motivated and placed personal friendships above the allegiance to his offices and the citizens it served."

The grand jury also said that instead of using the general counsel's office for legal work, the JEA had hired Tommy Greene's brother, Ray, as outside counsel to buy land for the coal-fired plant. JEA staff had been acquiring land since 1971 and had added a staff member to its right of way section in anticipation of the property purchase for the coal-fired plant. McQuaig had recommended against soliciting proposals from other firms.

After reading the grand jury's findings and facing the newspaper headlines, Godbold was shaken and incensed. "The past several months have been very difficult ones for me," he said.

He asked for the resignation of all JEA board members. The mayor said he came to that position "after considering everything from jumping off a bridge to resigning." The mayor said he wanted to review each JEA member's performance and said he would interview them one by one. He also considered asking for Schneider's resignation but decided against it after reviewing the general counsel's overall performance.

If any JEA member refused to resign, the mayor said he would have the person removed through a city process that required a two-thirds vote of the City Council.

Godbold proposed major changes in the city's professional services system and the creation of a committee on ethics.

The city's system for selecting consulting firms called for the Professional Services Evaluation Committee to receive all proposals, then select the top three firms and send its recommendations to the mayor.

Godbold, who always wanted to keep an arm's length between the selection process and himself, had McClure pick one firm from the three and then send his recommendation to the mayor. After the grand jury report, the system was changed so that three firms would be recommended and ranked by the committee. The firm ranked first had to be given the first opportunity to negotiate with the city.

The *Jacksonville Journal* editorialized that Godbold was to be commended for his response to the grand jury report. "For his forthright response we think the mayor deserves praise," said the newspaper.

Looking back forty years later, Godbold said, "I wanted to be fair to everybody and I didn't want anybody to feel like I owed them an obligation, that their donation I could do well without. Nobody gave me the kind of money that they ought to expect me to do more than listen to their problems. I didn't feel an obligation to any of them. I thought I ought to be fair to everybody and I did everything I could to spread out the business to people who never got it before."

Any sense by the mayor and his team that the state grand jury report was bringing the nightmare to an end was misplaced. Just as the state grand jury ended its work, U.S. Attorney Robert Merkle announced that a federal grand jury was being convened to examine the awarding of municipal bond contracts in Jacksonville.

Everybody around Godbold, even most of Jacksonville, knew the popular mayor wasn't his energetic, positive and dynamic self as a result of the past several months. When news first broke of the investigation in February, Godbold began limiting his public appearances. Knowing that a federal investigation and more negative headlines were ahead, people worried about Jake and the impact the loss of his leadership would have on the city's great momentum and progress. There was concern that many of the programs he championed would fall apart without his dogged and visionary leadership.

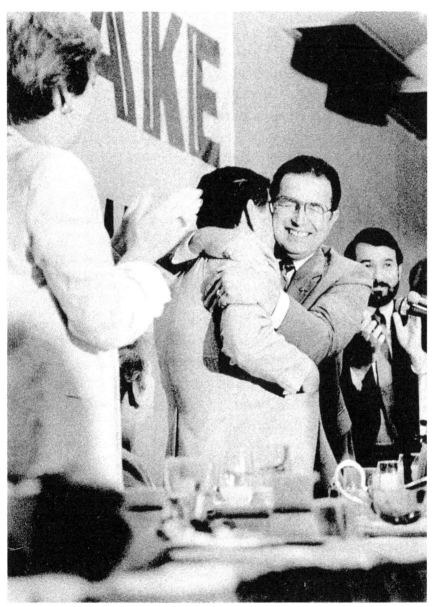

Breakfast host and friend Bill Mouro hugs the mayor.

THE NIGHTMARE BEGINS

Nobody who knew him believed Jake had done anything wrong. But many felt he had been too trusting of his friends.

August 21, 1985, three weeks after the grand jury report, at a 6:30 a.m. breakfast I organized, 700 supporters jammed into the ballroom of the Sheraton at St. Johns Place to give Godbold's spirit a boost. Those attending said they wanted to show their appreciation and were hoping to repay some of the energy and enthusiasm the mayor had given them during his six years as mayor. They wanted Godbold to return to his former highly visible leadership role.

State Sen. Arnett Girardeau, the first African American elected to the Florida Senate, was one of a dozen speakers who stood beneath a huge banner that read, "Thanks Jake for Being a Great Mayor." He praised Godbold and said, "…if Jake Godbold is not up to steam and working the way Jake Godbold likes to work, this community suffers."

"Jake got us moving, really moving," said another speaker. "He restored our confidence in ourselves and gave us a can-do spirit."

"I hope this acts to recharge his batteries and give him the confidence that the people are with him," Chamber president Bill Nash told the newspaper. The breakfast, he said, "is like a revival."

Godbold was touched. He told the newspaper, "It certainly boosted my spirits and made me feel a lot better. I'm very proud of it and proud for my family."

For perhaps the only time in his political life, when it came time to conclude the breakfast, Godbold kept his remarks short. "Thank God that some of you have reminded my son and my wife and me that we have done something good because there a been a few months lately that I, myself, was beginning to doubt." He didn't stop there before giving his supporters a taste of the Jake they love. "You must make sure

Labor leader John Bowden encourages Jake at the breakfast.

we still dare to try," he said, regaining some of his fire. "You must make sure we still take our chances. We cannot afford, as the 19th largest city in the nation, to drift backwards. We can't afford not to dream as we have in the last six years."

Chapter 33

—————◆◆◆—————

THE NIGHTMARE GETS DARKER

ROBERT "MAD DOG" Merkel was the chief federal prosecutor for the Middle District of Florida. He got his nickname because of the relentless and aggressive way he pursued people he thought were breaking the law. He also got the name "Mad Dog" because he was often called abusive and a bully by defense attorneys who frequently asked for Justice Department investigations into his behavior.

Merkel successfully prosecuted Carlos Lehder Rivas, the Columbian drug lord who was responsible for 80 percent of the cocaine being smuggled into the United States. He also got an indictment of Panamanian military ruler Gen. Manuel Noriega.

Shortly after becoming the U.S. Attorney operating out of Tampa in 1982, Merkel determined to root out what he perceived as corrupt behavior by city and county officials serving in his jurisdiction. That put a target on the back of every mayor in the Middle District of Florida, including Jake Godbold.

The media reports and state grand jury investigation of alleged misconduct in selection of underwriters and legal counsel for municipal bonds issued in Jacksonville was like blood in the water to Merkel. The F.B.I. began its own investigation in March 1985 and the ink had hardly dried on the state grand jury report in August 1985 before Merkel launched his own federal grand jury probe.

Just the announcement of the investigation was a major blow to Godbold, his staff and leaders in the community, who feared it would drive an already beat-up Godbold underground coming so close on the heels of the state grand jury probe. The city's progress, they worried, would come to a standstill.

Merkel's probe extended beyond the four targets of the state grand jury investigation: Godbold, McClure, Greene and McQuaig.

In June 1986 the federal grand jury started reviewing every record in the Duval County Courthouse going back to 1974 that had anything to do with attorneys Greene, Paul Harden and R. Lee Smith, along with former city councilman Rodney Hurst. It also asked for the same information for the wives of Greene, Smith and Hurst as well as for the Greene, Greene, Falck & Coalson law firm. The subpoena for the records was the 67th issued by the federal grand jury in less than a year.

Lee Smith, a former Greene partner, was the lead partner in the law firm of Smith, Davenport, Bloom and Harden, a group of young attorneys who shared about half of the space in the spacious 26th floor office with the Greene firm. He served on the Jacksonville Transportation Authority from 1979-1985, including three terms as chairman. Smith had been Godbold's campaign treasurer in 1979 and 1983.

Harden, 34, had been chairman of the city's planning commission from 1981-1984.

After review, the records obtained on Smith and Harden weren't out of the ordinary. But Hurst's records were a different story. They revealed that Hurst, who served on the council from 1975-1983, had been sued 24 times for allegedly not paying debts between 1974 and 1983.

The federal grand jury had been investigating Jacksonville's city government for 15 months. Most of Jacksonville, especially the mayor, was hoping than when its term ended in October 1986, four months away, the huge dark cloud which had been hanging over the city would finally go away. For Godbold, it was depressing and exacting a heavy toll. Rick Catlett, his aide who was a constant companion, witnessed the effect up close. "We would go to Tallahassee for meetings and check into a hotel and he wouldn't come out," Catlett said. "I'd go to his house to pick him up and he wouldn't want to go. I learned that dark side. It's real hard when someone is depressed like that to get them to realize that this is just a small segment of what is going on."

"It was a very difficult time for all of us," said Martha Barrett, Godbold's press aide who also handled the mayor's calendar. "Having that unknown on him…and the media…it was worrisome to say the least. It was just a hard time."

As difficult as it was for Godbold, he fought hard not to give in to his urges to just shut down. He got strength and comfort being around people, average citizens, who felt like they knew Jake well and wanted only the best for him. He especially drew on the love he had for senior citizens and often went to their meeting places and events to get a boost in his spirits.

Good things continued to happen in Jacksonville despite the gloom brought on by Merkel and his grand jury probe that frequently made the newspaper headlines. Gloomy or not, the last half of 1986 was typically busy for the city as well as for the mayor.

Large crowds were showing up at the newly opened Southbank Riverwalk, movie companies continued to make films in Jacksonville, and 120,000 attended the city's annual July 4th celebration downtown.

Godbold reopened a renovated Hemming Plaza in the heart of the city with a celebration. He spoke to civic organizations, cut ribbons and even pitched in a softball game between his staff and the Chamber of Commerce in August.

Godbold also presented his final city budget to the City Council in July, telling the council members he was tired and his back hurt, but that if he wanted to taste victory, he had to continue running hard until his term ended in a year. The mayor also reminded the council—and the community—of some of the accomplishments during the last seven years. "When I was elected mayor in 1979, I saw a Jacksonville that could become one of America's great cities…and I believe it has." Then, he ticked off just a few things from a long list: 183 new companies, 88,000 new jobs, completed or planned $1 billion in new construction downtown, the tax base almost doubled since 1979 and building permits increased 200 percent. It was vintage Godbold.

Perhaps moments like that gave Godbold a temporary escape from the reality of the federal investigation swirling about him. The investigation had broadened from looking at how the city awarded municipal bond consulting contracts to include the city's pension fund, zoning, other city business dealings and the Duval County Property Appraiser's office.

In September 1986, the grand jury subpoenaed the travel records of Godbold and key members of his staff, McClure, Barrett, Catlett and Henry Stout. In October the travel records of McQuaig were subpoenaed. Then, 72-year old property appraiser Robert Mallard was indicted by the grand jury on 18 counts including lying to the grand jury, urging potential witnesses to lie and destroying official files.

Mallard entered a plea of not guilty.

Beginning in September 1985, Merkel waged a campaign to have State Attorney Ed Austin turn over the state grand jury testimony of Godbold, McClure and McQuaig, but Austin resisted and U.S. District Judge Susan Black sided with Austin.

When the 18-month old term of the grand jury ended in October, Merkel did what Godbold and much of Jacksonville hoped he wouldn't. He extended the term another six months, prompting *Times-Union* columnist Robert Blade to opine, "The grand jury and the lawyer responsible for it are warping the process."

In December 1986, under advice of his attorney Lacy Mahon, Godbold said he would not testify before the federal grand jury, invoking his constitutional right under the fifth amendment that protects a citizen from being compelled to be a witness against himself. McClure, Greene and McQuaig also said they would plead the fifth if called to testify. Later, the mayor said, "If I had my choice, I would probably have gone over to the federal grand jury, but I haven't been asked. It means your attorney tells you, 'Don't do that…you don't want to go over there.' I don't know what his reasons are."

Godbold's decision to invoke his fifth amendment right drew an expected amount of criticism, especially from some members of the City Council who said it hurt his credibility.

As if Godbold didn't have enough problems, when 1987 started the *Times-Union* reported that Judge Black, who would ultimately decide if Merkel could get his hands on the state grand jury testimony, was the guest of the mayor in his private box for the Gator Bowl game just played. The judge went with her husband, Lou Black, who had been invited by Godbold. Another guest was State Attorney Austin.

Godbold did not attend the game.

Twenty months into the investigation, Godbold was weary. "I really mean it when I tell you that I don't understand it. If I can't run it (city government) straight, nobody can. I've been as hard working and dedicated as anybody possibly can be. It's something that's been going on too long; it certainly has an effect on your people, yourself, and your family."

With six months remaining in his term, Godbold couldn't escape the constant drip, drip, drip and the pressure wrought by the investigation. He spent time reflecting, often sharing his thoughts with the press and others. "I just want to be a good mayor. I don't want to make a lot of money. I don't want to go away and become a big lobbyist. I hope I will be known because I turned the city around," he said in mid-January.

Later, in a speech to a local civic club, he said, "My problem was, how the hell do you make this city proud of itself? How do you build spirit and pride? Nobody believed we could do anything. We weren't excited about ourselves. Now," he said, "we're the fastest growing city in the state and we're in one of the fastest growing states in the nation."

He used another speaking opportunity before the Meninak Club to give advice to the next mayor, who would be elected in the 1987 spring election. The next mayor, he said, will have to confront the problems of the growth of the past seven years: transportation, parking, housing for the poor, public safety, garbage disposal and sewer shortcomings.

Finally, on February 23, the grand jury returned indictments against Greene for bank fraud and against Stout, a former aide to Godbold. Stout was charged with six counts of lying to the grand jury about his knowledge of attempts by Godbold, McClure and others to influence the selection process for hiring consultants for city contracts.

Greene was charged in a five-count indictment involving bank fraud and making false statements to obtain personal loans, nothing at all to do with the almost two-year old investigation of alleged City Hall corruption. After a week-long trial, he was given two, two-year consecutive sentences. Greene, 54, spent 26 months in a federal white-collar prison. He could have been sent to prison for up to 30 years and given a $50,000 fine.

Later, Greene said the U.S. attorney continuously squeezed him in an effort to get something on Godbold. "They figured if they could do something to me, if I can give them bigger fish, they would let me go. I didn't have a bigger fish to give them. There wasn't anything I would say to them under any circumstances that Jake did something wrong. He never did. I would tell them that he was afraid of his shadow. He wouldn't do anything wrong for love or money. I couldn't tell them what they wanted to hear and I served 26 months in jail for that. They got me," Greene said, "when I was settling a judgement for underestimating my net worth on a bank application."

While in prison, the feds didn't let up, said Greene. Once, they brought him to an F.B.I. office. In a large room, "they had every financial record I ever had in my life. It was a helluva investigation. They spent a lot of money, but they couldn't get Jake because there was nothing there they could get him for," he said.

The grand jury said Stout, 52, lied when he said he was not involved in selecting consultants, that he had not tried to influence votes of city employees on the Professional Services Evaluation Committee, and that he never told committee members which firms should be finalists for city contracts. Despite testifying under a grant of immunity, the grand jury said he had lied during three separate appearances.

In returning the indictments, Merkel said they should not be taken as an assertion that Godbold or McClure engaged in criminal conduct.

During his eight years, Godbold's staff was both hard working and cohesive—with one exception. Stout worked long and hard, but he had no interest in working well with others and was a constant source of friction among the Godbold team. He had worked for McClure when McClure was a department head under Mayor Hans Tanzler. When McClure became Godbold's chief administrative officer, he brought Stout with him.

Godbold recognized Stout's issues with others. "He was our one loose staff problem," Godbold said. "He was a great asset to Don, but he was a liability to the staff. Henry probably knew as much about government as anybody did, but he didn't know how to handle it. He was very vindictive."

Stout did try to influence government decisions, including hiring choices, usually through intimidation, said people who worked for the city. Fortunately, it was pretty clear to everyone that the mayor would never have instructed Stout to call anyone regarding those kinds of issues.

In the mid-eighties, Godbold friend Tillie Fowler planned to run for the City Council. She phoned Godbold and said she had just received a call from Stout, who told her the mayor didn't want her to run. Godbold was incensed. He told Fowler that was not true and renewed his commitment to help her get elected. Stout was privately planning to run for the council seat himself.

When President Ronald Reagan was shot, Godbold tightened up on City Hall security out of a concern about copy cats. "Henry got this idea he should be armed, and he wanted to bring a Luger up to the office," Godbold said. "So, the staff came to my office and said, 'Please don't let him have a firearm up here on this floor.'" Joanne Carter, who had worked for Godbold when he was on the council, "stood up and said, 'I'm going to tell you something. I'd be the first one he'd shoot.'" The mayor made sure Stout remained unarmed.

Godbold wanted to fire Stout, but out of respect for McClure he kept him on staff. "I never pushed anything on Don. Don was such a loyal hard-working guy."

Following the indictments of Greene and Stout, Merkel said he might extend the grand jury once again when its term concluded in May.

As the days faded away before Godbold would no longer be mayor, the bad news continued to hammer at his spirit. He admitted to a newspaper reporter that the investigation had hampered his administration. It dominates his life, he said and causes him not to want to do anything. He backed away from doing anything that might be controversial and routinely avoided going to the office. When he did go in aides said he seldom stayed the whole day.

Business leaders said the grand jury had killed business deals for the city and crippled the city's leadership.

Once again, *Times-Union* columnist Robert Blade weighed in, writing, "He (Merkel) has spent enough time and money. It is time to get moving. The best government might be the least government, but this is getting ridiculous."

In mid-March, the Fraternal Order of Police and the Jacksonville Association of Firefighters threw a big birthday party for the mayor, in part to thank him for his leadership, but mostly to lift his spirits.

Just over a week later, U.S. District Judge Black reversed her earlier ruling and ordered the release of the 1985 state grand jury testimony by Godbold, McClure, McQuaig and Greene. But, in doing so, she leveled heavy criticism at the U.S. Attorney. "The court finds that there is no excuse for the conduct of the United States in the prosecution of this case," she wrote. "The court finds that the United States failed to diligently prosecute this case and has ignored the court's order delaying the motion to delay the filing of factual information."

Later, Judge Black granted a motion by Godbold and McClure to appeal her order.

On April 24, 1987, Godbold was able to step outside the controversy and participate in the long- anticipated opening of the first of two giant generators for the JEA's $1.6 billion coal-fired plant. It was a hallmark of his eight years as mayor. When he took office in 1979, Jacksonville's electric rates were the highest in Florida and second highest in the nation, primarily because the city was dependent on high priced OPEC oil. It was the first bear he faced, and the mayor had tamed it.

Godbold and the JEA had good news to share on multiple fronts:

- The first generator came on line 45 days early and $100 million under budget.
- As an investor-owned utility, JEA's partner, Florida Power & Light, would pay $5 million annually in property taxes.
- A refinancing of the power plant's bonds from 11.5 percent interest to 8.5 percent would save $1.4 billion over the thirty-year life of the bonds.
- Coal contracts were 40 percent under projections, saving ratepayers $27 a ton.

Five hundred of Jacksonville's top dignitaries were on hand for the ceremony and Godbold, the *Times-Union* reported, was the "ring master."

"What a challenge we have overcome. This is truly a great day for Jacksonville," he said, recalling those early days when rates soared and ratepayers revolted.

Godbold, who loved being mayor and never had an interest in holding any other elected office, was counting down the days until June 30 when he could cut out the lights and go home. In his final weeks, like the opening of the coal-fired plant, there were people and events to remind him why he enjoyed being mayor of Jacksonville so much.

On May 3, 1987, the Northeast Florida Builders Association and its executive director, Godbold's childhood friend Arnold Tritt, held an appreciation dinner for the mayor at the Prime F. Osborn Convention Center. Over 1,500 attended.

Comedian Red Buttons was a special guest. When he entertained the crowd, Buttons looked at Godbold and said, "Well, mayor, it's all over."

Red Buttons looks on as Godbold messes with his friend, Arnold Tritt.

"Thank God," Godbold replied.

When it was Jake's time to speak, he talked over thirty minutes, using the opportunity to make the crowd laugh and give them some valuable things to think about.

He also took time to chide Democrat Tommy Hazouri and Republican Henry Cook, candidates who were campaigning to replace him in the upcoming spring election. During the final weeks of the campaign things had turned ugly and Godbold said he was saddened by the mud-slinging that focused on religion and ethnic origin.

"It concerns me when you start dividing this community into religions," he said. "It concerns me when you start dividing this community into ethnic groups. A city is a city because of the cohesiveness of its religions, ethnic groups and races. The greatest challenge of future mayors will be to continue the partnerships we've started between the government and its people."

In closing, Godbold told the gathering that he wanted to be remembered for the contribution he had made to the human soul, for the compassion he had shown for the elderly, the poor, blacks and whites. "I want to be remembered for my ability to bring Jews and Arabs, blacks and whites, the elderly and the young together."

The mayor received three standing ovations during his speech.

On May 13, 1987, 43-year old former councilman Hurst was indicted for perjury, income tax evasion and mail fraud while on the council.

In addition to Stout and Hurst, the grand jury indicted city finance director Ray Clardy for lying to the grand jury about soliciting campaign contributions from his City Hall office. McQuaig was also indicted. All four were sentenced to time in prison.

After returning the indictment against Hurst, the grand jury disbanded, almost two years it had begun. However, the U.S. Attorney said other grand juries would continue the investigations. Finally, in January 1988, six months after Godbold left office, the investigation ended.

In his book "*Jacksonville, from civil rights to consolidation*," historian Dr. James B. Crooks wrote, "The exposure of the political favoritism, fraud and perjury were devastating to Godbold, a man whose personal honesty was not questioned. He had trusted his friends and colleagues and they had misused him."

Chapter 34

KEEP ALL YOU CATCH

IF JAKE GODBOLD was born to sell, he was also born to fish.

"I started fishing when I could ride a bicycle," says Jake. As a young boy, the Trout River on the northside of Jacksonville was his favorite spot. He would pedal there every chance he got. "They had a long dock and I'd get some shrimp and fish off there with a pole."

He developed a habit then that has stayed with him all his life. Jake does not know the meaning of "catch and release." On those bicycle fishing trips sitting on the dock over the Trout River, he would fill up his bucket with little fish and bring them home. "It didn't matter how small they were. Mother said, 'Don't throw them back. If they're big enough to bite, they're big enough to eat.'"

As an 8, 9 and 10-year old boy, during the summers, Jake would visit his grandfather's farm just west of Lake City, where he would work for money, first raking tobacco and later cropping tobacco in the fields.

"The whole time I was hanging out with my cousins and fishing in all of the fresh water lakes there."

When he got home with his bucket of small fish, his mother would clean the fish and fry them. "She'd pat you on the back and hug you around the neck for bringing the fish home."

Perhaps it was the implicit permission from his mother to ignore fishing's unwritten rule of catching only what you can eat and throwing back the small fish that caused a contradiction in the normal way Godbold lived, always walking a straight line and playing by the rules. You could say that when it comes to fishing, he sometimes leaves his personal honesty behind.

When Jake and Jean Godbold were first married, they lived in a small house in the Gateway community, not far from the Brentwood Projects where he grew up and near Jake's Gateway Chemicals office.

When they had enough money, they bought a house farther out in a community called "The Cape." It was one of the first developments in far north Jacksonville, almost to Nassau County. It was also an area that offered nearby fishing opportunities in the rivers and waterways, as well as the Atlantic Ocean.

Jake still lives there. "We moved out here so I could be near the river and fish."

Over the years, his fishing buddies have pretty much remained the same: Dickie Burnett, Arnold Tritt, Warren Alvarez, Tom Crews and his son Ben Godbold. Godbold is well known for never throwing a fish back, always carrying multiple rods with him, and often buying out a bait store. If the fish are biting, he doesn't want to have to stop fishing because he's out of bait.

Among his long-time favorite places to fish are the fresh water lakes on the 1,200-acre Thousand Oaks Ranch owned by the late J.B. Coxwell, a close Godbold friend and political ally. The lakes are stocked with trophy bass, bream, catfish and crappie. The gates at Thousand Oaks are locked, but Coxwell gave Jake a key so he can fish whenever he wants, which has sometimes been two and three times a week.

His friend Burnett often accompanies Godbold in his visits to Thousand Oaks, which is in Brooker, Florida about an hour west of Jacksonville. "He always wants to get the bait on the way," says Burnett. "He'll go in and ask, 'You got shiners?' and the guy will say, 'Yes, I got all you want.' And Jake will say, 'I want all you got.' So, we'll end up with $100 worth of bait and I'm supposed to pay half."

One of the best fishing places at Thousand Oaks is Lake Helen, where a large gazebo provides shade. "We get there and he's probably got 20 rods. I'm dragging stuff out and Jake goes on down to the lake with five rods. I'm hauling the bucket of shiners and all this stuff and I look down there at the gazebo and he's taken all the places with his five rods." When the trips are over, Burnett confesses, "We have a cooler full of good eating bass and another cooler full of trophy bass that you would normally have mounted, but that he is going to have filleted."

For decades, when Jake has caught a cooler or two of fish, he takes them to the Trout River Fish Market off North Main Street and on the Trout River. There, the owner. Jake's cousin Marvin Nipper, has the fish filleted; the filets are placed in the Fish Market's cold storage, where they remain until Jake has a fish fry attended by dozens of his friends.

Shortly after Coxwell established a new fishing rule at his ranch that all "lunkers" caught in his lakes had to be thrown back, Jake, Burnett and Tritt went to Thousand Oaks for a day of fishing. A "lunker" is a large fish of 8 pounds or more.

Even though he may have a cooler overflowing with freshly caught fish, if you ask Jake if he's caught anything, he will say, "No."

According to Burnett, "Jake caught a large bass, a monster, and I put him in the cooler. Later, we went to one of the smaller lakes to catch some bream. That's when Bubba (ranch manager Bubba Boykin) came up and talked to Jake. 'Have you caught anything?' Bubba asked Jake. 'No, we haven't caught a thing.'" Bubba walked away and went over to where Arnold was fishing. In a while, he came back.

Apparently, Arnold had talked to Bubba about the big fish. 'Mayor, I'm a little disappointed in you,' Bubba said to Jake. Jake responded, 'Why's that?'"

It's not unusual for Jake to unbutton his pants when he's sitting in his chair along a lake bank with more than one rod in the water. One day at Thousand Oaks, he was with Burnett, Tritt and his son Ben fishing in one of the smaller lakes when Burnett moved to another location on the lake and began catching bass. Jake decided that Burnett was in a better spot and picked up his chair and rods and moved that way. Soon, says Burnett, "He hung into a pretty good bass. He started running up the bank to pull the bass in and his pants started coming down." Instead of stopping to fasten his britches, Jake told Tritt to pull up his pants. "Tritt told him to go to hell," says Burnett.

In 2003, Godbold and Coxwell worked hard to help John Peyton get elected mayor of Jacksonville. Shortly after the election, Coxwell felt that Peyton had gone back on a promise not to hire a certain individual on his staff because the new mayor immediately gave the individual a high-level position. Coxwell went ballistic and began criticizing Peyton to friends and in the media. He asked Godbold to write a letter to the editor of *The Florida Times-Union* blasting Peyton. "I told him I couldn't do that as a former mayor," says Jake.

Jake refuses to let big bass get away, even if it means he loses his pants.

Shortly afterwards, Godbold and a couple of his friends drove up to the gate of Thousand Oaks only to find they couldn't get inside. "The guy at the gate said, 'We changed the locks and Mr. Coxwell doesn't want me to let you on the property,'" Godbold recalled.

He came back to town and phoned Coxwell. "You can kick my ass, stop doing business with my company, and do whatever you want to. But don't take my fishing rights away from me," he said. Eventually, Coxwell gave Godbold a new set of keys.

Chapter 35

Chapter 35

MAKING MAYO AN OFFER
THEY CAN'T REFUSE

"ONE FROZEN WINTER day in Rochester, Minnesota, Mr. (J.E.) Davis said he was sitting his behind on a cold slab in the Mayo Clinic. That's when he told the chairman of Mayo he should move the clinic to Florida 'where I won't have to come up here to this frozen country every year and have these physicals,'" recalled Mayor Godbold.

Ten years later, on Friday October 3, 1986, Davis and Godbold, along with Rev. Billy Graham and Mayo Jacksonville CEO Thane Cody, stood in front of 600 invited guests and several hundred Mayo employees, all sitting under a white canopy, to dedicate the first ever satellite Mayo Clinic, a $35 million facility that had been built on 140 acres of land donated by Davis along San Pablo Road and J. Turner Butler Boulevard. It was the first Mayo expansion in its famed 78-year history.

Davis told the crowd that on that frigid day a decade earlier he had razzed his examining doctor about what he called a short-sighted marketing strategy on building a world-class medical center in so frigid and isolated place as Rochester.

Rev. Graham had been traveling to the Rochester-based Mayo Clinic for over thirty years. "Hospitals have been closely associated with Christianity, for Christ's teaching and healing gave rise to compassionate medical care. This facility we dedicate today stands in that long and noble tradition of skillful and compassionate care," he told the crowd.

For Godbold, the Mayo Clinic satellite was another feather in his cap; one more time as mayor Jacksonville would surprise the nation, associate the city with excellence, and forever change the landscape of Northeast Florida.

But like most of the major projects completed under his watch—coal-fired plant, Riverwalk, Metropolitan Park, Prime Osborn Convention Center, Gator Bowl renovation, a downtown renaissance—opening the Mayo Clinic only happened after a long struggle and overcoming numerous obstacles. "It surprised me," said Godbold. "I thought this would be a project that wouldn't harbor any controversy at all.

J.E. Davis was a philanthropic, business and political goliath in Jacksonville as well as in Florida and throughout the south. He was the retired chairman of Winn-Dixie Stores, a highly successful business started by his dad. But, when J.E. was 26-years old, his father died unexpectedly at age 54, thrusting Davis and his three brothers—M. Austin Davis, A.E. Davis, and Tine W. Davis—to the front line of running the company. J.E. became chairman and CEO. Although the transition took place at the height of the Great Depression, Winn-Dixie expanded and grew quickly.

At the time of the Mayo dedication in 1986, Winn-Dixie was a grocery empire with nearly 1,300 stores and almost $10 billion in annual gross revenue. As Winn-Dixie prospered, Davis and his family gave tens of millions of dollars to colleges like Jacksonville University, Stetson University in Deland, along with historically black colleges, including Jacksonville's Edward Waters College. The Davis family put its fortune to work for numerous charities and non-profit groups. Davis and his wife, Flo, were founding benefactors for Mayo Medical School and in the Clinic's annual report, they were listed as major benefactors.

Certainly, in Jacksonville no one was bigger, more important and more respected than J.E. Davis. It was widely known that when major local political candidates began their campaigns, they wanted their very first financial contribution to come from Davis. Having him listed as "number one" was seen as an indication of strength and a source of pride.

By 1979, Davis had convinced the Mayo board of trustees they should take a serious look at Jacksonville for expansion. Godbold was the newly-elected mayor, but he fully understood the incredible impact it would have on Jacksonville—and in advancing his aggressive vision—if Mayo landed in his town.

Davis, he said, needed a couple of things to happen to facilitate a move by Mayo: water and sewer would have to be laid to that vast area of undeveloped real estate off JTB from Phillips Highway to the Intracoastal Waterway. In addition, Davis wanted a JTB east bound off ramp built at San Pablo Road. Doing those two things would not only facilitate Mayo, it would open up thousands of acres of prime land for development.

Shortly after Davis persuaded the Mayo board to think about expansion, Mayo officials began making "courtesy calls" on Jacksonville to study the feasibility of putting a clinic there. Former State Sen. Bruce Smathers, son of powerful ex-U.S. Senator George Smathers, escorted the Mayo guests around town. George Smathers had been a member of Winn-Dixie's board of directors and a close Davis ally.

When word of the Mayo visits got to members of the Duval County Medical Society (DCMS), local doctors got restless. Some were resistant, viewing the entry of the Mayo Clinic into the Jacksonville health market as a threat to their own economic security.

The DCMS addressed several questions to Mayo, including what effect the clinic would have on an existing shortage of nurses and other allied health professionals, and to what extent the clinic duplicates existing regional referral centers. Another area of concern would be a point of controversy throughout the years-long process of Mayo's expansion. The DMCS wanted to know what plan Mayo had for Florida medical licensure for its physicians.

To the frustration of DCMS chair Dr. Charles B. McIntosh and other local physicians, Mayo did not respond immediately to the society's questions. Until a decision about expansion is made, Mayo said, it could not answer the questions.

Many Jacksonville physicians were flat out opposed to Mayo. Dr. Sanford Mullen said what many doctors were saying privately, "We don't think the Mayo Clinic can offer anything we don't already have."

Sensing the growing opposition in the medical community, Godbold took to the speaking circuit, talking to civic and business clubs to drum up support. He said he would ask the City Council for a resolution of support. The mayor said the Mayo Clinic would be good for the economy, drawing thousands of visitors annually to Jacksonville. But, DCMS chairman Dr. McIntosh said, "You can't get the economy of medicine mixed up with the economy of hotels and motels."

McIntosh reinforced the medical community mantra. "I feel they have the name of Mayo to offer," he said. "But, from a strictly medical standpoint, they can offer very little in terms of services which are not already being provided here."

The Florida Times-Union disagreed with the doctors in an editorial on July 8, 1980. "Jacksonville and Mayo would both benefit from location of a regional branch of the famed clinic in the area. The welcome mat should be left out and prominently placed."

Not every Jacksonville doctor was in the "no" column. One wrote in the medical society's monthly newsletter, "It places the medical community in an unfavorable position to express opposition to those efforts. It would constitute a bad public relations maneuver, and it would be interpreted as a self- serving move to stifle competition."

Godbold was fearful that the medical community opposition would derail any plans that Mayo might have about moving to Jacksonville. The public, he said, won't take kindly to doctors who blow Jacksonville's chances to make a name for itself in medicine. Mayo, said Godbold, would pass up Jacksonville if the community is in opposition. "There are too many people and communities who would like to have Mayo for them to go where a segment will start shooting them and tearing them down."

He put the target directly on the DCMS. "Personally, I feel the only obstacle to bringing Mayo here is convincing the medical people that Mayo will overall be good for the community," adding, "I think there are going to be those people who put selfish interest before the community. There are an awful lot of medical people in favor of it who don't want to say it publicly and go against their brothers. I think the ones who oppose it are the ones who aren't secure in their fields."

As July 1980 came to an end, the Mayo Foundation trustees said they had decided against expanding in Jacksonville. In a telegram, Mayo listed several concerns, including significant financial risks, staffing problems, and "unpredictability of future government regulations in the practice of medicine which might impact adversely on the project." The telegram said Mayo was also worried about licensure problems for its medical and paramedical personnel because Florida's regulations were among the toughest in the country.

At the time of Mayo's decision, several members of the DCMS were circulating a petition urging opposition to the expansion.

Godbold was shocked and disappointed, but said Mayo officials had shared the news with him when the trustees made their decision. "If this one thing could have happened, maybe it could have really turned this town around. It could have really gotten us started."

Chamber of Commerce president Earl Hadlow said Mayo's decision was, "disgusting."

Years later, Godbold said, "All of a sudden, it was snatched away." Godbold thought the medical community in-fighting, along with some resistance in the state legislature, is what kept Mayo away. Not willing to give up, he reached out to Davis. "I said, 'Mr. Davis, I'll do whatever it takes. Let's overcome this thing. I'll go to the governor. I'll go to the legislature. I'm starting to brag about bringing them in, and now, I'm going to fail, you're going to fail, we're all going to fail.'" Davis told the mayor not to worry about it. "I'm going to make them an offer they can't refuse," he said.

The Professional Golfers Association (PGA) had moved its national headquarters from Washington D.C. to Ponte Vedra, Florida in the late seventies. The PGA headquarters was just across the Intracoastal Waterway from the Davis property. Dean Beman, PGA commissioner, had lunch one afternoon with Rick Catlett and me. Dean said he had a message he wanted us to take to Jake. He said, "You tell the mayor to do whatever he has to do to get the Mayo Clinic to move to Jacksonville."

Noting the PGA headquarters presence, Beman told us that if Mayo joined the PGA by locating in Northeast Florida, it would transform the area. "Right now," Beman said, "all of these heads of industry go to Rochester, Minnesota for two days for their physicals and get out of there as fast as they can. If the Mayo Clinic comes here and the PGA is already here, those people will come to Jacksonville and bring their families for two weeks. They can get their physicals, stay on the beach, play golf and take their kids to Disney World." Beman then predicted, "They'll start buying property and moving their businesses here."

Davis, Godbold and others continued their pursuit of Mayo, out of the headlines and behind the scenes. In 1982, Davis sweetened his offer to include $6 million that he and others had collected in a fundraising campaign. Davis told Mayo it had five years to build on the site or the land would be turned over to another medical-oriented project.

In April 1983, Dr. Eugene Mayberry, chairman of Mayo's Board of Governors, delivered the commencement address at Jacksonville University where Davis had donated millions of dollars. At that time, Mayberry said that Mayo had not eliminated the notion of expanding to Jacksonville.

Over a year later, DCMS officials were told by the American Group Practice Association, to which Mayo belonged, that Mayo planned to locate satellites in six Sun Belt cities. Jacksonville and Scottsdale, Arizona were expected to be the first two sites. Russ Barker, deputy executive director of the Association, said, "It's true. I don't know how far along they are, but it was announced in their publication in June that Jacksonville would be one of two pilot sites." Barker said the information was relayed through an interview with Mayberry. Mayberry said Mayo Jacksonville would be initially staffed with twenty physicians.

In July, Mayberry wrote the DCMS that plans were being made to have a group practice in Jacksonville and Mayo welcomed an opportunity to have a discussion before the plans became final.

On August 21, 1984, more than four years after Mayo's first flirtation with Jacksonville, Godbold made what he called, "the most exciting announcement of my lifetime," at a press conference to reveal Mayo's plans to open its satellite clinic by late 1986.

Mayo said it would build a $10 million facility with a group practice of 20-30 physicians, which would be transferred from Rochester, along with 80-100 paramedical and staff personnel. The clinic, said Dr. Thane Cody, vice chairman of Mayo's Foundation Board, will be out patient. He also said Mayo had, "no intention of building a hospital, buying a hospital, or running a hospital. We are strictly an outpatient organization. We do plan on supporting the local hospitals in every way we can."

Cody also said Mayo plans to expand very rapidly if the demand is there.

An enthusiastic mayor told the media, "The goal, they tell me, is to develop the Jacksonville facility to the point where this city becomes the medical center of the Southeast and the possible equal in treatment and capacity to the Rochester clinic. That's their goal—not mine. But, I love it." In Rochester, Mayo had 1,600 salaried physicians and a total workforce of nearly 14,000.

Davis was on vacation at the time of the announcement, but the Davis family was represented by his nephew Wayne Davis. "My family's small part in bringing this great institution to Northeast Florida will be of little significance in contrast to the enormous benefit that we expect to accrue for the city and the citizens of Jacksonville," he said.

The announcement only heightened the anxiety of many of Jacksonville's doctors who were very worried about competition with Mayo for patients. Neurologist Dr. Jacob Green was blunt. "I'm concerned for myself and our group on the negative economic factor."

Others took a different view, saying Mayo's decision was a compliment to Jacksonville's high quality of physicians and hospital facilities.

On September 22, 1984 the *Times-Union* editorialized, "There are many who regarded the attempt to have Mayo locate a clinic in Jacksonville as an impossible dream on the part of J.E. Davis and his family, especially after a hoped-for announcement failed to materialize four years ago. However, Davis persisted and the dream is on its way to becoming a reality." Then, the editorial echoed what Godbold had been saying since 1980. "For Jacksonville, the advantages are many. The most obvious is the prestige of being selected as the first expansion site away from the Minnesota locale where it was established 77 years ago."

By the time of the Mayo announcement, the previously undeveloped vast tracts of land off JTB called Southpoint were beginning to show some signs of change. When JTB was constructed in the late seventies, it was often derided as the road to nowhere, built to give rich people living at the beaches and Ponte Vedra quick access to downtown. But, already there was a new St. Luke's Hospital and the University of North Florida opened as a four-year college in the area. "The development that's happened out there is nothing compared to what's going to happen, especially after this announcement," said Godbold.

Jacksonville business leaders were counting on Mayo's presence to attract high-tech medical industries, increased airport traffic, restaurant sales and hotel and motel registrations. "History will show the 1980s as a major area of economic growth in Jacksonville, and a major ingredient of that growth has not yet begun to make an impact, but it soon will," said a *Jacksonville Journal* editorial. "…the broad effects on Jacksonville's economy—effects that go well beyond the area of health care—are just beginning to be widely understood."

Responding to the urgency of Mayo's planned opening in October 1986, the Jacksonville Transportation Authority (JTA) sped up planning for JTB improvements by nine months. The plans included construction of an east bound ramp from San Pablo Road, and widening the remaining portions of the expressway. The JTA also planned to build another bridge over the Intracoastal Waterway.

The thousands of acres of Southpoint land around the clinic site were controlled by just a handful of owners: the George Hodges family, the Bryant Skinner family, Gate Lands Co. (owned by Herb Peyton), and the J.E. Davis family.

"Some people thought Mr. Davis was crazy offering that free land out there, but he knew what he was doing," said Godbold. "Mr. Skinner used to tell me, 'Before you became mayor, I used to have cows and cow shit. Now, I have money.' That's because he started developing all that land out there. So, did Hodges and the others."

When the city began running water and sewer out to the Southpoint land, the FBI questioned if it was being done for the developers. "We got criticized for doing it, but everybody ought to thank God that we had the vision to do that," said Godbold.

Prior to Mayo, the Southpoint property was taxed as low-priced agricultural land. In 2017, its office towers, insurance campuses, hotels, corporate headquarters, medical facilities, shopping complexes and housing developments had a real property just value of nearly $11 billion dollars and paid about $90 million in annual property taxes.

But, just as political officials and business leaders were celebrating Mayo's announcement, members of the Jacksonville and Florida medical community were turning their guns toward Tallahassee in a major effort to blow up Mayo's effort to get an exemption for its out of state physicians from the state's stringent licensure examination requirements. Both the

DCMS and the Florida Medical Society, through their high-paid lob-byists, focused their efforts around the message that giving Mayo the exemption was anti-competitive and would set a precedent that could lead in the future to exemptions for unscrupulous doctors.

Under the bill in the legislature, Mayo would receive a 90-day tem-porary license for visiting staff physicians by registering with the State Board of Medical Examiners. It would also bestow "licensure by en-dorsement" to full-time Mayo Jacksonville doctors if they were certi-fied with appropriate medical specialty boards, provided they pass an oral examination within their specialty.

Mayo said the legislation was important so that medical resources in Rochester would be available to share expertise in Jacksonville. "But, with the laws of the state of Florida right now, we would not be able to do that without having them come down and take the licensure examination," said Greg Orwell, general counsel for Mayo Medical Resources. Arizona, where Mayo planned to locate a second satellite, already allows the waivers, said Orwell.

In the Florida Senate, Sen. Mattox Hair of Jacksonville was the bill's prime sponsor. Jacksonville Rep. Steve Pajcic led the battle in the Florida House. In the House, the bill had been in the Regulatory Reform Committee for three weeks. Most of the action by the com-mittee was conducted behind closed doors in the conference room of House Speaker James Harold Thompson. The discussions began on May 8, with only a short time remaining in the legislative session.

On May 10, 1985, under a bright blue sky, Gov. Bob Graham, Mayor Godbold, Paul Volcker, chairman of the Federal Reserve System and a trustee of the Mayo Foundation, Dr. Eugene Mayberry, chairman of the Mayo Clinic Board of Governors, and Dr. Thane Cody, chief executive officer of Mayo Clinic Jacksonville, all turned shovels full of raked dirt to break ground for the clinic. The *Times-Union* said the event was like "a garden party in the middle of nowhere."

Because the site was still isolated, 350 invited guests were transported in vans a mile down a dirt road to the future clinic's site.

J.E. Davis was present and very much the center of attention, receiving a standing ovation when he approached the podium to speak. "Jacksonville has a leg up on becoming the center of medical excellence in the southeast," he said. "This is a great day in medical history."

When Godbold spoke, he thanked Davis and Mayo officials. "What a fantastic thing this is for Jacksonville," he said.

While the governor didn't address the bill before the legislature in his remarks, he did confide to members of the media he was in favor of it and predicted it would be approved.

Meantime, back in the legislature, after three closed door meetings with groups opposed to the bill, on May 14 the House committee passed compromise legislation, 12-4. The organized doctors continued their opposition. Lobbyist Scotty Frazier said the Florida Medical Society was concerned about competition among clinics. "You are being asked to give corporations preferential treatment to maximize income," he said.

Frazier predicted that if Mayo got the exemptions, the issue would not end there. He predicted that the Cleveland Clinic and the Ochsner Clinic in New Orleans would expand into Florida. Frazier argued that if the state assists hospitals with expansion it impacts the business of other Florida-based clinics and hospitals. "These people are being deprived of their income because of the competition from the medical centers you have helped," he said.

Pajcic said the compromise bill was not all he wanted, but that it would

Mayor, Gov. Graham and J.E. Davis break ground for Mayo Clinic.

help Mayo, allowing up to 35 Mayo physicians to earn special Florida licenses to practice solely at the Mayo Clinic if they passed an oral exam in their specialty.

On May 24, with the clock ticking on the last days of the legislative session, the House passed the bill, 54-44 and rushed it to the Senate. It was supported by all of the House members of the Duval County Legislative Delegation. Later that day, the Senate passed the bill, 27-7. Jacksonville Sen. Joe Carlucci joined the no-voters.

By the time of Mayo's dedication on October 3, 1986, 2,700 patients had already signed up to have their two-day exams. They were from Florida, thirty additional states, and six foreign countries. Mayo predicted it would have 15,000 patients in its first year.

Despite Dr. Cody's earlier declaration that Mayo would not build or operate a hospital, in the more than three decades since it opened, Mayo has grown significantly, adding the Mayo Clinic Hospital in 2008. It has 304 beds, 22 operating rooms and a full-service emergency department as well as care in over 35 adult medical and surgical facilities.

The nationally-ranked Mayo Clinic Jacksonville today is a campus that includes the Cannaday Building, the Davis Building, the Mangurian Building and the Mayo Building. Mayo conducts laboratory research on neurological diseases in the Birdsall Medical Research Building, and cancer research in the Griffin Cancer Research Building. It has 547 staff physicians and scientists and a total of 5,804 clinic and hospital staff.

In addition, the Inn at Mayo Clinic is a hotel with 78 spacious rooms and suites that connects directly to the Mayo Clinic Medical Center by a climate-controlled walkway.

Chapter 36

LIGHTS, CAMERA, ACTION

JUST BEFORE GODBOLD became mayor in 1979, Florida Gov. Bob Graham reached out to Jacksonville film producer Lou DiGuisto. Graham wanted DiGiusto to conduct a feasibility study and write a white paper that the governor could use to motivate the Florida legislature to rebuild the film and television production industry in the state. "He saw it as great business to go after," said DiGuisto. "Disney and Universal had contacted him about building studios in Orlando."

As mayor, Godbold was always looking for something new, something different to promote Jacksonville and get his town excited. He made sure the welcome mat was always out. New ventures and visitors were met with open arms.

Jacksonville Information Services Officer Dale Eldridge heard about DiGuisto's project. She told the mayor and recommended that the two of them meet with DiGuisto. "Jake picked up on it right away. He knew the history and Jacksonville's heritage as the 'Winter Capital of Film,'" said DiGuisto. Between 1913-1916, during the silent movie era—before Hollywood was Hollywood—30 production companies made films there. That all ended when local leaders made it impossible for the production companies to do business because people were objecting to fake fire alarms so fire truck scenes could be filmed, wild west shootouts during church services, and the lifestyles enjoyed by many people in the film business.

"Being the great sales person he was, Jake said, 'We can do this again,'" DiGuisto recalled.

In January 1981, Godbold created the Mayor's Advisory Commission on Motion Picture, Television & Commercial Production by executive order. With Graham's aggressive approach, Florida had become the third largest film producing state in the nation, with a $1.2 billion economic impact, and Godbold wanted Jacksonville to have a piece of the pie.

The mayor tapped DiGuisto to be the commission's first chairman, and he named Eldridge to head the Mayor's Motion Picture & Television Production Office which had a measly budget of $15,000. For once, there was no big Godbold press conference to announce the new film office or tout its plans. "We said we were going to keep it quiet until we had something," said DiGuisto.

After visiting a couple of existing motion picture offices in the state to see how they were organized, Eldridge and DiGuisto developed a marketing plan and traveled to Los Angeles on several occasions to meet with production heads of every major motion picture studio to pitch Jacksonville. "They loved it when Jake came out," said DiGuisto. They also traveled to New York City to meet with television production companies.

With no money for incentives, Eldridge and DiGuisto were touting Jacksonville's climate, a variety of locations for filming, available low-cost production talent, and most of all, full city cooperation and support.

For the city to lure any movie production to the city, having a local film office was critical, said Eldridge. It also helped, she said, that when her office landed a commercial in 1984 for French automaker Citroen, she and the city were able to deliver big time. The production company wanted to feature a large number of horses running through various places in downtown, including down the Main Street Bridge which crossed over the St. Johns River. Eldridge was able to deliver 200 horses, plus wranglers, for two days without costs to the production company. She also managed to get the State of Florida to shut down the Main Street Bridge for two days.

Overnight, the 200 horses were kept in the parking garage of the Daniel State Office Building across the street from City Hall. That caused a big clean up job for the city's pubic works department. "It was such an amazing example of the city's cooperation that it was covered nationally by Entertainment Tonight," said Eldridge.

As a result of that story, word began spreading in the industry that Jacksonville had out its shingle for movie business and companies that produced films there could expect and receive total cooperation and assistance.

That brought to town Nederlander Television & Film Productions in October 1985 to film "Intimate Strangers," a CBS television movie starring Stacey Keach and Terri Garr. Gladys Nederlander was executive producer for Nederlander, which she co-owned with her husband, Robert Nederlander. Robert Nederlander and his brothers owned several Broadway theaters in New York City.

The two main production sites for "Intimate Strangers" were Fort George Island north of downtown (which doubled for Vietnam) and

Orange Park west of Jacksonville (which doubled for Annapolis). "The only location they had to pay for was a sailboat," said Eldridge, which was unheard of in the industry. "They shot 21 locations in as many days, also unheard of," said Eldridge. And, like in most businesses—and certainly in film production—time is money. "This had a tremendous ripple effect," Eldridge said.

It seemed the entire city was engaged in courting the movie business. Everybody wanted to cooperate, and, of course, many people wanted to be in a movie. A lot of them got their chance.

Nederlander quickly followed "Intimate Strangers"—which was the third most viewed CBS television movie ever—with another film produced in Jacksonville, "Vengeance, the Tragedy of Tony Simo," starring Brad Davis. To welcome the Nederlanders back to town, Godbold, Eldridge and DiGuisto finally had the press conference they had been putting off. The mayor told Gladys Nederlander that because of her high praise for Jacksonville throughout the film industry, Jacksonville was becoming well known.

Nederlander responded, "We came here originally looking for an aircraft carrier and found this county full of warm and beautiful people who wanted to be so cooperative and helpful." Her husband, Robert, told Godbold, "The cooperation we've received is something we can't describe." He said his organization had made 40 movies. "In this city we feel as if we're wanted and that's important for any organization."

"It's a clean industry," Godbold said, "and it means a lot to our city."

"We were great at hosting and taking care of the key players like directors, production managers and stars." said DiGuisto. "Jake was part of that and he did anything that Dale and I asked him to do. You could count on it."

On July 15, 1986 the *Jacksonville Journal* wrote, "Movies are returning to the city, bringing with them big-time stars and big-time budgets."

Movies were coming back. The Nederlanders returned to Jacksonville for a third movie. In addition, the production manager for "Intimate Strangers" came back and made two television movies, and the movie's assistant director returned to film "Brenda Starr," starring Brooke Shields, Timothy Dalton and Charles Durning.

Over 650 people showed up for a "Brenda Starr" casting call at the Sheraton Hotel. The line stretched out into the parking lot on a hot, blistery July day.

Godbold presented Shields with a Key to the City on location for a jungle setting at Hanna Park. "That was the only time I remember Jake coming onto a set," said Eldridge. "He was always supportive and gracious, but he was far from starry-eyed. He looked at the film business as smart economically. It poured in a lot of money and took nothing away but the film."

Mayor presents Brooke Shields with Key to the City.

Protecting Shields from the paparazzi during her six months in Jacksonville became almost a full-time job for Eldridge. She especially remembers her encounters with photographers from the National Enquirer. "They had tried to take pictures of her for the entire six months. She had gained weight and they were trying to say she was pregnant," Eldridge recalled. "They never got the picture despite the fact they stayed in the same hotel."

By the end of July 1986, the word was out about Jacksonville. Eldridge told the *Jacksonville Journal* that she was currently scouting locations for 15 feature length movies, two television films and two major commercials. "Jake was a brilliant sales person, not only on the front end, but he could close the deal," said DiGuisto. "Then, after the sale was made he made sure we took care of everybody. Because we took such great care of the people who came down here, they came back."

Chapter 37

—∾—

A Chicken Farmer
Made It Happen

Dr. Roy Baker was much more than a renowned Jacksonville cardiologist. Baker, who started his practice in Jacksonville in 1953 as Florida's first pediatric heart physician, was a visionary. In the 1970's, he was a driving force behind the creation of Jacksonville's Rescue System that led to Jacksonville being dubbed the safest place in America to have a heart attack.

He also helped adapt NASA technology for monitoring the EKG of astronauts to transmitting EKGs from moving ambulances to the emergency room.

As Mayor Godbold's friend, the heart doctor acted as Godbold's family physician, responding any time Jake contacted him about everything from a bad cold to an aching back.

In the 1950s, Jacksonville had been considered as a site for Florida's first medical school. However, many Jacksonville doctors opposed the idea so the hospital was located in Gainesville, home of the University of Florida (UF). Jacksonville's University Hospital opened as an eight story, 425 bed facility in 1971, and in 1982 it became a private not-for-profit hospital and contracted with the city to provide indigent care.

For years, Dr. Baker tried to create a partnership between University Hospital and the University of Florida's Shands Teaching Hospital to locate an urban campus for its medical school in Jacksonville.

Then, in 1979, Dr. Baker's buddy, Godbold, was elected mayor of Jacksonville.

Godbold and his chief aide, Don McClure, attended a U.S. Conference of Mayors meeting in Washington shortly after taking office. "For two days, we talked a lot about hospitalization and medical care," said Godbold. On the plane home, the mayor told McClure, "Everybody is getting out of the hospital business and the only two mayors that are still in the business of hospitals are Maurice Ferrer of Miami and me, and Ferrer is trying to get out. It seems like to me we need to get our ass out of the hospital business or we're going to go broke."

Godbold decided to join Dr. Baker's effort. "We need to convince the University of Florida to come in. We're the closest large city to Gainesville and Shands. We need to get them to marry us and run the hospital like they have Shands."

The mayor got with Dr. Baker. "Everyone agreed that was the direction we should go in," said the mayor. As chairman of the board of the city's public hospital, University Hospital, Dr. Baker knew he had a partner in the mayor's office who would move Mt. Everest to improve Jacksonville, something a medical school would certainly do.

Godbold formed a 20-member coalition that included Jacksonville legislative, City Council, medical and community leaders to begin talks about merging University Hospital with Shands Teaching Hospital. Dr. Baker was named committee chairman. The Jacksonville coalition saw the merger as a way to transform University Hospital into a full-fledged teaching hospital with high-quality medical care that would bring it prestige with the ability to attract more paying patients. Most of University Hospital's patients were indigent.

Just 13 months after being sworn in, Godbold called a meeting in his City Hall office with University of Florida President Bob Marston, Dr. David B. Challoner, vice president of health affairs for the UF Health Center, Dr. Baker and other members of his local coalition. "Jacksonville and Shands would benefit by the merger," said Godbold. "There are all sorts of medical programs in Gainesville that need an urban outlet."

President Marston said the university would welcome "some type of in-creased relationship between the two institutions," but Marston made it clear he wasn't enthused about the notion, saying it would cause ma-jor issues and problems. For one, Marston asked if University Hospital would be willing to cut its ties to city government and instead be run by a nonprofit corporation, similar to the arrangement between Shands and the university. A hospital, he said, can "plunge the university into debt in a week" because of the complexities of patient billing. The uni-versity, he said, would not take the lead in a merger. Baker responded that the City Council and state legislature would have to approve of University Hospital becoming a nonprofit corporation, but he said his team was studying materials from Shands to make that happen.

"We are an illegitimate teaching hospital and we want to be legiti-mized," Dr. Baker said. University Hospital was the only one of five teaching hospitals in Florida that didn't have an affiliation with a medi-cal school.

"There were a lot of people on the Shands board that didn't want this to happen," said the mayor. "They felt like we were just trying to unload this hospital on them and we'd back out altogether. We wouldn't abandon University Hospital. We'd still have to put so much money in indigent care, but they should operate and run the hospital and put their number one people there and use it as a teaching hospital."

After the initial meeting in the mayor's office, talks continued for five years, but Shands officials always found reasons not to move forward.

Then, in spring 1985, state Rep. Sid Martin of Gainesville called Godbold. "Martin was about 6-6 and he was a chicken farmer," recalled Godbold. "He had seen me on television and figured I was a country boy like him. He used to send me a basket of eggs all of the time."

"Mayor Jake, it's time to bring this to a head. We got all the stars in the right place," Martin told the mayor. "We got your man Pajcic (Rep. Steve), who is chairman of the budget subcommittee. We got the Speaker of the House (Rep. James Harold Thompson). And, we got Marshall Criser (University of Florida President who was from Jacksonville), who is very receptive."

Jake said, "Sid, that's great and I'm excited about that. But those bastards at the university are not going to let that happen."

"That's alright," said Martin. "You got some bastards with you. You bring your bastards and I'll bring my bastards and we aren't going to leave until we get this done."

With Rep. Martin providing the lead, Godbold, Dr. Baker, city finance director Gene McLeod and Rep. Pajcic traveled to Gainesville for a meeting with Martin, Criser and Shands officials.

The meeting started early in the morning, went through a working lunch and into the afternoon. Godbold, Dr. Baker, Criser and Dr. David B. Challoner, vice president of health affairs for the UF Health Center were there the entire time. "Criser just sat there," said Godbold. "He didn't engage in any of the discussions or arguments." Florida House Speaker Thompson, Rep. Pajcic and Rep. Martin all spoke in favor of the merger. "But the Shands people kept throwing up these fears and objections," said the mayor.

Around 4 p.m., Criser said he wanted to speak his piece. He stood up and told Dr. Challoner, "The speaker wants this done. The finance chairman wants this done. The legislator who represents Gainesville wants this done, and I want it done. How long will it take you to get this done?"

Dr. Challoner "started talking about weeks and months," said Godbold. "That's when Criser took his fist and hit the table. He said, 'Goddammit, I'm an attorney and I can get this done in two hours. I want you and Baker to sit here the rest of the night if it takes it, but don't leave until you have a written agreement. We'll work out the details later.'" Criser then exited the meeting.

Godbold drove back to Jacksonville. "About 11 o'clock that night, they called me and said it was done. We were married."

On May 1, 1985, it was announced that the University of Florida and University Hospital had worked out a tentative agreement to make the city-owned hospital an urban campus of the Florida Medical School. The agreement would have to be signed within 30 days and must be approved by the Jacksonville City Council, the State Board of Regents, and the board of the University Hospital.

The call from chicken farmer Rep. Martin had ended a five-year impasse.

Rep. Pajcic said, "It's going to move it from what it is now, an institution people are reluctant to come to use to one that people will be very anxious and willing to use. They'll get some of the best medical treatment available."

For Dr. Baker, it had been a vision and a quest that lasted for more than five years. He was in a celebratory mood. "I think it's historic for the city of Jacksonville. It's going to give us instant prestige and an image change we desperately need. The future's so bright it's unbelievable. I think all of the goodies start today." The medical school, Baker said, "should have been in Jacksonville 30 years ago."

Under the agreement, University Hospital would become a branch campus within three years and the University Hospital board would be expanded from ten to 15 members with five appointed by the University of Florida. In addition, the city would continue to pay for indigent care, $19 million a year at the time of the agreement.

Today, UF Health Jacksonville has more than 400 faculty physicians and offers services in nearly 100 specialties. It also has one of the South's top trauma centers.

Chapter 38

THE ULTIMATE CYMBAL CRASH

YOU COULD EASILY argue that Thursday June 25, 1987 was the ultimate cymbal crash for Mayor Godbold, bringing together on one grand stage everything he had worked for and the whole kit and caboodle that symbolized his eight years as mayor of Jacksonville, a run that would end in just another five days.

But what a way to go out!

It was the grand opening celebration of the Jacksonville Landing, the 7.5-acre festival marketplace on the St. Johns River that was the centerpiece in Godbold's "billion-dollar decade" of downtown development. If there was ever a way to put a giant bow on what Jake had done to turn his negative thinking town from a sleepy city seemingly without dreams to a vibrant metropolis comfortable on the world stage, it was the Landing's gala opening celebration. Marching bands, torch bearers, dancers, singers, a boat parade, fireworks cascading down from the Main Street Bridge and the release of thousands of balloons. And, in true Godbold-style, four Jacksonville television stations telecast the ceremonies live at 8 p.m.

Times-Union writer Bill Foley wrote that the opening was the "last grand gala hurrah for a Godbold team whose successes re-shaped the central city. Downtown Jacksonville transformed from a spot of dry rot…to a strip of glistening development on both sides of the river. It was, as the mayor said, a billion- dollar decade, and the city was resuscitated."

It all got jump-started almost eight years earlier, when Jacksonville shocked itself and the nation as over 50,000 screaming, cheering people packed the Gator Bowl to tell the owner of Baltimore's NFL team, "WE WANT THE COLTS!" In between that hot August 17, 1979 night and this glorious, equally warm evening on the river in downtown, Godbold had expanded and renovated the worn-out Gator Bowl, built Metropolitan Park, the Southbank Riverwalk, resurrected the boarded-up Jacksonville Terminal into the Prime Osborn Convention Center, sparked the development of the Enterprise Center and the Prudential Insurance headquarters, and the construction of the new Southern Bell headquarters and teed it up for the new Omni Hotel which would open shortly after he left office. In addition, construction would finally begin on the long-sought Automated Skyway Express (ASE), linking the convention center to the new Omni Hotel and the Landing.

"The illusion of 1979—50,000 people holding matches in the Gator Bowl in hope of something better— had become a reality," wrote Foley of the Landing opening.

Godbold, who had been battered for two years, first by a state grand jury investigation, followed by a probe from a federal grand jury, was buoyed and walking on air. The Landing was his exclamation point. "Godbold, obviously touched by the welcome of the crowd, made like a Presidential candidate and gave much the same speech he has the last two days," reported the *Times-Union*.

As always, when the mayor addressed the crowd, estimated at more than 20,000 crammed into the Landing courtyard and every conceivable space, he recognized those business leaders who first offered to join his team two days after he was sworn into office in 1979. He recalled his meeting with bank president Albert Ernest and developer Preston Haskell who were representing the Chamber of Commerce. "They told me I could cut ribbons or I could stick out my neck and take chances. I decided to stick out my neck and take chances," he said.

"Through our partnership, we have built a new renaissance in downtown Jacksonville. We have built a centerpiece today, not a corner piece. But, we took those first steps down those new roads armed only with our visions."

Two days after the Landing opening, *Times-Union* writer Foley recalled the days when Godbold's team painted Coastline Drive in front of the Daniel State Office Building to celebrate local achievements, had organized reactions to national tragedies like the holding of hostages in Iran, promoted Broadway plays in the Civic Auditorium, and welcomed the President of the United States. "It grew in sophistication over the years with jazz festivals and river days and country music shows that go off like clockwork nowadays. In eight years, they've become the fabric of the community."

During his eight years running the city, Godbold often called on lessons he learned during 13 years on the City Council by bringing council members in on the ground floor of most everything he did. At the opening of the Landing, the mayor continued to stroke members of the council. "Dreams can never materialize unless the mayor can round up ten votes."

And, of course, he re-told the story of "Little Train that Could." "We began to have the attitude that we can do it, we can do it, we should do it, we must do it," he said.

But, just as with every project Godbold championed and built, realizing his early dream of a festival marketplace in downtown didn't come easy. First envisioned when he took chamber leaders on a trip to Baltimore and visited Harbor Place in 1979, it took over four years of hard work and negotiations from when he announced the plan in February 1983 to the project's opening in June 1987.

Baltimore's fabled mayor, Donald Schaefer, was someone Godbold wanted to emulate because of the way he had led his city back from worn out urban rubble to become a great American city. Baltimore had a big challenge," Godbold recalled. "Go backward or go forward. We learned so much from Schaefer. He had such a good team. He built Harbor Place and I wanted to copy that." Schaefer told Godbold to get Harbor Place developer, the Rouse Co., involved.

When the mayor first unveiled his idea, he talked about a three-block open air shopping center that would be built on both city-owned property near Independent Square and downtown land owned by the Charter Co. When it opened, the Jacksonville Landing sat on 7.5 acres of what had been city-owned parking lots.

In 1982, Godbold started taking Mayor Schaefer's advice and used his salesmanship to persuade the nationally-recognized Rouse Co., from Columbia, Md., to spend $100,000 on a feasibility study of the local retail market to determine if a riverfront market would pay off. The firm had designed and built Harbor Place in Baltimore and The Grand Avenue in Milwaukee. It would later construct Faneuil Hall in Boston and South Street Seaport in New York City, as well as other markets in major U.S. cities.

Baltimore had 2.5 million residents, Milwaukee 1.5 million, and Jacksonville had just 500,000. Rouse wanted to know if a city of one-half million people could support one of its cutting-edge projects.

Rouse spokesman Scott Fitch said, "The study will take months and will be started right away." It would be "a very defined piece of arithmetic to determine what kinds of sales such a project would generate, look at the competition, and how much it would cost to build," said Fitch.

Following the study, the Downtown Development Authority (DDA) sought interested developers and in August 1983 three national firms responded: Rouse, Evans Development of Baltimore, and Halcyon Ltd. of Hartford. Godbold was ecstatic. A very confident DDA director Jim Gilmore said, "There is no way we can fail. We've been talking to these people for a long time. We've got top quality developers and we're ready to make a decision."

All three developers had four issues: public financing, market management, street and sewer improvements in the area, and getting complex project approvals from city officials.

While Godbold had built a relationship with executives at Rouse, he said he would support the firm selected by the DDA. A DDA subcommittee was formed to select and recommend one of the three firms to the full authority to prepare a design and finance package. Members of the subcommittee were banker Ray Norton, investor Ronald Belton, and Mary Alice Phelan, a local civic leader and sister of Godbold aide Martha Barrett. Their recommendation would be reviewed by the DDA and it would have to be ratified by the mayor and City Council.

Gilmore said the firm chosen would be based on its track record, financial strength, time and scheduling, and the developer's description of what can be done at the site.

Just when the subcommittee scheduled a meeting to recommend a developer, the process had a hiccup.

After learning that Evans president Charles Evans had spent two weeks in Jacksonville lobbying DDA members, city officials and the media, Rouse executive vice president Michael Spear asked for a "time out." Interrupting his vacation, Spear rushed to Jacksonville. He said he had received phone calls from civic leaders and city officials wanting to know if Rouse was serious about the project. "There was a suggestion that I should get down and reaffirm our commitment to the city and this project," said Spear.

The subcommittee meeting was postponed.

Godbold let Spear use the mayor's conference room in City Hall to meet with the press. "Jacksonville is special because of its size," Spear told the media. "This is the number one city we are looking at. This is a prime city."

All of that sent Halcyon president Michael Buckley into a rage, calling the whole thing, "a preposterous method of choosing a developer." Buckley pulled Halcyon out of the competition.

"We've decided to withdraw because of the substantial publicity generated by the two other competitors. It's clear that the Rouse Co. is preferred and that the Evans Co. received a substantial amount of recent publicity. This is not the kind of forum that we believe is conducive to doing a major real estate deal," he said. "There is no way I would select a developer based on who can make the most noise or can get his name in the paper most. We're not going to be part of that circus."

The *Jacksonville Journal* entered the controversy when it editorialized, "The last thing downtown needs is another shopping area that attracts few people after 5 p.m. and on weekends that it becomes a haven for transients and drug dealers who frighten off even a few shoppers."

On August 22, 1983, without discussion and in two minutes, the

DDA chose Rouse to develop Jacksonville's festival market. In addition to Baltimore's Harbor Place and Milwaukee's Grand Avenue, Rouse opened South Street Seaport in New York City a month earlier, and would be opening Faneuil Hall in Boston, and Gallery & Market in Philadelphia.

Rouse said Jacksonville's $35-$40 million development would take two years once construction started. Negotiations with the city and work prior to construction could take another two years, including site preparation. That meant the project should open in the summer of 1987. On everyone's top of mind was the fact that Godbold would leave office on June 30, 1987, setting a pretty definite target date.

The final product, Rouse said, should be 100,000-125,000 square feet and would be built on riverfront parking lots, west of the Main Street Bridge. The lots were owned by the Jacksonville Transportation Authority (JTA). JTA chairman John Lanahan, who was City Council president when the lots were turned over to JTA by the city, said the JTA would return the lots to the city for the development.

With all of the parking lots being used for the development, a problem surfaced that would plague the Landing project for three decades. "Where are visiting shoppers going to park?" Rouse insisted from the beginning that the project would not work without adequate parking.

Then came that "Here we go again," moment. Both Rouse and the DDA said that Coastline Drive would have to be closed. Some feelings were still raw from when Godbold wanted to close the riverfront street two years earlier to build his downtown esplanade on the same city parking lots. No one was anxious to wage that public battle once again.

Rouse vice president Alton Scavo told the DDA that Coastline Drive separated the public from the river and had to be eliminated between the Civic Auditorium and the Main Street Bridge.

On October 1, 1984 it was like Deja vu. Dr. Samuel M. Day, who had led the public fight against closing the drive in 1982, wrote a letter to the *Jacksonville Journal*. "Two years ago, our citizens let it be known in no uncertain terms that there was an overwhelming desire to keep Coastline Drive open. Judging by the people who approach me daily, that overwhelming opinion still prevails," Day wrote. "I implore the people of Jacksonville who spoke with such a unified voice two years ago to let Mayor Jake Godbold and members of the City Council know their views and let us keep Coastline Drive open."

Council members, still smarting from the earlier fight, were skeptical. When Gilmore made the DDA's case to the council's public services committee, he said closing the drive was "absolutely critical." Council members Eric Smith and Terry Wood were hesitant. Councilman Ed Holsinger said closing the road was not an option and promised to do everything he could to block the proposal. Committee chairman Gifford Grange named himself a one-man subcommittee and refused to release the road closing bill until he saw the full development plan.

In the meantime, the city and Rouse were locked in intense negotiations. The two sides were at loggerheads over financing for the $40 million development and the amount of money each would invest. Rouse wanted the city to pay most of the costs, then lease the development back to the developer with both sides sharing in the profits. Godbold had a different idea. He wanted a partnership where Rouse and the city would put in the same amount of money.

"We've made some offers and now they're coming back with some counter offers," said Godbold. "Every day it seems we're getting a little closer, but I have to tell you that it's been really tedious. It's been tough negotiating." The city had made its best offer, he said.

As the battle heated up over the closing of Coastline Drive, the mayor drew a line in the sand. In a meeting with the media, Godbold said the City Council would close the road or kiss downtown Jacksonville good-bye. Closing the drive, he said, is essential to development and development is essential to downtown. "We are going to close Coastline Drive. We can't have anything downtown without closing Coastline Drive. We would lose festival shopping and if you lose festival shopping you can close downtown."

As negotiations with Rouse started moving the two sides closer, in November 1984 the council approved a bill for $19 million for the Rouse project. $15 million would come from new excise bond money and the remaining $4 million would be from savings from another bond issue.

Just before Thanksgiving, Gilmore told the public services committee that the city would maintain ownership of the land and Rouse would pay annual property taxes on the buildings. In addition, Rouse would pay a lease fee that had to be set. He also said the development would create 1,500 jobs.

Coastline Drive, Gilmore said, would be closed from east of Hogan Street to west of Newnan Street, but would remain open from the Seaboard Coastline Building in front of the Civic Auditorium to Hogan and from Newnan behind City Hall and the Courthouse.

"This is the most exciting cornerstone of downtown development in a long time," Gilmore said. "This will place us in the upper rank of American cities."

In a reversal, councilman Holtsinger made the motion in the public services committee to close Coastline Drive and the committee approved the bill. "I looked at it long and fairly," said Holtsinger. Councilman Aubrey Daniel, a railroad executive, was the lone dissenter. That's when

Godbold received a huge heads up on why it had been so difficult during the esplanade battle to get the council to sign off on closing the road, and why the Rouse plan to shut down the drive was meeting council resistance.

One day, Godbold's director of Public Works, Al Kinard, told Godbold that Richard Sanborn, president and chief executive officer of CSX railroad (formerly Seaboard Coastline) had been fighting the closing "behind our backs." The railroad, and its CEO, wielded a lot of political power in Jacksonville. Godbold and Sanborn were close friends.

The mayor was livid. Sanborn's behind-the-scenes interference had caused him to lose the state and federal funds for his esplanade.

"I picked up the phone and I called Sanborn. I was very, very angry. I don't remember getting that mad at anyone and chewing his ass out like I did his." Godbold reminded his friend he knew the railroad and the city had an agreement that was made years earlier when the city built a viaduct across the railroad near the Gator Bowl. The railroad would pay to maintain it. "I have letters from years back and it's been falling down and we're about to make you fix it and bring all of that out," the mayor said to Sanborn. That's when Sanborn suggested they get together and try to work things out. "Maybe we can," replied Godbold.

The mayor sent Kinard and Henry Mock, the city's traffic engineer, to meet with Sanborn. During the meeting, they learned that around 75 percent of CSX employees used Coastline Drive as a preferred route to and from work. It was a quicker way to access the Mathews Bridge into Arlington. That was the source of Sanborn's private opposition to closing Coastline Drive. "They came back in two hours and had worked out a simple plan that could have been solved for years," said Godbold. The city turned Pearl Street adjacent to the CSX headquarters, which ran north and south, one way coming in during the morning and one way going out in the afternoons. It opened a quicker access to and from the Mathews Bridge.

Finally, the *Times-Union* weighed in, editorializing, "Closing Coastline Drive will put an additional burden on Jacksonville's downtown traffic, but is the right move at this point in the continuing improvement in the downtown area."

On November 27, with Dr. Day as the lone public speaker opposed, the City Council voted to close the drive once construction began. Holtsinger said closing Coastline Drive would be a boon to downtown development. In signing the bill on November 29, Godbold said, "If you knew what I know, you would really realize what an impact closing Coastline Drive will have on this community. We have literally been besieged by developers. We want to make the river available to people, not as a 30-second glimpse, but as a lovely and leisurely view from the vantage point of a table, chair or picturesque sidewalk."

Five days later, Godbold was joined by Rouse president Mathias J. Devito to sign an agreement in principal for the $43 million unnamed festival market to open in June 1987, before Godbold left office. "We will do our best to have the festival market reflect the very best of Jacksonville," Devito said. The deal included:

- $10.3 in city improvements and a $10 million loan to be re-paid by Rouse six months after the development opens;
- The city's commitment to build an 800-vehicle parking garage next to the festival market;
- Rouse's agreement to build a 125,000 square foot taxable festi-val market with 120-145 shops; and
- Rouse's agreement to pay a $100,000 annual lease for 45 years with an option to renew for another 25 years.

Under the agreement, both sides agreed to work in good faith to have a contract in place by April 30, 1985.

The *Times-Union* reflected much of what was being felt in the community. "It has been a long time since Jacksonville's downtown area was teeming with activity," the newspaper editorialized. "But, at one time, it was a magnet for people, a 'fun' place to be. Now, with an agreement between Mayor Jake Godbold and the Rouse Co., downtown promises once again to be the heart of the city upon completion in June 1987 of the festival market place that will be the core of the revival of downtown Jacksonville."

Now that the city and Rouse had an agreement in principle and Godbold had the support he needed to close Coastline Drive, moving closer to a contract and preparing the site for development became the focus.

Godbold could hardly contain his excitement, especially at the prospect that new development and more tall buildings seemed on the horizon as a result of the festival market. Right before Christmas, Henry Faison, who built the Enterprise Center that became headquarters for the Florida National Bank, signed an agreement with Omni to build a hotel next to the Enterprise Center and across from the festival market. Godbold, unauthorized by Faison, let word slip out about the hotel, then tried to walk the story back. Omni and Faison would not comment.

On Christmas Eve, the city said a draft contract might be ready for review by the DDA the third week of January 1985, which would put the project ahead of schedule. A city taskforce headed by McClure and Gilmore had been negotiating constantly with Rouse since the agreement in principle was signed on December 4.

Throughout the negotiations, Rouse didn't hesitate to initiate back channel discussions by letting Godbold, McClure or DDA chairman Roland Kennedy know when they felt they couldn't agree to something, or were trying to sweeten the deal for themselves. One day, Gilmore accidently caught them. "I was up in the mayor's office walking down the hall and I heard them talking on the speaker phone. McClure asked me to come in. Rouse was giving them an ear full, said Gilmore. "I jumped up and down and told them not do to it. I said it was a bluff so Rouse could get more than they need." Godbold and McClure listened to Gilmore, held their ground, "and Rouse backed down."

Elevating the hype about Rouse, the *Times-Union* ran a huge story on June 16, "The Urban Wizard," that touted the developer. It was the first article in a six-part series written for the newspaper by Edward Gunts of the *Baltimore Sun*. Boosting the company's success, the story listed Rouse projects: Tabor Center in Denver, The Shops at National Place in Washington D.C., South Street Seaport in New York City, and Harbor Place in Baltimore. Festival markets in those cities "have become symbols of hope for aging cities still reeling from a generation of economic, social and racial problems. In city after city, the story is the same. For shopping, dining and entertainment, downtown is once again the place to be."

Rouse was about to unveil a new project in St. Louis, with projects on the drawing board for New Orleans, Miami, San Francisco, Seattle, Atlanta...and Jacksonville.

The only problem with the great press for Rouse was it made members of the DDA, as well as council members, nervous that Rouse had so many projects in major cities that Jacksonville wouldn't get the attention it needed from the developer. But not Godbold. If anything, he relished having Jacksonville in the conversation with those other major U.S. cities.

Just after July 4, 1985, Rouse and the city had an agreement for approval by the DDA and the City Council. It was a 45-year deal for 7.5 acres that included free rent for the first five years. The city's investment would be $25 million that included $10 million in city financing and $10 million for public improvements. The city would also provide a short-term city loan to help start construction of the project that would be paid back at 5 percent interest 18 months after the project was complete.

The agreement required Rouse to raise $19 million in private financing and put in $1 million of its own money. Rouse's share of the development cost was $31.5 million. The developer also retained an option to purchase or lease a riverfront parking lot east of the Main Street Bridge.

There was one part of the agreement that was non-negotiable for the mayor. As mayor he had instituted a minority set-aside program to ensure minority participation in city contracts, and he was a supporter of affirmative action. He made sure the agreement required Rouse to award a minimum of 10 percent of contract work to minority contractors.

On July 18, the DDA approved the deal unanimously and without discussion, sending it to the City Council for review.

Council finance chair Eric Smith said he was excited about the project, "but we're going to make sure we get the best deal possible for the Duval County taxpayers."

Rouse was pushing council approval so it could take control of the property by October 15. That's also when Coastline Drive would be permanently closed. Five weeks later the 253-page contract was approved by the council, 16-1 with only Holtsinger voting against it.

Despite the two-year uproar over the closing of Coastline Drive, when the time came to shut it down, it happened without fuss. On September 30 the city posted some signs that announced the road would close at 9 p.m. on October 1. Police reported that hardly anyone noticed. The city also closed the city parking lots at the same time.

On October 18, the city and Rouse held an official ground breaking that included bands, balloons and fireworks. The *Times-Union* reported, "Friends, colleagues, business leaders and political and social luminaries joined the mayor outside a blue and white striped tent on the erstwhile parking lot to break ground for the long-sought festival market, known henceforth as The Jacksonville Landing." Godbold was joined by council president Bill Basford, DDA chairman Roland Kennedy, councilman Gifford Grange, McClure, Gilmore and Charles "Bucky" Clarkson, chairman of the chamber's Central Jacksonville, Inc.

Clarkson, who had worked for Rouse in Baltimore and remained close to its top executives, played a key role in convincing Rouse to build in Jacksonville.

"This is our greatest dream. This is the project that will bring our Northbank and Southbank together into our total town," said Godbold. "You are going to see more and more projects develop around here, this market place, because Rouse is successful and this is where people want to be."

Rouse senior vice president Spear touted Jacksonville. "We set out to find one community in America. We literally looked across this nation, from coast to coast, and your community was the one place our company sought to try for a project of this size. What we are building here is for Jacksonville."

On January 15, 1986—right on schedule—Rouse started setting up on the site and began soliciting tenants and vendors. It expected to have 50 percent specialty stores on the Landing's first level, plus twenty push carts. Upstairs, shoppers would eat at 20 over-the-counter food operators.

By mid-August, the structure was framed out with steel girders and most of the roof in place. People crossing the Main Street and Acosta

Bridges could finally see the horseshoe shaped market taking shape. Twenty percent of the merchants were committed, including local shops The Body Shop, Jarrod's and Special Effects. On August 20, Rouse vice president John Noggle conducted a hard hat tour for the media and pronounced the Landing on schedule.

Godbold got his own tour after Labor Day with chief aide Don McClure by his side. As Noggle showed the mayor where the shops and restaurants would be located, Godbold was as excited as a kid on Christmas morning. But, as enthusiastic as he was, Godbold knew the challenge ahead. "It's not complete until the people come in the front door and put a smile on their faces. Then, it's all going to be worth it," he said.

But there was still a big, unanswered question: Where are shoppers going to park? To help solve the issue, four months before the Landing was to open, the City Council voted to lease 800 parking spaces to Rouse in the new Water Street parking garage. But that left quite a hike for visitors to the Landing.

In late February, Rouse stepped up its efforts to recruit black tenants. Seventy-six percent of the space was committed, but there was not a single black-owned shop.

On March 9, Rouse was confident in its construction schedule and set the grand opening date for June 25, 1987.

Expecting 1,500 new jobs with a $7 million annual payroll, in April Rouse placed a three day hold on jobs so that economically disadvantaged applicants could be interviewed before any $4-$4.50 an hour jobs were advertised.

When the Landing opened its doors with great fanfare on June 25, the list of retail and food options did not disappoint. Shoppers were surprised and thrilled by stores like The Limited, The Gap, B. Dalton

Booksellers, Banana Republic, Victoria's Secret, Sharper Image, Laura Ashley, Footlocker, the Fudgery, and G.H. Bass Shoe Store. Little did most people in Jacksonville know that those high-profile shops opened in the Landing because Rouse leveraged its other festival markets in much larger cities. In other words, you want to be in our markets in Baltimore, Philadelphia, Boston and New York, then you will be in the Jacksonville Landing.

After all of the opening night fanfare, Mayor Godbold and his wife Jean retired to an upstairs restaurant that was overflowing with happy, celebrating people. All day long, Jake had been able to see smiles on the faces of thousands of people as they came into the Landing. Now, it was Jake's time to take a deep breath and feel good, not just about this special night, but about the last eight years.

The mayor had reserved his own long table where he was joined by close friends and his top aides. It was a final gathering of many of those who had been by his side through two elections and the transformation of Jacksonville. It was a happy time, but everyone sitting there also knew, and regretted, that in just a few short days, it would be over. There were no more drums for Godbold to beat.

As the always approachable mayor was besieged and interrupted by fans and well-wishers, finally, he thought, it was all well worth it.

And, it was one helluva way for Jake Godbold to say farewell.

(Author's note: On February 20, 2019, Mayor Lenny Curry and Landing owner Toney Sleiman ended years of hostility and litigation when the two men reached an agreement for the city to purchase the Landing for $15 million, some $10 million more than Sleiman paid for the marketplace in 2003. The sale, which was approved by the City Council, included an additional $1.5 million to demolish the 31-year- old structure.)

Chapter 39

———— ❦ ————

TALES BY AND ABOUT THE STORY TELLER

(Author's note: Jake Godbold is a great story teller. You could say that his waking life is one tale after another. And most of his friends and associates have stories about him to share. Below are just a small sample of those stories out of a trove of what could be told.)

IN 1981, RICHARD Bowers became director of the city's Department of Housing & Urban Development (HUD). The federal government had recently removed $14 million from the city that was to build public housing in west Jacksonville. In addition, federal HUD owed Jacksonville $5 million for maintenance on existing public housing. There are two versions of what happened, one by Godbold and the other by Bowers. Both are worth sharing.

Bowers and the mayor took their grievances to Sam Pierce, the secretary of federal HUD, who promised to try and work out a solution to restore the city's money. "Jake's attitude was, 'Let's just give them the

Jake serves food to members of the M.O.B.

keys and wash our hands of public housing,'" said Bowers.

According to both Godbold and Bowers, a second meeting in Washington D.C. followed, this time with Lamar Baker, the assistant secretary of HUD, a tall distinguished gentleman wearing what both men described as a $3,000 suit. "The guy was at the head of the table, Jake was on the left and I was on the other side." Councilmen Forrest Boone and Terry Wood also accompanied the mayor.

Here's where the tales take their separate turns. Godbold said that prior to making the second trip to Washington, he told Bowers to get the keys to every HUD housing unit and put them in a Winn-Dixie grocery paper bag. Once they got into the meeting, Godbold explained his utter frustration and anger with trying to maintain HUD housing without any maintenance money from the federal government.

Softball has been his passion; here in a game against the Chamber of commerce.

Jake conducts River City Band that he named the city's official ban

Showing the "largest fish" at the senior fish-a-thon.

Jake with seniors at the Jacksonville Beach pier.

A meeting of the M.O.B. with Jake in the Mayor's conference room.

"These are your damn housing units and you don't want to pay to keep them up, so I am giving them back to you. We can't afford to keep them up." Godbold says he then instructed Bowers to dump out the keys on the assistant secretary's desk. Once that was done, Godbold says he and Bowers left the office and headed to the elevator. "He got to us before the elevator door opened and asked us to come back and talk to him about our issues," said Godbold.

Bowers tells it differently. "When the mayor tells you to take them (keys) up there, you take them up there." He thinks Godbold's memory is interesting, but he differs in his own recollection. "The assistant secretary had been general counsel for Equitable Life Insurance in New York City. He met us in the secretary's office," said Bowers. "We sat down and Jake started talking to him about public housing. Jake would pat him on the arm and touch him. He shared with him his concerns, and then Jake got into, 'I was raised in public housing, my dad was a paint foreman and he went blind, my mother boiled peanuts and we

JAKE!

sold them for five cents a bag.' Jake gave him the full Jake treatment and you could see this guy melting."

After the meeting "We walked out of there with the $14 million, plus the $5 million they owed us," Bowers said.

Metal rocker Ozzy Osbourne, well known for his drugged up and drunken binges while on concert tours, brought his act to Jacksonville and the Civic Auditorium. During his performance Osbourne exposed himself to the crowd. They loved it. Mayor Godbold didn't and he barred Osbourne from ever performing in Jacksonville again.

A couple of years later, Godbold learned that Osbourne was returning for another concert despite being banned. Godbold received a call from a reporter for *Rolling Stone* magazine asking why the mayor was so opposed to having Osbourne perform in his town. "I talked to them and told them in a nice way that the guy had come here once and I had warned him that if he did that, if he got up there and exposed himself to these young people he would never be allowed to come back."

The reporter said, "A modern city like Jacksonville and you're telling *Rolling Stone* that you are barring Ozzy Osbourne from coming to your city?"

"I'm telling you that Ozzy Osbourne is not coming to Jacksonville and pull his ding-dong out and play with it in front of these kids. Do you understand that?" Godbold asked.

"Yes, I do. What's your name?"

"Don McClure," said the mayor, referring to his chief aide.

Earl Crittenden was head of Southern Bell Telephone Company in Jacksonville. The company's headquarters was an aging building in downtown, where Bell's continued presence was badly needed in Godbold's campaign to redevelop downtown Jacksonville. Word was getting around that Bell wanted to build a brand-new headquarters. Crittenden confirmed that in a meeting with the mayor, but said the company was thinking of relocating to Orange Park, an adjacent city in another county.

"I said, 'Oh my God, that will destroy me before I get a chance to swing,'" said Godbold. Crittenden said he was opposed to the idea as well. "You've got a great story here of what we are doing and how well we are all working together to make downtown development happen," Crittenden told the mayor. If he could get a meeting with the president of Southern Bell in Atlanta, would Jake go with him? Crittenden asked. "Man, I'd go anywhere because that would slow down our enthusiasm if this gets out."

The two men traveled to Atlanta and met with the president of the company. "We laid out what we were doing. We had to convince him that we weren't going to let downtown go backwards." The Bell executive "got enthused and he believed us," said the mayor. Once again, the salesman mayor had closed his deal. Southern Bell constructed a multimillion headquarters tower in downtown.

During Godbold's first term, the city-backed agency responsible for attracting tourists to Jacksonville hired a new executive director. He was from Kansas City, Missouri. One day, he made a courtesy call on the mayor, primarily to introduce himself and feel out what kind of support he could expect from Godbold.

The new executive sat in a chair directly in front of the mayor. I sat to the mayor's left and the city's public relations director, Dale Eldridge, sat on Godbold's right.

At this point, you should know that the St. Johns River, generally considered Jacksonville's greatest natural asset, cuts directly through downtown. Running 310 miles before it empties into the Atlantic Ocean, the river is a great source of pride in Jacksonville. Godbold had fished in the river since he was a young boy.

The tourism executive said he had a great idea that would revolutionize Jacksonville and be a sure-fire way to attract thousands of visitors to the city. Both Godbold and I listened intently.

"I think we should rename that river to Jacksonville Lake," he said, sending a tingle up the mayor's spine. "It's not really a river. It's more like a lake."

Godbold turned to me and said, "Do you want to go first?" I only said, "Why don't you go ahead and put out a press release announcing that idea?"

Then the mayor trained his guns on the new tourism chief. He told him it was about the dumbest idea he ever heard, and if he ever heard it again he would personally chase the man out of town.

"Mayor, that feels like a threat and I don't respond well when there's a gun to my head." At that point, Godbold leaned forward in his chair and put his arms on his desk. "I don't have a gun to your head," said the mayor. "I have a goddamn knife to your head."

When the mayor wanted to make a point, his ind index finger would pierce the air.

A couple of weeks later, President Carter came to town and after he left, I took some members of the Secret Service to my favorite watering hole, Ye Olde Tyme Tavern. Shortly after we arrived, the phone in the booth in the corner of the bar rang and it was answered by the female bar tender. "It's the mayor," she said to me. When I got on the phone, Godbold proudly announced, "Well, that son of a bitch is gone."

In 1926 Pio Bozzi and John Ganzi opened the first Palm Restaurant in New York City. It quickly became the place to be for musicians, actors, artists, writers, tycoons and political figures. In the early 1970's at the request of then Ambassador to the United Nations George H.W. Bush, the family of Palm founders opened another restaurant in Washington D.C. and introduced their infamous four-pound lobster to the menu.

JAKE!

Once Godbold was mayor in 1979 and became a frequent visitor to the nation's capital, he was introduced to the Palm and it quickly became his favorite restaurant away from Jacksonville. It had everything he liked: great food, terrific service with his own favorite waiter, a place where his entourage could gather for business conversation, and best of all, a setting that was a hot spot for the biggest political stars in Washington. The walls of the Palm back then and continuing today were filled with caricature paintings of national politicians. Jake became such a popular customer that his own likeness was added to the wall in a prominent place right where you entered the front door.

In 1980, as Jacksonville was in hot pursuit of federal funds to pay for its downtown Automated Skyway Express (ASE), President Reagan appointed Miami lawyer Art Teele as director of the Urban Mass Transportation Administration (UMTA). Godbold quickly became Teele's new best friend.

On one of his visits to D.C. to lobby Teele for money, the mayor and Teele, along with Congressmen Bill Chappell and Charlie Bennett, HUD director Richard Bowers, attorney Tommy Greene and a couple of others visited the Palm for dinner.

(To help understand this next scene better, you need to know that Congressman Bennett was widely known as a "prude" and "straight-laced," both in the halls of congress as well as back home in Jacksonville. You must remember this was long before cell phones and the ability to create instant videos for social media).

Seated next to Godbold's table were four young men celebrating the upcoming marriage of one of them. "We were having a great time," said Bowers, "when this beautiful woman came around the corner dressed totally in black. She had on those tall pumps." The woman, Bowers recalled, "took a long leg and put it up on their table." She had a piece of paper tucked into her garter, said Bowers, which the guest of honor carefully removed. The woman had a tape recorder that she placed on the table and turned on. Suddenly, at the table next to the mayor of Jacksonville, two congressman and the powerful director of UMTA, the hit song, "Stripper," started blaring and the woman began removing her clothes.

"It stopped everything in the Palm," said Bowers. Bennett quickly excused himself and left the restaurant. "She stripped down to pasties and a G-string and everybody clapped and cheered." Bowers said watching the reaction of the people at his table was "more fun that watching the stripper."

Godbold's favorite waiter was standing behind the mayor enjoying the show. "Jake didn't seem to be very comfortable," said Bowers.

By the way, each member of the mayor's group—except Bennett—ate one of the Palm's four-pound lobsters at $14 a pound.

Betty Holzendorf was Godbold's liaison to the City Council. The mayor called her brilliant. She also happened to be African American and her frequent foul mouth matched Godbold's.

Holzendorf said the best time she ever had with Godbold was during a campaign event at "Booker the Bone Cooker's," a barbecue joint in the heart of the black community at Moncrief Road and 36th Street. "There was this flatbed truck and bands playing. The crowd started coming. Well, me, living out there and knowing the community, I was watching out to make sure nothing would happen." During the event, Holzendorf said Godbold's young, white, Catholic press aide Martha Barrett came over to her.

Barrett told Holzendorf, "A guy came up to me and said, 'Do you want a coke?'" Barrett said she told him, "No, because I never drink coke. I have not had a coke since I was 12-years old. I don't drink coke." He said, "You don't drink the coke I have." Well, the guy had offered her cocaine, said Holzendorf.

Holzendorf went to Godbold. "I said, 'She's going to get killed.' He said, 'No, Martha will be all right.'"

When future mayor John Peyton joined the Godbold staff as an intern he was assigned to Holzendorf. "I will never forget sitting in a room with Jake and Betty," he said. "They were peeling boiled peanuts and cussing like sailors. They were mad at somebody and that person got called every name. I think they forgot I was in the room. I was thinking, damn, this place is rough." Peyton learned a valuable lesson. "These are the people you're mad at one minute, and you're hugging them around the neck the next, and you're working on a project with them."

It was eye-opening for young Peyton and a look inside the life of Jake. "I had never been in an environment where you can hate the son-of-a-bitch one minute and embrace and love him the next. I thought, these people are crazy in this business. Why would anybody sign up for this?" Twenty years later, as a candidate for mayor, Peyton found himself asking Godbold for his endorsement, which he received.

Denise Lee began her political career as a young volunteer working on campaigns out of Tallahassee. When she returned home to Jacksonville, she got a job in 1979 in the Godbold campaign working alongside

Holzendorf in the black community. After the campaign she went to work for the mayor, then was selected by the City Council in 1982 to fill the remaining term of Sallye Mathis, who had died of cancer. Lee served 18 years on the council, followed by four years in the Florida Legislature, and another eight years on the council, leaving office in 2015.

"I was on the council and Betty called me and told me to come to her office." Holzendorf took Lee to a meeting in the conference room where Godbold was holding court to discuss a minority set-aside program he intended to institute to give minorities an opportunity to share in city business. The chairs around the table were filled with white business-men and Godbold was at the head. Lee took a chair in the back of the room. "They didn't want it (the set-aside). Arnold Tritt (executive director of the Northeast Florida Builders Association and childhood friend of the mayor) was talking shit," Lee recalled. "Jake leaned up on the table. He hit the table and said, 'Arnie, I tell you what. We're going to have set aside. I got my balls. You put your balls on the table.' Then everybody started talking about balls."

Lee was thinking, "Why am I here?"

After the meeting, she went to Holzendorf's office and asked why she invited her to attend the meeting. "Everybody was talking over my head," said Lee.

Holzendorf said, "What are you talking about?"

"Well," Lee replied, "everybody was talking and everybody had balls. I felt out of place because I didn't have any."

"Say that again," said Holzendorf. Lee repeated what she had just said. "You want some balls?" Holzendorf asked.

"Well, not necessarily. But I don't think you should invite me into a meeting and everybody else is prepared and I'm just sitting there and I felt out of place."

"Bitch, you want some balls?" "No."

"Do you have a penis?"

Lee thought, "This lady is so nasty." "No, I don't," she said.

"Well, that's the only way you're going to get some balls."

Over the years, Lee has developed an uncanny imitation of Holzendorf and she loves sharing this story with both friends and strangers.

Joe Forshee was a strong-willed councilman who represented north Jacksonville, a blue-collar section of Jacksonville. He called himself a "gentleman farmer," and he was one of Godbold's closest friends on the council. "Joe," said Godbold, "was a thorn in everybody's side. He was spoiled and arrogant and mean as hell sometimes." Other times, "He was the sweetest person in the world," Godbold said.

Forshee was "probably one of the best councilmen for his district that I ever saw, except for Denise (Lee)." Forshee was council president while Godbold was mayor. "One day, somebody said, 'Mayor, if you want to meet with your public works people, go out to Joe's house on Wednesday.' Every Wednesday he had the heads of public works, feeding them spaghetti and meat balls and telling them what he wanted them to do in his district."

Forshee "had more power out there than I did. But we let him get away with it and kept him happy." He was the kind of guy, said Godbold, "that liked to feel important and he'd make you pay if you didn't make him feel important."

Forshee was always trying to get Godbold appointments fired. "I would say, 'Joe, you may be right. But I don't know all the things you know about this person. You go back and write me a letter and tell me why you think I should move this guy and have your secretary bring it up here. You have to sign it and I'll investigate what you're claiming.' He never once did that."

Ed Ball was 89-years old when he died in 1981. He was a crusty, whiskey-drinking, bare-knuckled legend, not just in Jacksonville but across Florida and throughout the nation. A *New York Times* article in 1979 said Ball "had the reputation of a tart-tongued, hard-nosed conservative financier."

Railroad baron, banker, newspaper publisher and in control of the vast Alfred I. Dupont business empire, Ball was both revered and feared.

He worked out of his office in the Florida National Bank Building in downtown and walked back and forth to his residence in the Robert Meyer Hotel across the street. Ball didn't own a car.

In 1978, when Godbold was president of the City Council and Ball was 86, Mayor Hans Tanzler held a meeting in his city hall office with unhappy residents living near the stinking Buckman Street sewage plant. They were pleading with the mayor to do something that would give them relief from the stench. It was covered by the press, including local television stations.

Godbold attended the meeting and at one point, when he sensed that Tanzler was not responding to the residents' requests, Godbold stood up and strongly suggested that Tanzler show more concern and give the residents some help. The confrontation was shown later that day on the 6 p.m. television news. Ball, who was no fan of Mayor Tanzler, saw what Godbold had said.

He phoned Godbold and invited him to meet with him in his hotel residence. "I was nervous about going over there and having a talk with him," Godbold said. "I was a young man and he was a legend."

Godbold confided in his friend, council secretary David McNamara, who said he had met Ball and would go with him. "We went over there one afternoon late. Mr. Ball came into the hotel lobby and he had his Palm Beach hat on, a white suit with his coat over his arm." Ball invited the two men up to his suite.

"He wanted to talk politics and he wanted to talk me into running against Hans. I wasn't ready to run for mayor."

Ball enjoyed Jack Daniel's whiskey and had a bar in his suite. He usually started having cocktails at 5:30 every day. He was also known to say he didn't trust any man who wouldn't take a drink with him. That afternoon, as Ball poured his Jack Daniel's, he asked Godbold and McNamara what they wanted to drink. Neither of them had ever tasted whiskey. They fumbled for an answer. Undeterred, Ball poured both a glass of Jack Daniel's.

When Ball proposed a toast Godbold attempted to take a small sip. It sent shivers over him. He had to escape. The future mayor excused himself, left McNamara, caught the elevator down, and then walked around the block. McNamara made an apology for Godbold and politely exited to join Jake.

In year-one of his first term as mayor, Godbold determined that members of his staff weren't doing a good job communicating with the public. "We weren't getting the message out on where we wanted to go and what we were accomplishing," said the mayor. Godbold met with his chief aide, Don McClure. As mayor Godbold said he couldn't be the lone spokesman for the government. "There are too many people and I can't use all of my time just making speeches and being a salesman."

Godbold and McClure hatched a plan that each of his aides would make talks to service clubs and other community organizations and they had to do it several times each month. Everyone did a good job, with one exception, Leon Green, a liaison to the Florida legislature and City Council. When time came to give out raises McClure determined that since Green had not held up his end of the speaking strategy, he would not get a raise. Green, a long-time personal friend of the mayor, was incensed.

"Leon came in and raised hell with me," said Godbold. "I told him that Don makes the decisions about raises. I take his recommendation and I'm not going to overrule Don—and I never did." Instead, he called McClure into his office to tell him about Green's complaint. "Don showed us the records with what all of the other aides had done compared to what Leon had done. Don then told Leon that when he caught up with the others to come in and discuss his salary."

Godbold also had a policy with his staff, members of the City Council, or anyone else who came to him and complained about someone else. "I would not talk to them unless the person being criticized came in and I was told the story in front of them. That eliminated a lot of bull shit."

Godbold had a habit of ignoring aides and others who he felt had screwed up or angered him. Aide Glen English, who was the staff jester, started calling it being "put in the deep freeze." At one time or another, almost everyone working for the mayor felt the chill. "He thought we were disappointed when he put us in the deep freeze," said aide Rick Catlett. "What he didn't know is, sometimes we were happy to be in the deep freeze."

Catlett came into the 1979 mayoral campaign after losing in a primary election for a City Council seat representing Arlington, a section of east central Jacksonville that borders the St. Johns River. As campaign manager and strategist, I scooped him up and put him to work. Following the successful campaign, Catlett worked on my staff after Godbold appointed me the city's energy czar. Catlett then became a key member of my special events team.

On the occasion of the second Mayport & All That Jazz Festival in October 1981, Catlett was assisting me. During the afternoon he took a boat across the St. Johns River to pick up the mayor on the northside of the river at the ferry slip. The ferry was out of service because of the festival. Glen English drove Godbold to the ferry slip in the mayor's city car. "I go over there," said Catlett, "and Glen said, 'We have a flat tire.' I told them not to worry about it. 'Get in the boat and I'll take you over to the festival.'"

Godbold told Catlett to get the tire fixed by the time he returned to the car later in the day. "I called motor pool and said, 'Hey, this is Rick Catlett in the mayor's office. The mayor's car has a flat tire at the Heckscher Drive ferry slip. We need ya'll to come out and fix the tire." When English and the mayor returned to the northside ferry slip later in the day, the tire was still flat. "That was not good," said Catlett.

"Rick didn't understand that if somebody gave him an assignment and he gave somebody else the job, he needed to see that it was done. Once he turned it over, he washed his hands of it. That's not how it works," said the mayor. Catlett was handed a short suspension.

As mayor, Godbold pulled every lever and formed every partnership he could to develop downtown. One of his biggest, but often unknown, partners was Dr. Homer Lindsey, Jr., pastor of the enormous First Baptist Church that took up several blocks of downtown. "Lindsey had put in everything that church had and bankrolled that end of town for a long time when nobody would put a dime down there," said Godbold.

Downtown department store institutions Mae-Cohens, Furchgotts and J.C Penny's had moved out of the north end of downtown near the church. "The only one that stayed and put a lot of money in was Dr. Lindsey."

The dynamic pastor, who followed his father as senior pastor in 1975, visited the mayor one day and let him know that First Baptist was all in for his efforts to revitalize the downtown area. "I'm not going to be loud. I'm not going to be foolish," Lindsey told Godbold. "But, I want you to know that whatever you need from me and my congregation, I'm with you. I want you to remember that we stayed when nobody else did."

The mayor and the Baptist preacher met often, usually in Lindsey's church office. "We'd have our conversation and prayers. He always supported me from the pulpit on every project we did in downtown." Lindsey was a big supporter for building Metropolitan Park on the river because "he thought it would be a place for people to go in a family environment."

In the summer of 1978, about a month before Jake Godbold became president of the City Council for the second time, voters in California approved Proposition 13, an initiative that limited the amount of property tax that could be collected to one percent of the property value. The results of that election sent shockwaves through local governments, fearful that a ripple effect would sweep their own communities and severely hamper a local government's ability to pay its bills, much less invest in things like infrastructure and economic development.

Godbold was one of those who got the message. One morning around 9:30, just after the California vote, he went to one of his favorite breakfast places on Lem Turner Road. When he walked inside, Godbold saw a dozen water services and JEA employees having breakfast. He went ballistic, drove to City Hall, and called two members of the mayor's staff and the council auditor to a meeting in his office.

Referencing Proposition 13, Godbold said, "If city employees are not getting that message, they've got their heads in the sand." Two days later he proposed a freeze on city hiring.

When he became mayor, city employees knew that Jake would routinely ride around city projects to see if the employees were working. Pity the poor soul who was slacking or goofing off.

Godbold was constantly rallying Jacksonville, preaching about being positive and ginning up the spirit he believed was needed to move the city forward. In February 1980, he spoke to the conservative Southside

Businessmen's Club and compared Jacksonville to the children's fairy tale, "Little Engine that Could."

"You remember the childhood story about the little train," he said. "As the engine began to climb up the hill the train creeped along. 'I think I may be able to do it, but I don't think I can. I don't think I can.' But as he got up towards the top and he built up steam, the train engine began to say, 'I can do it. I can do it.' That's how Jacksonville is beginning to sound," the mayor said.

"The boilers were stoked with Colt Fever and people began to have the attitude that, 'We can do it. We can do it. We shall do it. We must do it.'"

Mayor often had breakfast with members of the Mayor's Older Buddies (M.O.B.)

JAKE!

The Mathews Bridge opened in 1953 as a route for motorists in east Jacksonville and the beaches to access downtown in the west, and then return to the east. The bridge was backed by bonds and paid for by toll revenues.

Over the years, as Arlington and the beaches increased in population, traffic on the bridge escalated, especially during morning and afternoon rush hours. In 1981, the tolls remained on the bridge, despite arguments that the bonds had long ago been paid. Because of the increase in vehicle traffic caused by the thousands of people working in downtown, as well as the tolls which were collected at the east end of the bridge, traffic during morning and afternoon rush hours was horrendous. Motorists using the bridge were frustrated and often infuriated by the delays.

The bridge carried an estimated 55,000 vehicles daily, including almost 10,000 between 7 and 9 a.m., and 4 and 6 p.m.

In Arlington, 25 groups under the umbrella organization the Arlington Civic Association took their complaints to City Hall and Mayor Godbold. Godbold, who had already been thinking of making the bridge one-way during rush hours, met with the group. "One of our chamber leadership trips we had been on, one city had a bridge they made one way for the same reason," Godbold recalled.

When the mayor asked why Jacksonville had never tried the one-way approach, the city's traffic engineer, Henry Mock, said a test was discussed five years earlier. "Why didn't you try it?" Godbold asked. "We just never got around to it," Mock replied.

In typical bureaucratic fashion, Mock told the mayor the Jacksonville Transportation Authority would have to hire policemen which would require overtime pay and barricades would be needed. Godbold told Don McClure, his chief aide, "Take a pad and figure out how much it would cost for barricades and how much for police. Let's do it." The crowd was pleased.

After the meeting, Mock met Godbold in the hall. "Mayor, do you really mean to do that, or was that just for show?" he asked. Godbold grabbed Mock by the ear and said, "I want to do it so bad I'm going to chase your ass off it doesn't happen in the next few days."

WJCT Channel 7 is Jacksonville's public television station. In the 1970's the station moved into a new headquarters on Festival Park Avenue, adjacent to Metropolitan Park and across the street from the then Gator Bowl.

Godbold's battles with WJCT president Fred Rebman were never ending over Metropolitan Park. Even after the newly-built park was opened, there were frequent clashes between the mayor and the public television chief. Jacksonville civic leader Preston Haskell was chairman of the Jacksonville Visitors and Convention Bureau and, to conclude his year of leadership, he planned a dinner under the big canopy over the stage at Metropolitan Park. Haskell took the mayor to the park to show him what he planned to do. Haskell then told Jake that Rebman was charging him $2,000 to use the facility, which he said was less than it would cost to hold the event at a downtown hotel. Haskell was happy.

Jake was outraged and told Haskell, "This is a public park and you don't have to pay. You pay to clean it up and pay for catering. Rebman was not authorized to charge you anything." The mayor told Haskell, "I'll handle it." Godbold then phoned Rebman. "This is the very damn thing the Interior Department was afraid of. You can't do that. Don't let me catch you doing that anymore."

Later, city recreation department director Julian Barrs advised the mayor that Rebman had locked the gates at the park to keep out visitors. Once again, Godbold phoned Rebman. "Julian tells me you put a chain on the fence and nobody can get in the public park." Rebman interrupted, "You don't know the story. These damn blacks are coming in there and they get out on the dock and make a mess out there."

"What are they doing?" Godbold asked.

"They're fishing out there," replied Rebman.

"That's what that dock's for," said the mayor.

"They throw their trash out," said Rebman.

"Well, we'll put some trash cans out there," said Godbold.

"That won't do any good. They throw their shrimp bags and stuff on the dock," Rebman shot back. Godbold said he would have two recreation workers clean and wash down the dock twice each week.

"You can take the chains off within 24 hours or I'll come down there with Julian and cut that lock off." Rebman removed the lock and the city furnished garbage cans along with two recreation workers to wash the dock.

Chapter 40

The Spirit Lives On

It has been more than three decades since Jake Godbold was mayor of Jacksonville. Through the years, his fingerprints have remained all over the city he loves. Many of his visions still remain and are integral to the kind of community Jacksonville is today. Others have been altered, some improved, some have disappeared.

The Gator Bowl was razed in 1994 to make room for a brand new, state-of-the-art, NFL-ready stadium that has operated as home of the Jacksonville Jaguars, continues to host the annual Florida-Georgia game around Halloween each fall, and is the site of the TaxSlayer Bowl each New Years. It is now called TIAA Bank Field.

Of course, the foundation laid by Godbold starting in 1979 finally yielded a long-sought NFL team in 1995 when the league decided to award the city an expansion franchise, eventually named the Jacksonville Jaguars.

Converting the boarded-up Jacksonville Terminal into the Prime F.

348

Osborn Convention center saved a historic building, but the inability to ever attract a first-class convention hotel cramped its ability to fulfill the big goals envisioned by Godbold and other city leaders. Today, the convention center is used primarily by local organizations for events. The city continues to wrestle with whether Jacksonville needs an expensive convention center, and if it does, where it should be located.

Thirty-nine years after its highly successful inaugural in 1980, the Jacksonville Jazz Festival continues to attract large crowds and world-class musicians to downtown during the Memorial Day weekend each May.

The retail world changed for all the once-glamorous Rouse festival market places in some of America's major cities and the Jacksonville Landing was no exception. In 2003, Rouse sold the struggling Landing for $5 million to Jacksonville strip mall king Toney Sleiman. The city's promise to provide 800 nearby parking spaces never materialized and Sleiman has had contentious relationships with two of the last three mayors. The city has failed to keep up with needed maintenance at the Landing. If Godbold were mayor, he would probably declare it a slum and figure out how once again to make the Landing site a valuable piece of downtown's heart.

University Hospital, now UF Health Jacksonville, is one of the finest teaching hospitals in the Southeast with over 400 faculty physicians and offers services in nearly 100 specialties.

In the more than three decades since it opened, Mayo has grown significantly, adding the Mayo Clinic Hospital in 2008.

Recognizing how important the Southbank Riverwalk had become in almost 30 years of existence, in September 2013 the city demolished the original wood planked riverwalk and replaced it with a concrete structure that opened in February 2015. Godbold's vision for a second riverwalk on the St. Johns River's northbank started becoming reality in the 1990s under Mayor Ed Austin and it was extended by Mayors John Delaney and John Peyton. The Northbank Riverwalk stretches from the Fuller Warren Bridge on the west past the Acosta Bridge, in front of the Jacksonville Landing, under the Main Street Bridge and down to Berkman Plaza on the east.

The one thing of which Godbold is most proud has nothing to do with brick and mortar. Instead, it is the burning spirit he ignited in order to change Jacksonville forever. No longer a city that didn't know how to dream, or a place whose own residents didn't like living there, today Jacksonville continues to be a dynamic community that believes it belongs on the big stage and is unafraid to set its aspirations high.

Like all cities, Jacksonville has its issues related to education, crime and infrastructure. But, more often than not, its leaders tend to work together to find solutions. That notion of partnerships to make things happen and the collective attitude of the "Little Train That Could" is Jake's legacy.

Chapter 41

ACKNOWLEDGEMENTS

ONE OF THE things that Jake Godbold has always preached is the value of partnerships to get things done and make things happen. This book is a prime example, meaning there are many people to thank.

It begins with Godbold himself who spent hours throughout weeks patiently sharing much of his personal and political life with me. At times it was exhausting for the 85-year old former mayor who suffers daily from severe arthritic pain.

Of course, interviewing Jake, while important, was a small part of the story. So many people were involved and integral to his incredible success. Some are no longer with us. But I managed to talk with about sixty people who eagerly told me their own memories and Godbold stories.

When Martha Barrett was his press aide, she and another aide, Fleury Yelvington, kept huge scrapbooks for eight years filled with every single article that had anything in it about the mayor. For years after Godbold left office the scrap books languished in a closet in his company office. Those scrapbooks have provided a treasure trove of historic information for my research. They have now been turned over to the Jacksonville Historical Society.

Our daughter Natalie Brock once again served as my proof reader, a job that took many hours over lots of days. Great friend Richard Bowers, a history scholar in his own right, was my official reader and fact checker. I also owe a special gratitude to a pair of retired University of North Florida professors: Dr. James B. Crooks, a distinguished professor of history who read the manuscript for historical accuracy, and Dr. Richard Bizot, former head of the university's English Department who was meticulous in his thorough editing and helped ensure the book was readable.

In his wisdom, Dr. Crooks pointed out what he felt were important omissions in my telling of Jake's story. Here are two of them:

1. "Jake tried very hard to get an All-America City Award as Mayor Hans Tanzler had done (and Mayor John Delaney would later achieve) but failed. He failed because there was no growth management or impact fees on suburban development. Developers had free reign. He secured a 2005 Master Plan. but never enforced it. This was one limitation on his successes."
2. "He opposed the odors and spoke against them, but never attempted to regulate the paper mills or chemical plants like Mayor Tommy Hazouri did. Jake with all of his good intentions seems to me in his desire for economic growth to be beholden to corporate Jacksonville too much."

Carol Boone of the *Florida Times-Union's* editorial department facilitated my search of the newspaper's archives, and editor Mary Keli Palka allowed me to retrieve many of the photos for copy which appear in the book. To them and the *Times-Union*, thanks.

Finally, there are those individuals who stepped up to help fund this project. In the beginning, the idea to write a book about Jake was encouraged by J.B. Coxwell, a close Godbold friend, road contractor and Jacksonville icon. Coxwell offered to pay for the cost of the book. Unfortunately, he passed away in November 2017, just after I began. Jake and I both wanted to finish what we had started, so he turned to some of his friends for help. The response was overwhelming and indicative of the fondness and high regard in which he is still held. This is a list of those who stepped forward:

David Adams, David Allen, Mike Balanky, Bill Basford, Martha Barrett, Peter Bragan Jr., J.F. Bryan IV, Fred Bullard, Dick Burnett, Gene Callahan, Matt Carlucci, Pete Carpenter, Rick Catlett, Henry Cook, Harry Frisch, W.W. Gay, Chris Hand, Ceree Harden, Preston Haskell, Jacksonville Association of Fire Fighters, A. J. Johns, Bob Johnson, Teala and Ted Johnson, Marvin Lane, Steve Leggett, Wilford Lyon Jr., Dr. Lewis Obi, Steve Pajcic, John Rood, Kim Sadler, Al Safer, Bill Scheu, Hawley Smith, Lee Smith, Bobby Stein, Jay Stein, Chester Stokes, Arnold Tritt, Tom Wills, Josh Woolsey.

Then there is my wife Annette who surrendered the dining room table for a year so that I could lay out the huge scrapbooks where I conducted research. She also showed tremendous patience and kindness as I spent many days and nights away from home in Jacksonville during the research period.

To everyone, Jake and I want you to know how very grateful we are for your help and support. Mike Tolbert

ABOUT THE AUTHOR

IN ADDITION TO being a former aide and a friend of Jake Godbold for five decades, Mike Tolbert is an accomplished writer and successful corporate and political strategist. A former daily newspaper editor in Georgia, Tolbert came to Jacksonville in 1969 as a 25-year old political reporter for the *Florida Times- Union* and quickly got involved in campaign politics.

In 1970 he was press aide to former Florida governor Farris Bryant in an unsuccessful race for the U.S. Senate. He then reeled off wins as manager and/or chief strategist for a series of campaigns for Florida governor, Florida Cabinet, Florida Legislature, Congress, City Council and four Jacksonville mayors. He served on the staff of Mayors Hans Tanzler and Godbold, ran Mayor Tommy Hazouri's successful 1989 campaign to abolish tolls, and in 2000 he was an advisor to Mayor John Delaney's winning Better Jacksonville Plan referendum.

After a seven-year, $150 million effort to clean the polluted St. Johns River in downtown Jacksonville, in 1977 Tolbert created the River

Day celebration and convinced Mayor Tanzler to ski with the Cypress Garden skiers to prove the river was clean. In 1979 he produced Colt Fever, the first shot fired in Godbold's campaign to land an NFL team, and in 1980 he created the Jacksonville Jazz Festival at Mayport which attracted over 70,000 celebrants and continues as an annual signature event.

In 1983 Tolbert opened his own public relations firm. He and his wife Annette live on a horse farm in Brooksville, Florida.

CPSIA information can be obtained
at www.ICGtesting.com
Printed in the USA
BVHW081231120819
555664BV00023B/2278/P